"Dusty, Deek, and Mr. Do-Right"

"Dusty, Deek, and Mr. Do-Right"

High School Football in Illinois

Taylor H. A. Bell

University of Illinois Press

Urbana, Chicago, and Springfield

Frontispiece: Darryl Hicks (40) of Willowbrook
breaks away from a host of Glenbard North
tacklers during their 1987 game. Photo courtesy
of the Illinois High School Association.

© 2010 by the Board of Trustees
of the University of Illinois
All rights reserved
Manufactured in the United States of America
P 5 4 3 2 1
∞ This book is printed on acid-free paper.

Library of Congress Cataloging-in-Publication Data
Bell, Taylor H. A., 1940–
Dusty, deek, and Mr. do-right : high school football
in Illinois / Taylor Bell.
p. cm.
Includes bibliographical references and index.
ISBN 978-0-252-07731-9 (pbk. : alk. paper)
1. Football—Illinois—History. 2. School sports—Illinois—
History. 3. Football players—Illinois—History. 4. Football
coaches—Illinois—History. 5. Football teams—Illinois—History.
I. Title.
GV959.52.I5B45   2010
796.332'6209773–dc22   2009045140

Contents

"Dusty, Deek, and Mr. Do-Right"

1

The Players

Johnny Lattner:
Heisman Trophy Winner

Johnny Lattner, who once had his picture on the cover of *Time* magazine after winning the Heisman Trophy for his football exploits at Notre Dame, admits he experienced "one of the biggest thrills of my life" while playing basketball.

As a senior at Fenwick High School in Oak Park, he was an All-State tailback and
captained the football team to the Prep Bowl for the second year in a row. But he
also was the captain and leading scorer on a Friar basketball team that beat Tilden
at Chicago Stadium for the All-City championship.

"I enjoyed basketball as much as football," Lattner recalled. "After my sophomore
season in football at Notre Dame, I tried out for the basketball team. I didn't make
the traveling squad but when two players were declared ineligible, I was put on the
team.

"We're playing Navy and NYU in Madison Square Garden in New York and I'm
sitting on the end of the bench watching the girls and not paying attention. We're
losing by one point and Leroy Leslie, the team captain, fouled out and assistant
coach Johnny Dee called me to go in.

"I get the ball with 17 seconds to play, I score and we win by one point. [Famed
New York sports columnist] Red Smith, a Notre Dame guy, wrote how athletes could
play football and basketball. Leslie scored 32 points and I get one basket and get a
big write-up. The next year, I figured I'd flunk out if I played basketball."

In fact, Lattner loved basketball so much that he nearly passed up his trip to New
York to accept the Heisman Trophy because he didn't want to miss a basketball
game at Dayton.

"He asked, 'What should I do?' He invited his mother to go to New York in his
place. Then he decided he'd better go," said Bob Rigali, a Fenwick classmate who
roomed with Lattner at Notre Dame for two years. "He was serious about playing the
basketball game and not letting the other guys on the team down."

But his biggest disappointment came in football, when he fumbled at the goal
line with his unbeaten team leading 7–0 and Fenwick went on to lose to Schurz
20–7 in the 1949 Prep Bowl before nearly 58,000 witnesses in Soldier Field. It was
the second year in a row that Fenwick had lost in the Prep Bowl.

"I'll never forget that loss. Neither will the other Fenwick guys. That was my biggest
disappointment in football," Lattner said. "We beat St. George for the Catholic League

championship. We were better than 1948. We beat Leo, the preseason pick, and Mount Carmel, which was being coached by Terry Brennan in his first season."

Lattner, halfback Bob Rigali, quarterback Norm Canty, guard John Dwyer, and center Don Weaver were the hubs of the 1949 squad. Rigali, whose father had played for Knute Rockne, won the Tony Lawless Award (named for the Fenwick coach) for his academic and athletic prowess. Lattner was the second choice.

"He still talks about that fumble in the Prep Bowl," Dwyer said. "It still hurts him to think about that fumble."

In 1948, Lattner was an All-State end on a Fenwick team that also was unbeaten until losing to Lindblom and Dale Samuels 13–7 before 65,000 in the Prep Bowl. Because teammates Bob Rigali and Ed Lejeune were injured, Lattner was called upon to play a lot of halfback. But he couldn't do anything about Samuels.

"Samuels was a legend in the city," Lattner said. "They used him like a spread offense. We chased him all over the field. He'd stand 10 yards behind the line of scrimmage and throw the ball. I chased him all the time but never caught him."

Samuels tormented Lattner on defense, too. "I was deep on kickoffs. Twice after they scored I'm running down the sideline and a blocking wall formed in front of me and I thought I was going to break away for a touchdown. But Samuels tackled me twice," he said.

Lattner, the youngest of three children, grew up on Laverne and Madison, on Chicago's West Side. Former Austin star Bill DeCorrevont still was a legend in those parts. His mother lived in the Lattners' apartment building. There were 20 kids in the neighborhood who were his age. He had to learn how to handle himself.

"I was a big sissy and I got beat up all the time," Lattner said. "After getting knocked on my butt a lot, I figured I better start fighting back. My dad, who played baseball in the old Three Eye League, told me, 'You've got to be competitive.' So I started to play a lot of sports."

He became a gym rat and played basketball at St. Thomas Aquinas grammar school as a fifth grader. As a sixth grader, he became a tackle on the eighth-grade football team. He was going to enroll at St. Ignatius to play basketball and could have gone to Austin to play football for Bill Heiland. But his parents wanted him to get a Catholic education. Finally, he was persuaded to attend Fenwick because of Tony Lawless' reputation as an outstanding football coach. At the time, however, Lattner never dreamed the game would take him as far as it did.

"I never thought I'd play football in college," he said. "As a freshman, I would mop floors in the school on weekends to earn $1 an hour to pay for my tuition, which was $15 a month. My goal was to go to St. Benedict or St. Lawrence or Quincy, a small college. I didn't sense I could play big-time football in college—until the end of my junior year."

Lawless drove a busload of 20 players, including Lattner, to Notre Dame's spring practice. Coach Frank Leahy's assistant, Bernie Crimmins, took Lattner aside and said, "If you work hard and keep improving, we'd be interested in you." Up until then, Notre Dame had only been a dream in Lattner's mind. But Crimmins' message was great incentive.

After his senior year, Lattner had 100 scholarship offers. He said he almost went to Michigan because Lawless wanted him to go there and he would have been highlighted in Coach Bennie Oosterbaan's single wing. But Red Noonan, a Notre Dame bird dog who scouted players in the Chicago Catholic League, became friendly with Lattner's parents, who encouraged their son to enroll at Notre Dame.

"When I entered Notre Dame, they hadn't lost a game in four years. People said I'd only be a number, that I wasn't big enough [at 6–2 and 180 pounds] to play there," he said. "There were a lot of negatives but one incentive was to go there and see how good I was."

Lattner was used to tough competition in the Catholic League. Could Oklahoma be any tougher? The rivalries were intense. St. George of Evanston was Fenwick's biggest rival. Lawless and St. George coach Max Burnell didn't like each other. The Christian Brothers didn't like the Dominicans. Burnell worked his players until darkness to prepare for Fenwick.

On the West Side, it still was Fenwick vs. Austin. Lawless told his players, "If you beat Austin, you have a good team. But if you think you have a great team and lose to Austin, you're not that good."

"But the games against St. George at Hanson Stadium as a sophomore and junior and at Soldier Field for the Catholic League championship as a senior were as intense as any game I ever played in high school or college," Lattner said. "We hated each other."

Dick Butkus:
The Ultimate Competitor

The hundreds of quarterbacks and running backs who were terrorized by Dick Butkus during his Hall of Fame career would be surprised to learn that "Moby Dick in a goldfish bowl," as he once was so poetically described in an NFL highlight film, still gets mad at people who don't think he is a sensitive and caring person.

"He isn't a mean, growling person," said lifelong friend Rick Bertetto. "He never bit anyone's ear. There was a difference when Dick stepped on the field. It started a few days before a game. He'd go into his moods and try to build up a hatred for his opponent. But people thought that was who he was. Not so. He is sensitive and inquisitive about other people. He wants people to know his sensitive side."

Despite a successful post-football career that saw him become a celebrity endorser, broadcaster, an actor who starred in three weekly television shows, and the founder of a national program to address the issue of steroid abuse by young athletes, Butkus remains a very private person. In fact, because he dislikes going through airport security, he was influenced by Bertetto to purchase a motor home to travel coast to coast.

"Rick and I met in kindergarten," Butkus recalled. "We hit it off from the beginning. We had devilish twinkles in our eyes. We fooled everybody. People wondered, 'How can these kids succeed?' He was a social worker at Thornton Township High School. He could take kids away from drugs. We'd play handball at Fernwood Park and watch Uncle Johnny Coons on television at lunchtime. We've been close ever since."

In fact, Bertetto influenced Butkus to enroll at Chicago Vocational School (CVS) instead of Fenger or Tilden, where his older brothers and sisters had attended, or Mount Carmel or Leo. Because Coach Chuck Palmer had retired at Fenger after producing a city championship team in 1954, Bertetto talked his friend into going to CVS to play for Bernie O'Brien.

"I didn't know about him [O'Brien] at first," Butkus said. "But he seemed like a father figure. He took an interest in kids. He was such a good guy. He never swore. He was mad when he came close to saying 'damn.' He looked for kids who would do anything to improve. He couldn't cut them open to see all the desire they had but he loved to take someone who had ability and desire and see how good he could make him.

"He understood what football meant to a lot of kids who came out of south Chicago and didn't have much. He knew football was an outlet for a lot of guys, to get them away from the street gangs. He was able to take a lot of tough kids and teach them rules and how to funnel it on the football team. If you were looking for the ultimate coach, O'Brien was the guy."

Butkus grew up on 103rd and South Lowe in Roseland, not far from Gately Stadium. He skated in the winter and swam and played baseball in the summer. But football was the love of his life. From the outset, he relished the physicality, the running and tackling aspects of the sport. In his judgment, it was the best of all team sports.

Before his junior season, teammate Landis Rush joined the Navy, leaving an opening at the fullback position. Urged by Bertetto, O'Brien gave the 225-pounder a tryout.

"I played center, guard, and nose tackle on the freshman team," Butkus said. "As a nose tackle, I was free to roam, like [former Chicago Bears greats] George Connor and Bill George. They stood up and turned into linebackers. I played fullback, too. Selfishly, I felt I could do more for the team on offense. I didn't see anyone I couldn't beat out. I did all the kicking, too. I didn't want to get off the field. I even felt I could play quarterback in high school because I could throw the ball."

Even before Illinois assistant coach Bill Taylor convinced Butkus that he could make an indelible mark as a linebacker in college and the NFL, he realized he could play better on defense.

"A linebacker could impact the game. That's why I loved it," he said. "Linemen made blocks but the linebacker was in position to do more. That was exciting to me. I felt the way I performed made a difference in the game. Certain positions are more key than others. I don't like to say it but it's true. There are key players in key spots. At that time, linebackers and fullbacks were most important."

In 1959, he became the first junior to be chosen as the *Chicago Sun-Times* Player of the Year. His team tied Lane Tech 6–6 for the Public League championship but Lane

Tech had an edge in statistics and was awarded a berth in the Prep Bowl against Catholic League champion Fenwick.

"I don't recall much about the Player of the Year award but it was the first major achievement of my football career," he said. "Not making it to the Prep Bowl was another incentive for me not to get complacent and to work harder. 'Maybe someone is still out there working out harder than me,' I thought to myself."

In 1960, Butkus was injured. CVS lost to Taft 14–6 in the Public League final and Taft running back Al MacFarlane was named Player of the Year.

"It was a bummer of a year," Butkus summed up. "I felt I let everyone down. I was on the field all the time and I couldn't play up to what I could. I was banged up [he had a stretched ligament in his right knee] and I knew I couldn't perform up to expectations. It prevented me from having any lateral movement. After winning the Player of the Year award as a junior, everyone was pointing to me."

He chose Illinois because Notre Dame, his first choice, wouldn't accept married students and Illinois would. He was 15 years old when he met his wife, Helen. She was a student at Fenger, and then transferred to CVS. They have been married for 45 years. After being a two-time All-America at Illinois and starring for the Chicago Bears from 1965 to 1973, he was inducted into the Pro Football Hall of Fame in 1979.

"The second I saw him on the field at training camp, I knew my playing days were over," said Bill George, another NFL Hall of Famer. "Nobody ever looked that good before or since."

Despite his fearsome reputation, Butkus never participated in weight training in high school or college or even with the Bears. He worked construction, lifted cement blocks, moved furniture, and pushed cars.

"If I had it to do all over again, I'd train more," he said. "It would have helped me. It might have helped to cut down on the severity of my injuries. But strength training doesn't give you the skill to play a sport. At the time, before weight training became popular, I did what I thought I had to do to be better.

"For me, football was a great way of life. I found something I really loved to do and was able to do it. It ended too quick. You can't do it all your life. Then it's tough to find something to do after football. I loved every part of the game. It's like a toy. Kids love to play with toys. I never grew out of it. I loved it from the first time I saw it.

"I made sure football came first, even with my marriage. It was an edge I had on everyone. I would question if there was a guy who outthought me or dedicated himself more to football, how many days he thought about football. I had to have an overdose of football. There wasn't a day went by that I didn't think how I could get better."

Dave Butz: Illinois' First Goliath

Dave Butz was the first Goliath of high school football in Illinois, an intimidating and overpowering 6–6, 280-pounder in an era when 225-pounders were considered overweight. He defied the axiom that big kids were too slow and too uncoordinated to be competitive in sports. He was a Clydesdale who could run and perform like a thoroughbred.

"I was taller than my kindergarten teacher and always could reach higher to get stuff off a shelf," Butz recalled. "I was 6–5 in junior high school and 6–6 and 265 pounds as a sophomore in high school."

That's when Maine South varsity coach Marv Nyren approached Butz during a practice session, put his hands on his shoulders, and looked up at the towering youngster.

"Dave, you should consider a career in professional football," Nyren told Butz. "You have the size and speed of most NFL players right now."

"He was an inspiration, the best mentor I had," Butz said. "He gave me goals, something to strive for. I was languishing in mediocrity. As a sophomore, I started at offensive and defensive tackle. He was the one who encouraged me to do more. He didn't try to coach by humiliating you. He gave me a goal. I knew I wanted to be in sports.

"In the old days, we used to have Parent Appreciation Day at the school. You'd spend an entire day with your parents. And you had to wear a sport coat and tie. When we'd walk down the street, I'd say to myself, 'Dave, I hope I can play football long enough and well enough that I don't have to wear a sport coat and tie and have to work every day.'"

Butz was born in Lafayette, Alabama, on a cattle and poultry farm about 45 minutes from Mobile. His family moved to Park Ridge, a Chicago suburb, when he was nearly three years old. It was a bit of a culture shock. At the time, he didn't know money existed on paper. And shoes, socks, and underwear weren't part of his daily wardrobe.

He also suffered from dyslexia as a child. It wasn't discovered until he was about to enroll in high school. But once Nyren inspired him to become a big-time football player, he started to work harder, physically and academically, to prepare for college. When he graduated in 1969, he had 132 scholarship offers, including one from the legendary coach Adolph Rupp to play basketball at Kentucky.

Longtime friend and classmate Gary Posel characterized Butz as "a gentle giant" who was a legend in high school. He wore No. 77, Red Grange's number, and always was the biggest player on the field. In a basketball game against Niles West, he soared over 7-foot Gary Cartwright to jam the ball and shattered the glass backboard. In track and field, he set a state record in the discus of 180 feet, 4 inches, that stood for 19 years. In football, he once tussled with Deerfield's 6–5, 260-pound Jim Anderson, who later played at Northwestern.

"Playing three sports in high school was important to me," Butz said. "I wanted to play football because that's what I wanted to do. I went out for basketball to use my agility, to cover smaller guys, to get quicker and react. I can recall getting a rebound, throwing an outlet pass, and running down the court and putting the ball in the hoop. Basketball helped me to be a better football player."

He still insists his best sports memory of high school was scoring 32 points in a basketball game as a junior.

"I still have a copy of the letter-of-intent that Adolph Rupp sent to me in my scrapbook," he said. "I would have given new meaning to power forward. In three years on the varsity in high school, I never remember losing a tipped ball. But I felt I had more of a future in football, a more physical game."

Butz lifted weights to prepare for throwing the shot and discus in the spring. It bolstered his strength for football. But he was very proud to hold the state record in the discus for nearly two decades. He almost killed Coach Carl Magsamen when he hit him in the head with a discus.

"At the state meet, I had a bet with Coach Magsamen," Butz recalled. "I asked him, 'If I break the state record [in the discus], would you give me the biggest meal that I want?' Sure, he told me. That night, we went to a steakhouse. They said my steak was so big, they had to cut it and put it in two pans."

Despite a flattering offer from Adolph Rupp, Butz felt his future was in football, not basketball. He visited Alabama and talked to Bear Bryant. He noted that he outweighed Alabama's heaviest player by 52 pounds. He was personally recruited by Illinois' Jim Valek, Michigan's Bo Schembechler, and Purdue's Jack Mollenkopf.

In the end, he chose Purdue over Michigan. His uncle, Earl Butz, later a U.S. Secretary of Agriculture, was a professor at Purdue. The campus felt like home. He liked the players, including future NFL players Gary Danielsen, Darryl Stingley, and Gregg Bingham. But, he admits, had he been aware that Mollenkopf would retire after his freshman year, he would have opted for Michigan.

The recruiting experience taught Butz that football is a business, a valuable lesson that he would carry through his professional career.

"I was told I might be picked first in the NFL draft," he said. "But John Matuszak went No. 1. I went No. 5 to the St. Louis Cardinals. The Bears talked to me. Did I want to stay in Chicago? Yes, I told them, that's where I live. [Bears coach] Abe Gibron called me at my fraternity house at Purdue. I had some serious problems with [Cardinals owner] Billy Bidwill.

"The draft is one of the great monopolies that exist. I equate it to being a bricklayer. If you want to practice your trade in California but they draft you to go to New England, you can't go anywhere else. The Redskins still hold the rights to me. It is very restrictive."

After two volatile years with the Cardinals in which Butz had what he described as "severe contract problems" with Bidwill, who wouldn't talk with him or negotiate with him, Butz played out his option and joined the Washington Redskins in 1975. They tripled his salary and guaranteed his contract for three years.

He repaid them by playing out his 16-year career in Washington. He retired in 1988 after playing on three Super Bowl teams and being named to the 1980s All-Decade team. But he never forgot about his unpleasant times in St. Louis.

"Bidwill said my first preseason game was the best game I ever played for him," Butz said. "After I went to the Redskins, we played the Cardinals twice a year for 14 years. The Cardinals won only three times in 28 games. I played against the owner, not the players, for what he had said about me. I was naïve. I thought I had loyalty to the Cardinals. I didn't realize it was all business."

Mike Kenn:
Here's "Mud" in Your Eyes

As a senior at Evanston, Mike Kenn was an offensive tackle who stood 6–6 and weighed 192 pounds after a full meal. Many colleges said he looked more like a basketball player. They were reluctant to recruit a lineman who weighed less than many quarterbacks and running backs.

Michigan assistant coach Elliott Uzelac saw Kenn play lacrosse. He reported to Coach Bo Schembechler, "Bo, you've got to sign this guy. He can run."

But Schembechler was reluctant. In fact, Michigan had dropped Kenn from its A recruiting list and placed him on its B list. Evanston coach Murney Lazier was furious. He told Schembechler, "If you don't take him, don't ever bother to recruit any of my kids again."

Schembechler relented. He never regretted his decision. Kenn went on to become an All-American at Michigan, a 6–7, 275-pound offensive tackle who was the 13th selection in the NFL's 1978 draft. He played 17 years with the Atlanta Falcons before retiring in 1994. He was an All-Pro choice six times and played in five Pro Bowls. He started in 252 games and missed only 9 in his career.

"I had been told my entire life that I was too thin," Kenn said. "As a freshman at Evanston, they put you through two days of workouts without equipment to evaluate you. Then the best kids got their choice of gear. I was in the last group so I knew they didn't think very highly of me. When I got my gear, I had a helmet with a two-bar facemask.

"They put me in a one-on-one blocking drill against defensive linemen. I started to do well so they put more defensive linemen against me. I became a starter as a freshman and played my entire high school career with a two-bar face mask, something a quarterback would wear."

Kenn didn't start to gain weight until his freshman and sophomore years in college. It took a while for his metabolism to catch up. He would eat five large meals a day, including five sandwiches and mashed potatoes for lunch at the school cafeteria, but he couldn't put on weight. Finally, he grew to 242 pounds as a junior in college, then 258 as a senior, and 290 in the NFL. He thought of himself as a basketball player playing offensive line.

He credits Lazier for his development. His mother wanted him to attend nearby Loyola Academy in Wilmette, a school for boys. But Mike insisted on Evanston, his father's alma mater and a school where his friends were going.

He said he didn't know much about Lazier when he enrolled in 1970 even though Lazier was well established as one of the most successful football coaches in state history. Instead, he was in awe of the school.

"I tell people I went to a school with 1,200 graduates and 5,000 students," he said. "Evanston had two indoor swimming pools, 12 indoor gyms, an indoor tennis court and track, four cafeterias, four research centers—it was a phenomenal facility. The school had a great historical reputation. It was very good athletically and academically. It had people from every social and ethnic background, so complex and diversified. I experienced so many aspects of life."

Football was something he enjoyed doing, like participating in basketball, baseball, rugby, hockey, and lacrosse, but he insisted he had "no aspirations beyond trying to make the team" until he got older and realized he was better than everybody else. As a senior, he never left the field, playing offense, defense, and special teams. Lazier said Kenn was the best lineman he ever produced.

But it took time to develop. And Lazier, a great innovator, had ways of turning Kenn and others into productive players at the high school level, some into stars at the college and NFL levels. For openers, he started Kenn on a weight-training program and persuaded him to compete in lacrosse, which has often been jokingly referred to as Lazier's version of spring training for football.

"Murney invented dance aerobics but he didn't know it," Kenn recalled. "We used to do winter conditioning in the gym and run exercise drills. He came in with a phonograph. He planned the whole exercise with music, an hour at a time. It was choreographed, like the Rockettes. But you knew you would be successful if you committed yourself to what he wanted you to do."

As a senior in 1973, Kenn participated in perhaps the most famous game in Evanston history, a 3–0 loss to archrival New Trier that forever will be remembered as "the Mud Bowl" or "the Mouthguard Game." It was Evanston's only loss that season. The star of the New Trier team was linebacker Clay Matthews, who later starred at USC and was the 12th selection in the NFL's 1978 draft, one pick ahead of Kenn. They played against each other in the Rose Bowl, the NFL, and the Pro Bowl, and finally ended their careers as 39-year-old teammates in Atlanta.

But 1973 was unforgettable.

"I remember seeing mud on the top of my shoes before the game started, when I went out for the coin flip," Kenn said. "[New Trier coach] Chick Cichowski admitted they had wet the field and let the frosh-soph play on the field the day before. It was a mud bowl. We lost 3–0. We kicked a field goal to tie the game but the official under the goal posts threw a flag. He called our kicker, Jim Skinner, for not having a mouthpiece."

Kenn said he was lucky to be coached by Lazier and Schembechler, whom he described as "two significant personalities who were similar." Along with his father, he said they were the biggest influences in his life. In a racially mixed school that had several disputes over the years, including black athletes and parents and white coaches, Kenn said Lazier "was more color-blind than anyone I ever met."

"Lazier became a coach for the right reasons," Kenn said. "It wasn't about the glory, not about personal success. He became a coach because he cared about young people and wanted to have a positive impact on their lives. Through football—no sport is more difficult mentally and physically—he saw it as a way to mold young boys into young men.

"The standards and convictions he taught and insisted upon would reap positive rewards in each kid's life in the future. He wouldn't tolerate insubordination. If you were being insubordinate—well, that was an awfully long fence you had to run around the field. He wanted players who were committed. If you weren't committed to your teammates, if you didn't play at an appropriate level, he didn't want you. He taught you tools that allowed you to be successful at a high level."

Kellen Winslow: One-Year Wonder

Kellen Winslow recalls when his hometown of East St. Louis was "a different time than it is today." There were gangs but Winslow belonged to his own gang, a bunch of neighborhood kids whose lives revolved around sports instead of violence in the streets.

"It was a close-knit, very supportive environment," he said. "We walked the neighborhoods, wherever we wanted to go. We put together football games and baseball games and track meets and played all day long. They were organized by kids who were the leaders on the blocks. We lined our own fields and put bases down where we wanted to.

"I was 13 years old before I played in a baseball game that had a fence. My idols were Lou Brock in baseball and Jackie Smith in football. Everybody listened to Jack Buck and Harry Carey on the radio at night. The St. Louis Cardinals of 1968 and 1969 were my heroes—Brock, Bob Gibson, Curt Flood, Roger Maris, Steve Carlton, Mike Shannon, Orlando Cepeda, Tim McCarver."

Winslow grew up on the 400 block of 22nd Street. He and his friends would compete against the 500 block or the 400 block of 21st Street. They were so competitive that, one summer, after a church had been built on their old baseball field, one of the older kids taught everybody on the block to play chess. Four years later, four of the five members of the East St. Louis chess team were from Winslow's neighborhood.

Amazingly, the future Pro Football Hall of Famer didn't play a down of organized football until his senior year. His mother refused to sign a permission slip to allow him to play football in seventh grade. He tried out as a sophomore but was discouraged by the two-a-day practices in the summer heat and opted to get a good-paying job unloading trucks for United Parcel Service.

Finally, East St. Louis football coach Cornelius Perry came to Winslow's geometry class and recruited him at the end of his junior year.

"He pulled me into the hall and said he had watched me in gym class and saw me do things that other kids couldn't do," said Winslow, who stood 6–4 and weighed 200 pounds at the time. "He said I belonged on the football field. It sounded like fun. But I still went to work for UPS after he talked to me. He kept talking to me about coming out."

Even after he decided to go out, however, Winslow wasn't enthusiastic. During a two-a-day session in the heat, he approached Perry and Assistant Coach Jimmy Lewis and told them he was seriously thinking about quitting. They urged him to take off the second workout, go home and think about it, then come back the next day.

"They said they considered me a diamond in the rough, that after a year with them there was no reason why I shouldn't be in some man's college playing football," Winslow said. "I rode the bus thinking about it and came back the next day. It worked out. It turned out to be a life-changing situation. I decided to learn a lot about myself through sports. They saw something in me that I didn't see in myself."

Winslow had attended some football games at East St. Louis' legendary Parsons Field. But he admitted he wasn't aware of the great players who played there. His father liked to take him to the East St. Louis–Belleville games on Thanksgiving Day.

"I knew Parsons Field was a special place," he said. "We couldn't get on it when I was 10 or 11. It was a place of honor. When I finally got a chance to play there, I realized how special it was."

But when Winslow joined the football team in 1974, he said he was so green, he could have been a tree. "I didn't know a damn thing about football," he said.

"They had to push me on the field. I didn't know when to go out there. I was hit so hard on the first pass that I caught—I had never been hit like that—that I was in great pain and almost in tears."

But he stuck it out. Perry, Lewis, and Assistant Coach Bob Shannon, who later would guide East St. Louis to six state championships, changed his life.

"Much of my success I attribute to them," Winslow said. "If you want to know about a coach, talk to the players, not the fans or media. You would be hard-pressed to find a young person who played under Perry and Lewis who wouldn't tell you the same thing: They got kids to be the best they could be.

"They both should have had PhDs in psychology. They knew what to say, when to push and not push. So many coaches don't understand how to coach kids about what they need, that one size doesn't fit all."

In his second game against St. Louis Soldan, he was assigned to block a linebacker. The following Monday, Perry and Lewis sought out Winslow before the team meeting.

"They said, 'Wait until you see the film.' They were so proud of me," Winslow said. "They saw some development and growth in me. In the film session, they told my teammates to watch me. They lifted me up. I could have floated out of the room."

Winslow played on a great team. Two other players, tackle Cleveland Crosby and wide receiver Eugene Byrd, also played in the NFL. Twenty of the 22 starters went to college on some type of aid. Five went to Division I schools.

As a 6–5, 210-pound tight end, Winslow caught 17 passes for 300 yards and two touchdowns. But he didn't catch a single pass in the state championship game. He always will be remembered as the most celebrated member of the best high school football team in Illinois that never won a state title.

East St. Louis lost to Glenbrook North 19–13 in overtime in the first Class 5A championship. The last two passes were designed to go to Byrd. But he was covered so quarterback Maurice Tolson threw to Winslow. The first was too high. The second was intercepted by defensive back Brian Edwards. To this day, Winslow thought it was linebacker Jack Moller who tipped the ball away. No matter, the game was over.

"As I look back on it years later, my fault was waiting for the ball to get to me," Winslow said. "It hits the ground and you can hear the wind go out of the stadium from the East St. Louis side. It was deathly quiet. When it hits you that you lost the championship, I felt I let down my teammates and the school and the entire city. We were probably a better team on paper. But we didn't get the job done. If I could go back and change something, that's what I would change. I still get reminded of it to this day."

But it is difficult to be disappointed in a career that saw Winslow go from one season of varsity football at East St. Louis to All-America recognition at Missouri to the 13th selection in the 1979 NFL draft to the NFL's 75th anniversary All-Time team to the Pro Football Hall of Fame and the College Football Hall of Fame.

He also is a lawyer. He was encouraged to go to law school while he was playing football at Missouri. The school's vice-chancellor, Dr. Walter Daniel, the highest-ranking African American in the Missouri educational system at the time, planted a seed and recommended that Winslow should obtain a law degree. Later, while playing for the San Diego Chargers, he went to law school at the University of San Diego.

"I feel very fortunate. I have lived a blessed life," said Winslow, who currently is the director of athletics and student wellness at Central State University in Wilberforce, Ohio. "My ultimate goal is to continue to share life experiences that I had with youth. I'm at Central State because this is where I'm supposed to be.

"It is part of my giving back. Success is when opportunity meets preparation. You must be prepared to take advantage of things when they come your way. You never stop learning. You always are looking to expand your knowledge base. You are only as good as the people around you. You can't hang around people who aren't doing anything."

Winslow heeded Dr. Daniel's recommendation when he attended a meeting in Chicago during his NFL career. He was surrounded by people with PhDs and MBAs, doctors, lawyers, and accountants. He realized he might have been the best-known person in the room but he surely was the least educated.

"Fame is fleeting," he said. "I needed to get another degree. Law was an education, a way of thinking. I use it every day even though I don't practice law. It taught me to look at a situation, get down to the relevant facts, and find a solution to the problem, to see both sides of an issue. It taught me a lot about how the country works. It made sense to me. It's about people who come into your life and help guide you."

Like football coaches.

Don Beebe: 4.21? Are You Kidding?

It wasn't easy for Don Beebe to make a name for himself. He played football at tiny Kaneland High School in Maple Park, Illinois, which didn't win a conference championship until he was a senior in 1982. He sat out of college for three years, then played one season at little-known Chadron State, a National Association of Intercollegiate Athletics (NAIA) school in Nebraska.

In fact, if it weren't for Joe Thorgesen, Bill Giles, and a burning desire to run faster than anyone else, Beebe probably never would have had an opportunity to be the Buffalo Bills' No. 1 selection in the 1989 NFL draft, play for nine years in the NFL, and participate in six Super Bowls. Or have the football field at Chadron State named for him.

"I was a naturally fast but small athlete," Beebe recalled. "If I hadn't trained for speed in college, I probably would have stayed at 4.45 seconds (for 40 yards). Western Illinois saw my speed and offered a scholarship out of high school just on my speed. But, because nobody knew who I was, 4.45 probably wouldn't have been good enough to get drafted in the NFL. I had to be something special."

Special is running 4.25 at the NFL combine and 4.21 at the New York Jets' camp. Special is breaking the NFL record for the 40-yard dash and running as fast as the highly celebrated Deion Sanders in the 1989 combine.

Only the top 300 prospects in the country are invited to the NFL combine and Beebe, a 5–11, 176-pound wide receiver at Chadron State, wouldn't have been on the list if combine scout Bill Giles hadn't heard about a fast kid at a small school in Nebraska and made a trip to time him. Impressed, Giles extended an invitation to Beebe.

"One coach asked me if I had a black uncle," Beebe said. "No one could believe that a little white kid could run so fast."

It all began at Kaneland. Joe Thorgesen became head football coach in Beebe's junior year. Until then, Beebe had concentrated on track and basketball. He was runner-up in the 200-yard dash in the state meet but false-started in the 100 semifinals.

Football wasn't a priority at the school. Thorgesen produced only two winning teams in his first 13 seasons, then had 13 winning teams in a row before retiring in 2006, including state championship teams in 1997 and 1998.

"Thorgesen instilled love and passion for football like no one before," Beebe said. "Then my dream to play in the NFL became real for me."

At Western Illinois, Beebe switched from running back to wide receiver. Gary Crowton, once offense coordinator with the Chicago Bears and now an assistant under Les Miles at LSU, taught him how to run pass routes, how to catch the ball, and how to beat cornerbacks off the line of scrimmage. Later, with the Buffalo Bills, Hall of Fame receiver Charlie Joiner improved Beebe's pass-catching skills.

"Most important, he taught me how to be deceptive in route running, to make every route look like a go route, full speed, but you're really running three-quarters or seven-eighths," Beebe said. "A defensive back has to believe you are going deep. You have to make it look full speed but under control."

So how many football players can say they participated in six Super Bowls? In nine NFL seasons, six with the Bills, one with the Carolina Panthers, and two with the Green Bay Packers, including a victory in the 1996 Super Bowl, he caught 219 passes for 3,416 yards and scored 25 touchdowns. He also returned 81 kickoffs for 1,735 yards.

But he is best known for one of the most memorable incidents in Super Bowl history. In 1992, while the Bills were losing to the Dallas Cowboys 52–17 at the time, Dallas defensive tackle Leon Lett recovered a fumble and began to celebrate prematurely as he ran for an apparent touchdown. Beebe streaked across the field, knocked the ball out of Lett's hands, preventing a touchdown and regaining possession for a touchback.

After retiring from football, he opened his House of Speed in 1998. Four years ago, he became head football coach at Aurora Christian High School. Deeply religious, he said he launched his speed-training business "on the premise of teaching character, the right morals, and values through sports" and he finally was persuaded to get into the coaching profession at the high school level "because I wanted to be part of kids' lives in a more intimate way, day in and day out, and I wanted to use football as a vehicle."

Beebe could have returned to Buffalo to serve as receivers coach under Marv Levy. But he wasn't interested in the pro level. He wasn't interested in coaching at Northern Illinois or Aurora University, either.

"It wasn't the right fit," he said. "I don't look at things for money or prestige, but how God would want me to. Years ago, I applied for the job at Yorkville. But I was told I was underqualified. I felt God didn't want me there. Why Aurora Christian? [Athletic director] Don Davidson had approached me ten years ago when they were starting football. But I wasn't ready. But now I know this is where God wants me to be."

Beebe said he is coaching at a Christian school for a reason—to rear young boys into men of God, to teach them how to work hard, and to treat people right and with respect and honor—things he believes are lacking in society and most school systems today.

"Winning isn't that important," he said. "If you teach a kid the right principles, you will win football games."

So character is important, more important in his view than blocking and tackling. He concedes that some colleges will give a scholarship to any athlete if he has talent, regardless of his rap sheet. But he insists there is more emphasis today on character, especially in the wake of the Pacman Jones, Terrell Owens, Randy Moss, and Michael Vick episodes.

"Athletic skill is overrated," Beebe said. "You can find hundreds of kids who can run, jump, catch, and block. But you can't find a lot of high-character guys with that same ability. That's why the NFL draft is such a crapshoot.

"What is character? It's a person who, when you talk to him, looks you in the eye and is respectful. He is a 'yes sir, no sir' guy who has a firm grip on his handshake and shows up on time for meetings. On the field, he is relentless, doesn't pout or complain or blame others, doesn't hang his head, but runs and pursues and tackles until the final whistle."

Just like Don Beebe always did.

Russell Maryland: A Charmed Life

Russell Maryland admits he has led a charmed life. At the very least, fate had a lot to do with it. He never planned to go where he was going and he never understood how he got there. But it happened as if somebody had a game plan for every snap of the ball.

For example, Maryland grew up on the Southeast Side of Chicago, at 91st and Luella, near Chicago Vocational High School and Jesse Owens Park. Even though his father, a one-time pitcher in college, encouraged his youngest son to participate in sports, Russell preferred watching television and playing video games.

But his parents insisted on something better. They didn't like the neighborhood schools. They had sent their oldest son, Eric, to Whitney Young, a magnet school on the near West Side, and they wanted Russell to get a better education, too. They also wanted Russell to attend Whitney Young, which in a short time had achieved a reputation as perhaps the best public school in the city.

But Russell almost didn't get in. He wasn't invited to take the entrance exam. But his mother persisted. She wrote a letter to "the right people" and pleaded her son's case. He was allowed to take the entrance exam. He passed.

Later, after a good-but-not-great football career that saw him earn All-Public League honorable mention recognition as a senior, Maryland dreamed of playing at Notre Dame. Coach Gerry Faust showed some interest. But when Faust was fired after the 1985 season, Maryland was scratched from Notre Dame's recruiting list.

Brown and Dartmouth showed interest. But the only legitimate scholarship offer came from Indiana State. After visiting the campus, Maryland's father said it wasn't the right school for his son, that he'd pay for him to attend Chicago State if there were no other options. On signing day, Russell told Indiana State coaches that he had changed his mind.

"I was upset because I felt it was my only shot," he said.

But it wasn't. Unbeknownst to Russell, his father had sent a highlight tape to the University of Miami in Florida. Miami coaches said Maryland was "on our radar" as a junior, that they would recruit him as a senior. But he hadn't heard from them until . . .

On the night before signing day, highly recruited defensive lineman Mel Agee of Chicago Washington, who had made an earlier commitment to Miami, changed his mind and announced he was going to the University of Illinois.

Miami, with a scholarship available, called Maryland, who had a 3.2 grade point average (on a 4.0 scale) and ranked in the top 10 percent of his class. Coach Jimmy

Johnson, impressed by Maryland's tape, chose Maryland over a prospect who was less qualified academically.

"I was shocked when they offered me," Russell said. "Miami is one of the best programs in the country. Vinny Testaverde was there. It was the start of big things for me. I played on two national championship teams."

Looking back, would Maryland have been able to win the Outland Trophy as the nation's best collegiate lineman and become the No. 1 choice of the Dallas Cowboys in the NFL's 1991 draft if he had opted to play at Indiana State? Not likely.

"The main thing I learned was if you want to accomplish anything in life, you have to work at it," Maryland said. "At Young and Miami and with the Dallas Cowboys and the Oakland Raiders, I worked hard. It paid off. I was blessed to have been put in those situations, in organizations that knew what hard work was all about. All I needed was an opportunity because I felt if I worked hard I could make the most of it."

Jerald Prince, Young's football coach, was Maryland's first teacher. Russell still describes the summer of 1982 as "one of my worst summers." He wasn't in shape. He wasn't used to hitting and conditioning. Bear crawls at Union Park still evoke unpleasant memories. The whole experience turned him off to the game. Consequently, he didn't give much effort. If he could have quit, he would have. But his father wouldn't let him.

Prince, for whatever reason, saw some promise and potential in the youngster, who grew an inch or two, got a bit stronger, and turned some fat into muscle as a sophomore. Prince also uncovered a mean streak in the young man, a bit of nasty attitude, something every coach looks for in a defensive lineman. He promoted Maryland to the varsity.

"I wasn't a starter but I was feeling my way around," he said. "Football took a turn for the better for me. I knew what was expected of me. I worked harder."

As a junior, Maryland said, "I really got the hang of it. Now I was enjoying the game. I was doing better. We beat [perennial power] Lane Tech. It was a big deal for us. I was gradually getting better and better."

As a senior, he was starting as a defensive end and offensive tackle. "I had it down," he said. "As a freshman, it never crossed my mind that I would go to Miami to play football and be the No. 1 pick in the NFL draft. My parents wanted me to get a quality education. They weren't thinking about sports. But now I loved to play the game. And I felt I was ready to play in college."

Prince prepared him for what was to come. "What I took away from my high school experience was I learned how to be hard-nosed football player, a tough kid, very competitive. Lots of kids at Miami were like that when I got there, tough Florida kids. Prince taught me how to stick to something, not to quit," Russell said.

Maryland's first memory of stepping on the practice field at Miami was seeing Michael Irvin running 100 yards in spring drills with his shirt off, running 100 yards up and back, up and back, talking trash.

"He must be Superman the way he was running in front of everyone, I said to myself," Russell said. "I said, 'What the hell am I doing here?' It scared me a little bit.

I wondered if I belonged there. Miami was a shock. I was used to 60-degree days in Chicago and Miami was hot, hot, hot. After every practice, I wanted to quit.

"But the coaches kept my body into the experience and my mind out of the grind. What kept me going was when I was in the locker room with the other rookies, dog tired, letting the sweat drip off me, after 20 or 30 minutes, I'd say to myself: 'Russell, you made it through this day. Now do it tomorrow.' I did the same thing for the first 40 practices. I related to what coach Prince had taught me, how to stick to it and never quit."

Bryant Young:
A Future NFL Hall of Famer

Bryant Young still remembers what he describes as "the most humbling moment" in a splendid athletic career that saw him earn Athlete of the Year recognition in the Chicago area as a high school senior, All-America honors at Notre Dame, and a spot on the NFL's 1990s All-Decade team.

"I came into the state wrestling tournament ranked as the No. 1 heavyweight," he recalled. "In the semifinals, Brian Rose of Elgin Larkin pinned me. I was winning 5–2 in the second period and he catches me with a headlock and gets me on my back and I was pinned after 42 seconds of the second period. It was my only defeat in 30 matches."

But he recalls other moments that fill his scrapbooks with more pleasant memories—when the San Francisco 49ers traded up to select him as the seventh choice in the 1994 NFL draft, when the rookie tipped the ball and sacked the quarterback on successive plays against the Chicago Bears to thwart a scoring threat during a playoff game, when he sacked Dan Marino on the first two plays of the game on Monday Night Football, when he suffered a broken leg in 1999 and came back to play after only two days in pads.

"I learned that nobody will lay down for you and give you what you want," he said. "You have to work for it. When an opportunity presents itself, you have to take advantage of it, do the best that you can.

"When I talk to kids today, I tell them that they can't expect people to give them things. In high school, I had to work for everything I got. I learned how important off-season workouts are. I didn't realize it at the time. I enjoyed the off-season.

"For me, it was always a challenge and a sense of newness going into a new season. I might not have played as well as I wanted. But I always wanted to do better in the next season. It was a way of getting ahead of your opponent."

Sometime in the next few years, Young will be rewarded for his dedication, leadership, and numerous accomplishments when he is inducted into the National Football League's Hall of Fame in Canton, Ohio.

He has the proper credentials for enshrinement. In a 14-year career with the San Francisco 49ers, he was named the NFL Rookie of the Year in 1994, the NFL Comeback Player of the Year in 1999, was named to four Pro Bowls, started on the 1994 Super Bowl championship team, and was selected on the NFL's 1990s All-Decade team.

Equally as important, he won the 49ers' Len Eshmont Award eight times, more than any other player. The award is presented annually by teammates to the player who best exemplifies the leadership and inspirational and courageous play of Eshmont, an original member of the 1946 team.

"He gives us greatness," said Bill Walsh, the 49ers' late head coach and general manager.

It all began at Bloom Township in Chicago Heights. The youngest of three brothers, Bryant grew up on the east side of town, in a neighborhood infested by gangs and riddled by drug-related crime, in a town that at one time was voted "the most corrupt" in the nation per capita. Still, Bryant insists it was a good community to grow up in.

"My parents weren't sports fans. They didn't take us to sports-related events. But they did a good job of raising us," he said. "My father worked nights at the Ford assembly plant on Torrance Avenue. For a while, I was alone doing sports. If sports weren't there, they still wouldn't have had to worry about me. I steered away from trouble."

When he enrolled at Bloom, he wasn't aware of the school's distinguished tradition in sports—football, basketball, wrestling, baseball, and track and field. He didn't know about Homer Thurman or Leroy Jackson or Jerry Colangelo or Chuck Green, about the school's four state track and field championships in a row in the 1950s, about the 1957 football team that was regarded among the best in state history.

"I didn't embrace the history," he said. "I had heard about Lonnell Poole and Audie Matthews and Eddie Doxy and Derrick Walker and Kent Thompson. When I got there, I began to walk through the Hall of Fame and saw the people who came before me. 'Wow,' I said to myself. I realized the school had a long tradition in a lot of sports. It was good to be a part of it."

Young was a three-sport star in football, wrestling, and track and field. As a senior, he was an All-State defensive lineman in football, finished third in wrestling and third in the discus. Surprisingly, he didn't play organized football until his freshman year at Bloom. He played no sports at all in seventh grade. He was more interested in wrestling than football.

"I didn't embrace football until I began playing in high school," he said. "I didn't know what position to play. A friend suggested that I play fullback. When the coach said for all the linemen to go this way and all the running backs to go that way, I went with the running backs. Another coach stopped me and said, 'Young, you go with the linemen.' It was a challenge for me. But it hooked me. I was trying to get better at something that I wasn't too familiar with."

As a junior in 1988, his team was 8–3, including a second loss to Homewood-Flossmoor in the state playoff. Young reveled in the success. "I had the bug," he said. "I was starting to find out what my body could do and how good I could be if I worked hard." Under defensive coach Tom Holt, he realized he had the potential to be a dominant player. "I was helping to make a difference," he said. Colleges began to take notice.

In 1989, Bloom finished 8–2, losing in the first round of the state playoff. But Young made his mark. "I was hooked on football," he said. Notre Dame coach Lou Holtz visited his home. Michigan, Michigan State, Georgia, Illinois, and Tennessee also recruited him. He chose Notre Dame.

"It was a no-brainer," he said. "When I look back, I feel it was destiny. God had his hands on me. I took a field trip to Notre Dame when I was in eighth grade. I didn't realize the connection then. But I believe everything happens for a reason. At the time, Notre Dame was the biggest name of all the schools with a program that was good academically and athletically.

"For a guy who hadn't played organized football before high school, I had come a long way. It is amazing that I was able to achieve so much in such a short period of time."

Mike Alstott: Riding the A-Train

Today, many youngsters who aspire to greatness and careers in professional football or basketball hire personal trainers or join private clubs to enhance their physical conditioning, to get bigger, stronger, and faster, in order to attract college recruiters.

Mike Alstott had a better idea.

He prescribed a blue-collar approach. When he was 10 years old, he tied two automobile tires to a rope and pulled them down the street. He ran sprints in his yard. Later, he ran up and down hills in his neighborhood. And he pushed close friend and teammate Ryan Brown's Volkswagen in a cornfield and on back roads.

"We'd measure 100 yards and try to push the car as fast as we could," he recalled. "We cranked up the radio and motivated each other. We did it throughout the summer, 10 times a day, until we finished the length of a long road."

Alstott knew where he was going. His family had long been associated with Joliet Catholic. His older brother Mark had attended the school. Mike had attended Hilltopper games at Joliet Memorial Stadium and participated in pickup games with other young wannabes on a nearby field. All he could think of was wearing a Joliet Catholic uniform.

"There was no other place to go," he said. "I wanted to be part of a winning tradition. When you heard of Joliet Catholic, you thought of Coach Gordie Gillespie, his great legacy, winning, the state championship, Wednesday playoff games, Friday night under the lights. You didn't think about the great players. You just wanted to play the game.

"I was a part of it for years. When I was eight, nine, and ten, I remember seeing guys coming out of the locker room. I'd walk across the track and onto the football field. To me, it was bigger than the NFL and college at the time.

"I still think of the tradition, how much we bonded, the great teams. How many players went to college to play football? I can't count how many but we were a family together. As a senior, your goal was to be state champion. Nothing else mattered. It was a big letdown if it was anything less. Your team was measured by history and tradition, the teams that came before you.

"It was an awesome feeling. It set the tone for the future. It benefited me as I went on to college and the NFL. I understood what work was all about. We had good talent but we also had a lot of heart and passion."

Alstott earned his stripes. As a freshman, he played with the sophomore squad on Friday nights and with the freshmen on Saturdays. As a sophomore, he was promoted to the varsity for the state playoff. Gillespie, who had won nearly 80 percent of his games and five state championships in 26 years, had retired after the 1985 season. Alstott played for Bob Stone, who won 26 of 27 games and one state title in Alstott's two varsity seasons.

"We revolved around the coach," Alstott said. "He was a perfectionist. He orchestrated the team. Everything had to be strategized. He understood his players. He was a people person. He knew how to motivate us and get our attention. He prepared us well. When he moved on [to become coach and athletic director at West Chicago], it was sad."

But 1990 was a glorious season. Joliet Catholic was coming off a 10–2 season, Morris was ranked No. 1 in the preseason in the Chicago area and the Hilltoppers weren't projected to contend. But Alstott, a junior, running behind an overpowering offensive line led by Eric Gray and John Horn, propelled the Hilltoppers to a 14–0 record and another state championship. In the state playoff, they dispatched Morris 36–10, Rockton Hononegah 25–14, Woodstock 21–6, Leo and Player of the Year Corey Rogers 27–12, and Geneseo 21–20.

"It was a group that really came together," Alstott said. "Coach Stone gave me an opportunity to show what I could do. But you need players around you to let your skills stand out. That really started my career and helped me to mature as a young man. It helped to establish me for the future.

"Those were times we will always remember and never will forget, what we accomplished during the year. We still talk about those times. I still have close friends from that team—Gray, Horn, Ryan Brown, Don Laddas. It was special on Friday to go to school and wear the jersey and have a pep rally. At that time of my life, it was like the week before the Super Bowl. But we had it every week."

In the state final, Alstott executed what he describes as "the biggest play in my career and Coach Stone's career." After scoring on a four-yard run with three minutes to play, Stone called for Alstott to throw a pass for a two-point conversion. Alstott lofted a high pass that Jeff Bonebrake, a basketball player, leaped high to catch while making sure not to step out-of-bounds.

In 1991, Alstott was a popular choice as the *Chicago Sun Times*' Player of the Year. But Joliet Catholic won 12 games in a row before losing to Wheaton Central 28–6 in the state semifinals. In the season opener, the Hilltoppers rallied from a 24–6 deficit with six minutes left in the fourth quarter to stun Mount Carmel and Donovan Mc-Nabb in double overtime. Alstott ran around Simeon Rice's end to score the winning touchdown.

"I was Player of the Year but it left a sour taste," he said. "An individual award is nice but you like to have a gold medal hanging around your neck. We were so close but so far. Our expectations were to be state champion again. Second place is a lousy finish. It was a disappointing way to end my career at Joliet Catholic."

Despite his success at the high school level, many college coaches weren't impressed. They thought Alstott was too slow for the college game. He visited Illinois, Indiana, Wisconsin, and Purdue. And after he was selected on *Parade* magazine's All-America team, Florida State invited him to visit. But his mind was made up.

"Purdue was the best fit for me," he said. "[Former teammate] Eric Gray went there. We were close friends. He influenced me. And Jim Colletto was Purdue's first-year coach. I liked his split-back offense, which featured the fullback. I would have a chance to run with the ball, not just block. And I liked to play on grass."

Along the way, he picked up the nickname "A-Train," which referred to his bulldozing style of running. After graduating in 1996, the All-Big Ten fullback and Purdue's all-time leading rusher was selected as the Tampa Bay Buccaneers' fifth pick in the second round of the NFL draft. In 12 years, he was a four-time All-Pro choice and six-time Pro Bowl selection and starred on Tampa Bay's 2002 Super Bowl championship team.

"I didn't understand it at the time but when I look back on it, I have so much respect for Coach Stone and those who were there for us each day to make us better," said Alstott, who retired after the 2007 season.

"I see a lot of college players with great talent, more than me, but they lacked discipline and work ethic and didn't realize they were part of something special. I saw them fall off. They should have been in the NFL. But they didn't even finish their college career. They didn't make anything of their great talent."

He still wears his loyalty to Joliet Catholic on his sleeve. He still remembers when, as a sophomore, he stood in the hallway and boycotted classes with his friends when the school went co-ed with all-girls St. Francis and officials wanted to change the school nickname from Hilltoppers to Raiders.

"We had tradition. We didn't want to change the name of the school," he said. "We chanted in the hallway, boycotted classes, came together as a student body, and wanted the school to stay as it was. We believed in Joliet Catholic's tradition, all those years of history. That's why we're Joliet Catholic Academy today. We're Hilltoppers, not Raiders. We made a stand, like the same kinds of things we did on the football field. You never forget things like that."

Dusty Burk:
The Spread Offense Cometh

In the spring of 1994, Tuscola football coach Stan Wienke and assistant Tim Burk attended a clinic in St. Louis to learn about a spread offense that Bobby Bowden had introduced at Florida State. But they ended up at Glenville State College in West Virginia. And the offense they brought back with them has revolutionized the game of football.

"While we were in the lobby, somebody handed us a copy of *Football Quarterly* magazine, which had an article on Rich Rodriguez and his offense at this Division II school in West Virginia," Wienke recalled. "We had never heard of him or his school. He was running a no-huddle, shotgun offense, everything we wanted. Florida State was running parts of it with [Heisman Trophy winner] Charlie Ward. We called Rodriguez and arranged to go there during his spring practice."

After a track meet, Wienke and Burk drove 14 hours to Glenville, located in the heart of West Virginia's mining country. To get there, they weaved through mountains, ravines, canyons, and valleys for 40 miles along an unpaved road that was clogged with pickup trucks. Rodriquez, who later took his unique offense to West Virginia University and then to Michigan, sat with them and told them everything they wanted to know about the spread.

"We fell in love with it," Wienke said. "The run-and-shoot was too difficult because of the multiple reading of the defense. We didn't have enough time to learn the offense. It was too complicated. And we didn't have the capability of having a running offense because we didn't have a running back in school.

"We liked the spread. We liked throwing the ball around. The fastest way to get down the field was throwing the ball. It didn't require massive linemen to block and we didn't need a running back. What we needed were some skilled kids who were athletic and could catch the ball and make yards after they caught it."

Most of all, they needed a quarterback with some mobility who was a great decision maker. It helped if he had a good arm—but that wasn't a requirement.

They had the player designed to fit the mold. Dusty Burk, Tim's son, had been groomed to quarterback a no-huddle, pass-oriented offense since seventh grade. From the moment he began executing plays in a seven-on-seven league, Dusty felt like a kid in a candy store.

As a junior and senior, Dusty established state records for career total offense (9,911 yards) and season total offense (5,138 yards in 1997). He passed for 7,526 yards in his career and 4,052 yards in 1997, both fourth all-time. He also averaged 313.5 passing yards per game in his career, second all-time. And he threw 83 touchdown passes in his career, third all-time.

"We were fortunate because we didn't have to take a lot of time teaching Dusty to be a good decision maker. Some kids have it, some don't," Tim Burk said. "I felt Dusty was a special talent as far back as T-ball. He had been working on throwing the ball for years. From the time we started, we worked on throwing on the run, which many quarterbacks can't do. When you have the ability to run, it opens up so many more things in decision making. It drives defensive coordinators nuts."

Dusty's reaction to the new offense was "like getting the keys to the car." From the first snap, he knew it would be so much fun, and fun for everyone on the team. "My eyes were wide open. I wanted to go out on the field right then to start. I was eager to get going with it. It's every quarterback's dream to play in an offense like that," he said.

"From the standpoint of being the quarterback, you are the man in this offense. The team lives and dies on your shoulders. Some kids thrive on that pressure, some don't. That's what I wanted. It was all on my shoulders.

"My ability to pull the ball down and run or go to my second or third receivers was my big edge. I could sense the open areas of the defense. I had a feel for which windows would be open in the zones. I had a good feel for match-ups. I would start to run when I was flushed out of the pocket and still be able to throw downfield on the run. That was the most important thing."

Burk's favorite play was "right Florida." He would take the shotgun snap, take a three-step drop, invite the defensive ends to come after him, then spin out of the pocket and throw a comeback pass—"our bread-and-butter," he said—or take off and run. A backup guard stood next to him in the backfield. His only job was to block.

With Burk setting passing records, Tuscola advanced to the quarterfinals of the state playoff in 1996 and 1997 but never got any farther. In 1996, Tuscola lost to Villa Grove after beating them in the regular season. In 1997, Tuscola lost to archrival Arcola by 40 points. "The losses stand out," Dusty said.

But the opening game of his senior season stood out. Matched against Robinson, a Class 3A school, little 1A Tuscola felt it had something to prove. Tuscola won 50–40. The first quarter lasted 1 hour 15 minutes. Burk ran or threw on 68 of 70 plays, passed for more than 400 yards, and also played defense.

Oh, there were other pleasant memories—throwing six touchdown passes against Arcola as a junior and beating Casey-Westfield in overtime in a duel of 10–0 teams in the second round of the playoff in 1996. "That's the first time I had been in a game where the fans rushed the field. It was a great feeling," he said.

Tuscola enjoyed even more success with the spread offense when John Wienke, the coach's son, quarterbacked the team to a state championship in 2006 and second place in 2007. John passed for 3,300 yards and 34 touchdowns as a junior and 2,900 yards and 34 touchdowns as a senior. He committed to Michigan but, curiously, opted for Iowa when Rich Rodriquez succeeded Lloyd Carr as head coach. He felt Iowa's pro-style offense was better suited to his skills than the spread offense he had grown up with.

Unfortunately, Dusty Burk didn't have an enjoyable college experience. He always dreamed of playing at Notre Dame. But they didn't call. He visited Illinois, Iowa, and Vanderbilt. But they said he was too short. Illinois coach Ron Turner was brutally honest. He told Dusty that he wasn't good enough to be a scholarship player in the Big Ten because he wasn't big enough and would get killed. Turner gave a scholarship to quarterback Walter Young of Rich East, who became a receiver at Illinois.

Mississippi saw a tape, called, and said a coach would fly to see a practice and offer a scholarship. Before the coach was to board the plane, however, their first choice at quarterback made a commitment. So the flight was canceled.

"The recruiting process was disappointing and frustrating," said Dusty, who decided to attend Illinois State in December of his senior year. "I was getting letters every week but none meant a whole lot. At first, I had high hopes but then I began to understand the process. I thought it would be ISU or Iowa. Had Illinois offered, I'm positive I would not have taken it. Everywhere I turned, I was on the cusp of getting an offer but it fell through.

"At first, I didn't want to look at ISU because I didn't want to go to a 1-AA school. But I loved it. I got a chance to meet my wife, Julie. Then everything fell apart when Coach [Todd] Berry left for West Point. I realized the recruiting process is all business, hard for coaches and players. You don't know where you stand in a coach's eye. There are some coaches you feel you can connect with and others you don't."

Burk came in as a freshman at ISU in the third game, replacing injured starter Kevin Glenn, and led his team to the national semifinals. As a sophomore, Glenn returned and Burk was his backup. As a junior, Berry left and new coach Denver Johnson brought in a run-oriented offense. Burk never saw the playing field. Disappointed, he transferred to Truman State, a Division II school. On a 6–5 team, he ranked second in the nation in total offense.

"If I had it to do over again, a little part of me asks what it would have been like to play at a big school, to walk on and see what I could have done," he said. "But my first two years at ISU were more than I thought they could be. I was happy with my decision. Then things changed."

Kellen Winslow, now athletic director at Central State University in Wilberforce, Ohio, was a standout on the East St. Louis team that lost to Glenbrook North for the 1974 Class 5A championship, one of the most dramatic games in the history of the state playoff. Winslow later was an All-America tight end at Missouri and was inducted into the National Football League's Hall of Fame after an outstanding career with the San Diego Chargers. Photo courtesy of Central State University.

Nationally known recruiting analyst Tom Lemming (center) of CBS College Sports chats with Heisman Trophy winner Johnny Lattner (left) and Notre Dame football coach Charlie Weis during his annual banquet to honor high school players in the Chicago area. Photo by Barry Bell.

College and Pro Football Hall of Famer Dick Butkus greets old friends at a Chicago Vocational High School reunion for the class of 1961. Left to right, legendary football coach Bernie O'Brien, Mike Coffey, Butkus, and Rick Bertetto, Butkus' childhood friend. Coffey, Butkus, and Bertetto played on O'Brien's 1960 team that lost to Taft 14–6 for the Public League championship. Photo courtesy of Rick Bertetto.

Dusty Burk of Tuscola graduated in 1998 as the most prolific offensive performer in state history. Running out of a spread offense, he set total offense records with 5,138 yards in 1997 and 9,911 yards for his three-year career. Photo courtesy of Tim Burk.

2
The Coaches

Tony Lawless: "Sculptor of People"

Jim Maddock, who played football for Tony Lawless at Fenwick and Bennie Ooster-baan at Michigan in the 1950s, still remembers calling a play that might have ended his career, something you didn't do when the coach was known as "Furnace Face" because he got so mad when someone didn't follow his instructions to the letter.

Fenwick, nursing a 7–0 lead against DePaul Academy, faced a fourth-and-eight situation with 30 seconds to play in the first half. Maddock called for a punt. But as he broke the huddle, teammate Ed Shannon whispered in his ear, "Why not run around my end?"

Maddock took the snap, faked a punt, and ran around Shannon's end for a 60-yard touchdown (80 yards by Shannon's account). In the locker room at halftime, Lawless didn't say a word. After all, he didn't call the play.

"We expected him to say something," Shannon said. "He would have been all over us if the play didn't work. But it didn't come from him. He would never have called the play."

In the second half, Fenwick faced another fourth-down situation. Recalling how easy it was to fake out the defense earlier, Maddock decided to run around the opposite end for what he figured would be another touchdown. He faked the punt but was tackled for a five-yard loss.

"I come out and go where Lawless isn't," Maddock said. "He comes over to me and says, 'You jerk, you do that once a season, not twice in one game.' He was a builder of character, a sculptor of people. What he was really after was to build you into someone who knew who he was and where he was going, right from wrong, and send you on at an early age to what you had to do for the rest of your life."

Lawless was a master psychologist and a great teacher of fundamentals. When he retired in 1956, he was still teaching the Notre Dame box, Knute Rockne's version of the old single wing, while most strategists were coaching the T formation and the split-T and beginning to develop other option offenses.

"Alumni said to get him out of that [Notre Dame box]. But I became a believer because he could teach it," said former Glenbard West coach Bill Duchon, who played guard on Lawless' 1945 Prep Bowl championship team and later was an assistant on Lawless' staff from 1954 to 1959. "He was so good on fundamentals, blocking and tackling. He never passed up a teachable moment."

Shannon said you couldn't play football for Lawless for four years without learning the game. "The only reason I was able to play at Michigan was because all he taught me about the game became second instinct. At Michigan, I was ahead of a lot of guys, even All-Americans, because I knew more about the fundamentals of the game," he said.

Frank Reynolds, a 1955 Fenwick graduate who was a starting halfback on Terry Brennan's 1957 Notre Dame team that snapped Oklahoma's 47-game winning streak, recalled his first practice at Notre Dame.

"Brennan came up to me and said, 'You're from Fenwick. I know you know the fundamentals.' Lawless had a deep passion for the game. The No. 1 thing was he wanted to see you compete and give everything you had on every play," Reynolds said.

Most of all, Lawless was a winner. In 25 years, his teams won 80 percent (172–40–6) of their games and never experienced a losing season. Although he produced only one unbeaten team (8–0–1 in 1936) and only one 10-victory season (10–1 in 1949), he coached a dozen teams that lost only one game. In his first seven seasons from 1932 to 1938, he was 45–6–3.

Fenwick is all about Lawless and tradition, about Heisman Trophy winner Johnny Lattner's bronze shoe in the glass case in the hallway, about Olympic diving gold medalist Ken Sitzberger, about NBA star Corey Maggette, about hallways cluttered with football, basketball, and swimming trophies, about walls filled with photographs of All-State and All-America athletes, about Jug (detention on Saturday mornings), and about Dan O'Brien, a 1934 graduate who served as a coach, teacher, administrator, and athletic trainer at the Oak Park school for 73 years.

Born in Peoria, Lawless was an outstanding athlete. He led Peoria Spalding to the National Catholic High School Basketball Tournament championship in 1924 and later coached his Fenwick team to the national title in 1937. He played football and basketball at Loyola University and then was selected from a list of 250 applicants to be Fenwick's first football coach in 1929. He retired in 1976.

Lawless ran a tight ship. And he was supported by the man who hired him, Rev. Leo C. Gainor, Fenwick's principal.

Gainor told Lawless, "I was never an athlete but I do know that there is no better way of identifying and having Fenwick recognized than having a successful athletic program. I require that you tell me what I should do to support any concern you have and I'll see that it's done."

"There was no debate, no committee meetings, nothing. [Gainor] was in absolute control of every situation," O'Brien said.

On the football field, Lawless was judge and jury. Lattner said he was scared of him. So were most of his players. Dick Caldarazzo, a 1966 graduate who returned to Fenwick to coach the freshman football team, said Lawless was "a stern, tough man who ran gym classes with an iron fist. He was old school, as tough as the priests, if not worse. Most students didn't understand his brand of discipline. But he was Fenwick tradition."

"He was rough and gruff," Lattner said. "He didn't mix many words. He intimidated the freshmen. In spring ball, I was an end. I never was so scared in my life being out there with the varsity for 30 days. If I wanted to get ahead, I had to step it up and compete. I was only 15 years old and he was very intimidating."

Lawless tested his freshmen. He put pressure on them. He wanted to find out who could handle it and who couldn't. He ran the same offense year after year: the Notre Dame box, the single wing. His coaching techniques were unwavering and uncompromising. Do it my way or don't play, he said. His record proved he knew what he was doing. A lot of good athletes couldn't take his philosophy and refused to play for him. He didn't care.

"Looking back, it helped me to be a better athlete," said Lattner, who experienced the same coaching philosophy when he played for Frank Leahy at Notre Dame. "Lawless never put anyone on a pedestal. He never gave out too many compliments. But you knew where you stood with him. He was always trying to improve."

When things weren't going right, when someone fumbled or failed to execute a play properly, Lawless would turn to O'Brien and say, "The boys, Dan, the boys. You gotta have the boys."

"He was a stickler for fundamentals," said Norm Canty, who played with Lattner on the 1948 and 1949 teams that lost in the Prep Bowl. "You didn't want to make an error after he corrected you. He had the ability to see clearly every mistake that every player made. If you missed a block, he knew it. If you missed a tackle, he'd tell you how to do it right. He'd see something that somebody did and would stop practice and begin teaching. He produced teams that played the game to win and to do it correctly."

Rudy Gaddini, who played in the same backfield with Maddock and Shannon on the 1952 team and later played at Michigan State, recalled how Lawless taught his players more about life than Xs and Os. He still remembers many of the old sayings that the old Irish wit would recite.

"Gold is where you find it. Talent is talent, you can find it any place."

"You want to know how good he is? Put him in competition. Some can compete, some can't."

"What library do you go to and what book do you look at to get a map on life, how to conduct yourself? Conduct yourself as a gentleman all the time."

"If I knock you down more times than you knock me down, I win the race."

One time, Gaddini was having trouble in his religion class. The Sermon on the Mount had him stumped. He couldn't interpret its meaning.

"I was walking in the hall and Lawless brings me into his office," Gaddini said. "He said to me, 'I hear you're having trouble in religion.' I said I was. 'Are you going to church on Sunday?' he asked me. 'Yes,' I said. 'Are you honoring your father and mother?' he asked. 'Yes,' I said. 'Get out of here. You have no problems,' he said."

"But one thing he said that always has stuck with me was 'If you do something wrong, forget about it. Come back and do something right because people will forget about what you did wrong.' He was a complete coach. He coached everything, football and life."

Harvey Dickinson: Cradle of Coaches

Ken Koranda was an All-State running back on Hinsdale Central's unbeaten 1967 team, arguably the best in school history. Norm Chimenti was an All-State guard/linebacker in 1957. G. R. Thomas and Dick Purcell were two of the leaders on the 1954 team that allowed only 26 points in eight games, a school record. They can tell you a lot about Coach Harvey Dickinson's motivational skills.

"When I was a sophomore, we were going to play Downers Grove," Koranda recalled. "The day before the game, we had a team meeting in the cafeteria. Harvey was giving a talk. We wondered, 'What will he do to get us up for this game?'

"He walks into the room with a bucket, the Old Oaken Bucket that is the symbol for the Downers Grove–Hinsdale Central series dating to 1935. 'I want to read the scores of the games,' he said. He kept reading them all the way back to the 1940s. Then he put the bucket on the table and walked out of the room.

"We realized we hadn't lost to Downers Grove since before we were born. We didn't want to be the first class to lose to them."

Hinsdale Central beat Downers Grove 21–0. It was the first of five successive shutouts that closed out an 8–0 season. The Red Devils allowed only 27 points, one more than the 1954 squad. They were named the mythical state champion in Illinois. It was Dickinson's last season.

"He is probably the only coach I played for that when he said something, you knew it was going to work," said two-way lineman Skip Korty. "In 1967, we were tied four times at halftime. Three times it was 0–0. But he made adjustments at halftime. He would walk around the room and ask linemen what the opponent was doing, how they were lining up on us. Then he'd make two or three adjustments and we'd score two or three touchdowns in the second half to win."

The 1967 team was supposed to be the most inexperienced team that Dickinson had had in 10 years. It was picked to finish third in the West Suburban. Glenbard West was the favorite. There were no superstars in the lineup except Koranda, who was coming off a broken leg that he suffered as a junior. No one knew how good the team would be.

But Dickinson had some ideas. He moved some offensive players to defense. For his entire career, he had employed a 5-3 defense. But in his final season, he decided to make a change. He visited Notre Dame coach Ara Parseghian for three days and opted to install a version of the Irish's 4–4 for the 1967 season.

In the showdown with Glenbard West, Hinsdale Central prevailed 20–0 at homecoming. Three talented juniors—Ken Braid, Bruce Elliott, and Herb Briick—came up to the varsity to join a well-heeled group of seniors, including Koranda, Larry Grandy, Charlie Lewis, Joe Ramey, Roy Hart, John Schwitz, Jon Walton, Scott Robinson, Paul Frederickson, Roger Carlson, and Tom Vandndy.

Glenbard West boasted a dangerous passing game with quarterback Danny Halt and All-State end Mike Pickering. But Hinsdale Central's defensive line pressured Halt, Ramey shut down Pickering, and the Red Devils dominated the game.

It might have been the biggest game of 1967 but longtime sports columnist Bob Frisk of the *Daily Herald* in Arlington Heights said the best game he has observed in 50 years was the Arlington–Hinsdale game in 1959. Arlington, with quarterback George Bork and running back Mike Dundy, was 4–0 in the West Suburban; Hinsdale, with Vic Dutkovich and Hal Brandt, was 3–1. Trailing 26–13, Hinsdale rallied to win 27–26 on Dutkovich's touchdown run with eight seconds left.

Jim Kolzow was a safety on that Hinsdale team. Bork threw a 72-yard touchdown pass to Dundy on the first play from scrimmage, directly over Kolzow's head. "He never yelled but you could tell when he talked to you that you better get your butt going. He was always down to business. Do it right and you'll win the game," Kolzow said.

Dickinson was a very successful football coach. Before he was hired in 1940, the program had 10 losing seasons in the previous 11. In 25 years, his teams were 148–49–8. He was 81–13–3 from 1951 to 1962 with eight conference titles. In his last 17 years, he was 114–20–4. He once went three years without a loss. After going 4–5 in 1946, he posted 21 winning seasons in a row before retiring after 1967. He produced 15 All-Staters.

"He was smart and tuned you into the psychological aspects of the game," Purcell said. "But what stuck out in my mind is he always took blame when things didn't go well and we got credit when they did. We were convinced if we did what he told us to do, we'd be successful."

But perhaps his greatest legacy is the number of outstanding football coaches he developed—Jim Rexilius, Chuck Schrader, Dick Ohl, Gene Strode, Dale Foster, Bill Trescott, Bob Trevarthen, and Bob Thomas—and the number of nationally recognized coaches in other sports that he hired as athletic director, including Clare Riessen, Jay Kramer, Don Watson, Jodie Harrison, Tony Canino, Hylton Huseth, and Neil Krupicka. He was named the National Athletic Director of the Year in 1977.

"As good as he was, he didn't place himself on a pedestal," said Strode, who succeeded Dickinson as head coach and athletic director. "He was a players' coach. He had a great sense of humor. He had fun and the kids had fun. He wasn't a yeller or screamer. He wasn't profane. And he didn't embarrass his players or coaches. He appealed to your sense of pride in what you were doing. He let you know he thought you could do better."

Born in Browning, Missouri, Dickinson played football, basketball, baseball, and track at Culver-Stockton College. He coached at Pleasant Hill, Illinois, and Centerville, Iowa, before being hired at Hinsdale in 1940. He chewed grass in lieu of smoking cigarettes on the field, hated cold weather, Notre Dame, and the single wing, and never wavered from his slot-T offense and 5-3 defense until the end of his coaching career.

"He was a tremendous motivator but I didn't know it until I experienced it," Chimenti said. "As a senior in 1957, we were in a close game against York at home. There were a lot of college scouts in the stands. We played badly in the first half. At halftime, we went to the shed. No Harvey. He isn't there. The officials come in to let us know we have five minutes to get to the field. Still no Harvey.

"Then he walks in. The room is silent when the players see him. He pauses. He looks around the room. 'You are embarrassing yourselves and you are embarrassing me,' he said. Then he walked out. We outscored them 35–0 in the second half. Having his scorn was the worst thing in the world. He didn't have to do any more coaching than that."

Thomas, who was president of the class of 1955, recalls that when his class celebrated its 10th reunion, they voted Dickinson as the teacher who had the most profound influence on their lives—and the girls didn't play football.

"On the bus to Lyons Township, I'm thinking they have some good players I have to cover on passes," Thomas said. "As we're dressing for the game, Harvey came up to me and looked at my shoelaces. He untied them, then tied them again. 'I know you can keep up with the Caffey boys,' he said. Psychologically, he made us champions. He would get in your head and make you think there was nothing you couldn't do."

After giving the commencement address for the class of 2007 at Hinsdale Central, Braid stood on Dickinson Field and recalled what it was like 40 years earlier. He was a junior on the 1967 squad, an All-Stater in 1968, and later captained a team at Illinois.

"All I could think about these many years later, after playing for him in his last year, giving the commencement speech for these kids, it was a special moment. I was thinking how many days he gave us on that field. He was a mentor in life and football.

"He would say, 'Here is your job. You accomplish your job and let others do their jobs. Don't be doing somebody else's job.' The discipline did so much to help me at Illinois. I was so well coached. I didn't have to do somebody else's job. If someone didn't do his job, Harvey would take care of it."

Deek Pollard: In the Mold of Lombardi, Bryant, and Hayes

Donald "Deek" Pollard, sometime during the time he coached Pittsfield's football team to a state-record 64 victories in a row, was attending a spring practice at North Carolina State when he stopped at a local diner for a bite to eat. He noticed the décor was covered with old sayings and witticisms, a graffiti of stoic philosophy and trivia.

One sign said, "A society which will accept philosophy because it is considered a noble profession but scorn plumbing because it is considered a lowly profession is a society which will have neither theories nor pipes that will hold water."

"I never forgot that," Pollard said. "I don't know the author. But people who have success in anything generally in some form or fashion say they develop a philosophy. I've never operated that way. I've operated on principles. And my principles in football were simple.

"There is one thing you can control—the strength of the players you put on the field, both from a character and physical standpoint. If you want to restrict or reduce that to its simplest terms, the tough guys always win in football. You don't see a good football team that isn't physical."

"Physical" was the name of the game at Pittsfield. After starting 1–4–3 in 1965, Pollard introduced a state-of-the-art weight-training program—five benches, three power presses—and a wrestling program—his athletes lifted weights three days a week and wrestled two days a week—and created an environment that produced seven 9–0 seasons in a row and put Pittsfield football on the map. His teams were so good and so dominating that opponents kicked them out of the conference.

It wasn't easy. Pittsfield, the seat of Pike County, was the third-largest geographical school district in Illinois, stretching from the Illinois River to the Mississippi River. It was a farming community—the only industry was a shoe factory—and most kids played basketball. Football was a white-collar sport in a blue-collar town.

"I had to change the mind-set," Pollard said. "Kids learned I might be different but I'm honest. The best advertisement is word of mouth. I wanted to create an environment for every male student in the school so he knew if he could beat anyone one-on-one that he'd get a fair chance in football. All of a sudden, kids came from all the surrounding small towns to participate. You just had to be tough and willing to go through the program."

Some said Pollard was too tough. Forty years later, one of the best players he ever produced still holds a grudge and refuses to talk about his experience with Pollard. Today, walking through the halls of the school, there is scant evidence of the glory years of the football program that gave Pittsfield a national reputation—only one team picture (the 1968 team that was unscored upon) in the entrance area leading to the gymnasium.

"He was very intimidating," recalled Charles Hubbard, a fullback/defensive end on three unbeaten teams. "You found out quickly in practice that it was all business with him and no messing around. We loved it in two-a-days because after the first two or three days he was hoarse from yelling. With Deek, there were no politics. If you were the best player, you'd play, whether you were a city kid or a farmer, no matter who your father was. He recognized talent and never let anyone influence who would play.

"He had a set of rules. If you didn't like it, there was the highway. A lot of good athletes in school didn't play football because they didn't want to put in the time and effort. Most players didn't like him. They hated him all week long but loved him on the night of the game. But you always respected him because you knew he knew what he was doing. He demanded perfection out of everybody. He brought out the best in a lot of people, including me."

Michael Vega, a sportswriter for the *Boston Globe*, once wrote that Pollard had a personality that "could make a hobby horse cry." But everybody agreed that Pollard was ahead of his time. He obtained scholarships for young kids who grew up on cattle and hog farms who never would have gone to college—kids like Hubbard and Donnie Snyder to Western Illinois; Tom McCartney and Kevin Lowe to Illinois; John Ruzich to Michigan State; Dave Shaw, Mark Beattie, and Ron Ghrist to Missouri; and Tom and Steven Bunting to Utah.

"He got kids to play football who might not otherwise have played football," McCartney said. "He'd take a kid who weighed 280 pounds and slim him down. He'd take a skinny kid and get him up to 170 or 180. He did things that other people didn't do—weight training, film sessions, scouting. The football field was Pollard's baby. It looked like a putting green. He built a winning program and the people loved it. There would be crowds of 2,000 in a town of 4,000 for every home game."

Pollard was the Bob Knight of his day. His double sessions and summer workouts were brutal. Marginal kids who didn't want to work hard dropped out. His mission was to find 22 kids who wanted to play and make them winners. Lowe recalls baling 1,000 bales of hay in one day, then lifting weights for two hours. Pollard was determined that nobody would hit harder than his players or be in better physical condition. Parents bought into the program—and the philosophy and the success.

"He was in the mold of [Vince] Lombardi, [Bear] Bryant, and [Woody] Hayes," Lowe said. "He wasn't the type of person you talked to about an emotional problem. But you would run through a brick wall if he told you to. A lot of kids had a love-hate relationship with him. But you did what he said and did it his way because there was no other option."

Pollard almost never became a football coach. An outstanding athlete at Roodhouse, Illinois, he enrolled at Western Illinois to play basketball for Stix Morley. When football coaches Lou Saban and Red Miller approached Pollard about playing football, Morley vetoed it. His 29–0 team, missing injured star Walt Moore, lost to Tennessee A&I and Dick Barnett for the national small-college championship.

"Barnett was too good and too big. It convinced me that basketball wasn't going to be my forte. I was a short white guy who couldn't jump," Pollard said. "So I went out for spring football."

After leaving Pittsfield after the 1971 season—"I left the best team I had, the most talent, in 1972," he said—he coached at Western Illinois, Florida State, and Oklahoma State, then went to the NFL (Giants), then to the USFL (Denver, Chicago, Arizona), then back to the NFL (Browns), back to college (Central Florida and Boston College), then to the Los Angeles/St. Louis Rams in the NFL, Syracuse, and finally to the Arizona Cardinals. He retired in 2005, closing a 40-year career in football.

"Most people think coaching and winning at Pittsfield was easy but it wasn't," he said. "The administration always was looking for a loophole to keep things in proper perspective. They were anti-football, not the community. I got tired of it so I left.

"I couldn't get permission to go to a meeting to help form the state football playoff. Seventy percent of the student body didn't go to college but we had a college curriculum. One football player failed Latin. Latin? Why is he taking Latin? What success I had, the community has as much to do with it as I did."

Murney Lazier: Mr. Do-Right

A lot of racial strife and turmoil erupted at many high schools in the Chicago area in the late 1960s and early 1970s. Racially mixed Evanston, one of the state's largest schools, experienced its share of student and parental unrest. But Murney Lazier, known as Mr. Do-Right to his black football players, never had to make excuses for his conduct.

Oh, this isn't to say there weren't some crazies who called for his ouster, as they did for basketball coach Jack Burmaster and other white coaches. But most black parents and players supported Lazier. "He treats everybody the same, like dirt," one black player said.

"The black players gave him that nickname. It came from the Dudley Do-Right cartoon," said the coach's son, Shawn, who quarterbacked the 1971 powerhouse. "We knew regardless of our talent level, starter or not, black or white, no one was above the team. If you didn't do your job or made a mistake or not perform up to expectations, you would come out of the game, regardless of position. He treated me like any other player."

"Everybody knew he was a great coach and a tough coach—but he was fair," said Emery Moorehead, who starred on Lazier's great 1971 team and went on to play at Colorado and with the Chicago Bears. "He was the best teacher I ever had. I owe my career to his teaching of fundamentals.

"His legacy was the fact that he put guys in college and the pros. But he went beyond football. He produced a lot of guys who were successful in life. He taught them to be teammates, no matter if they were black or white. He taught lessons in life. If you were part of a team and played at a certain level, you would get opportunities. He said, 'If you get your grades, I'll get you an opportunity if you want to go to college.' So many kids went to college because Lazier made a call and got them into school."

Lazier was more proud of the number of athletes he sent to college than his coaching record. He sent 160 scholarship athletes to college, or an estimated $1.1 million in financial aid. Of that number, 52 percent were blacks but they comprised only 30 percent of the team.

"In all my years, I never counted noses," he said. "I never was concerned how many blacks were playing and how many whites were playing. But someone else was counting. When those figures were made public, that took care of that."

His record spoke for itself, too. In 18 years, from 1958 to 1974, his teams lost only 17 games. He recorded a .864 (125–17–4) winning percentage, third highest in state history. He produced 13 Suburban League champions, six unbeaten teams, and suffered only four losses in a nine-year period. In an era before the state playoff was adopted, six of his teams were named mythical state champion.

"Do it right or you didn't play," Lazier said, explaining his philosophy. "Race had nothing to do with it. Kids had rules to follow, skills to learn, and procedures to follow. If they do those things, they will play. If they don't, no matter who they are, they won't play.

"In those days, race was a problem. It was in the wind at Evanston. The Vietnam War was a problem. A lot of blacks were going to war and a lot of whites were going to college. There was a lot of turmoil in the community. Some blacks tried to accuse me of racism and told the black football players to boycott the team. But they wouldn't do it. They said there was no prejudice on the team."

Not on the football team. Lazier produced some outstanding players, including nine who reached the NFL. His All-Lazier team features Moorehead, Howard Jones, Mike Kenn, Bob Pickens, Jim Purnell, Joe Stewart, Doug Redman, Carlos Matthews, and Steve Greene. But a lot of 5–8, 150-pound youngsters made up the bulk of his rosters and several of them earned All-Conference recognition over the years.

"I believed a kid was never too small to play football, that if you had a heart and good work habits, you could play," Lazier said. "I recruited small players to make up the rest of the squad, to build them around a few very good players who might get college scholarships. We had very few big players at Evanston, rarely a lineman who weighed over 200 pounds."

Lazier learned how to be competitive at an early age. He was an All-State running back at Mattoon in 1942. He earned a scholarship to the University of Illinois. After serving in the Air Force in World War II, he returned to Illinois in 1946 and found himself on the 12th team with a lot of other veterans. They practiced on the golf course. He was on the 1947 Rose Bowl squad but missed the trip because he had to undergo knee surgery.

A magna cum laude graduate in physical education, the 25-year-old Lazier went to Oregon (Illinois) High School as head football and basketball coach and athletic director. After one year, he was hired by Evanston athletic director Leo Samuelson, who was impressed with Lazier's academic accomplishments. It didn't take him long to admire his skills as a disciplinarian.

"When I was at Evanston, there were more good athletes walking the halls than on the football team," he said. "But I wanted kids who wanted to work and we had those kids. I'd be in jail for some of the things I did then.

"One day, I was going to football practice and I had a shotgun in the back seat of my car. I was going to use it for motivation. I got stopped by a policeman. 'What are you doing with a shotgun in the car?' he asked. He told me not to take it out of the car until I got to the school. Today, I'd be in jail."

Lazier was big on motivation. Every Monday, if you thought you were better than the player ahead of you, you could challenge him at practice. If you won two of three, you won the spot. You could challenge every week if you thought you were better.

"He always taught that if you were fundamentally sound, you could play," Moorehead said. "He taught me to be more determined than anyone when I blocked. Most kids don't block, he told me. They know how to be the star, to run and catch, but they don't want to block. The pros want you to block. In the pros, what he taught me about blocking fundamentals got me to the top of the tight end depth chart."

In the end, it always was about the kids. He said the team belonged to the kids, not Lazier or the parents or the school administrators. But they had to make sacrifices to be successful—no vacations, no smoking or drinking or steroids, involvement in a year-round program that might include weight lifting in the winter and lacrosse in the spring. He made a commitment to his kids and he demanded that they make a commitment to the program.

"We did everything to be sure they would win," he said. "I didn't ask them to do anything I didn't do myself. Every kid was equal. There was no inequality in the program. I wouldn't dress a kid on Saturday if I didn't think he could play in the game. And I didn't recommend a kid to a college if I didn't think he could qualify. They felt I cared about them and worked for them so they worked for me."

Bob Reade: A Wise Decision

When Bob Reade interviewed for the head coaching vacancy at Geneseo in 1962, the school board president said the selection committee had two choices—drop the football program or hire Reade. They didn't know it at the time, of course, but they couldn't have made a wiser decision.

The outlook was bleak. The team hadn't won a game in two years. The school had to forfeit all of its sophomore games the previous season because not enough players tried out. Only 16 juniors and seniors showed up for the Reade's first season. He brought up three sophomores to fill out a 19-man squad. His goal was to win two games.

"When I interviewed for the job, they took me around the town to meet people," Reade recalled. "A former school board member told me, 'When you guys try to recruit a teacher, tell him it's just a great place to live.' I never forgot that. It has been special to us."

Reade, born and raised in Monticello, Iowa, played football and baseball at Cornell College in Iowa. Later, he coached at Maquoketa, Iowa, then at Beardstown and Plano in Illinois. His basketball team at Plano once lost 42 games in a row. So he knew something about losing. When he arrived at Geneseo, he had a plan for winning.

"I had to look up Geneseo on a map," he said. "But you have to realize that the excitement of building a program is tremendous. The challenge was something I looked forward to. In a lot of ways, we built this program like private schools build their programs."

Reade inherited a youth program that former coach Ted Lawrence had founded in 1958. Now it is more than 50 years old and one of the leading developmental programs in the state. Former coach Vic Boblett, who played on four unbeaten teams under Reade, said his family moved to Geneseo so he could participate in youth football. It was a community project. Everybody supported the program.

He established a freshman and junior varsity schedule and promised every kid in town that he could play every week. To attract numbers at the junior high school level, he created 22 starters. He lured 140 kids to participate in track and field and used it as his spring practice. He had only two rules—obey the law and behave like a gentleman.

"He put structure and discipline into the system," said Bob Orsi, who starred on three unbeaten teams in the late 1960s. "He got you to believe that his system could win—Delaware wing-T, repeat, repeat, repeat, do things to perfection. He knew how to bring players together, how to mold individual egos and talent and positions. If you had an ego, he had a way to drop it very quickly. You are part of a team, not a star player, he would say."

All of the players who formed the Green Machine, a phrase coined by *Quad-City Times* sportswriter Dick Brennan in the 1960s—Orsi, Barry Pearson, Vic Boblett, Rick and Steve Penney, Todd Watson, Jim Moberg, Steve Johnson, Ray Hansen, Rich Quayle, Ronnie Campbell, Dan Alexander, Doug Arnold, Mark Skelton, John Loucks, Steve Borkgren, Ron Mock—recalled how Reade, a devout Christian, reminded him of Vince Lombardi but was unassuming and quiet and had a way about him that made you want to perform.

"He set a standard for kids," said Steve Penney, an All-State running back on teams that were 26–1 in three years. "He made it clear from the start that if you got out of line, you wouldn't play and you wouldn't dress. You weren't going to stray. His philosophy was simple: practice hard, get it down so you do it better than anyone else, then knock them off the line and run down the field. Oh, and once in a while, we'll throw a pass."

Reade emerged as one of the winningest coaches in state history. In 17 years, his teams posted a 147–19–4 record, a .876 winning percentage, second only to East St. Louis' Wirt Downing on the all-time list. In the pre-playoff era, his teams were unbeaten in 52 games. In the post-playoff era, he won state titles in 1976, 1977, and 1978. In his last seven years, his teams were 73–5–2.

He left a grand legacy. Larry Johnsen Sr. was 77–14–1 in eight years, Vic Boblett was 36–9 in four years, and Denny Diericx was 120–30 in 13 years. Current coach Larry Johnsen Jr. is 44–12 in five years.

"He never talked about winning a game. He talked about execution and doing things the way we were taught," said Wayne Strader, who starred on the unbeaten 1976 state championship team and rushed for over 3,000 yards in his three-year career.

"He would tell us to 'run like a Geneseo football player, block like a Geneseo football player, tackle like a Geneseo football player.' He didn't care what Metamora or anyone else did. We would be all right if we did what we were supposed to do. I never heard him yell once. And I never heard him swear, not once.

"His pregame speeches weren't rah-rah but he touched all of us. We moved to Geneseo in 1968 and I didn't know anything about the football program until I went to my first game. I was hooked. There was an electricity in the air, so much community support. You looked up to the players. You wanted to be one of them with a

G on the side of your helmet. They were the Green Machine and you wanted to be part of it."

Reade, who later went to Augustana College and won four Division III championships and 60 games in a row, based his philosophy on fundamentals and discipline. Football wasn't a true democracy, he said. He treated everyone fair and equal but everybody—repeat, everybody—had to do it one way, his way.

"I always worried about how well we could do what we wanted to do, if we could execute what we wanted to do as well as possible, in high school and college," he said. "I told everybody: This is the way we're going to do it. I had control for one reason—I was the head coach and they wanted to play and they'd do what we asked them to do.

"Look at the programs that are successful. You know who is in charge. Everybody buys into one system, one way of doing things. You only have 25 seconds to call a play so you can't have a board meeting first. I never believed you could play potential. I looked for the doers who did it every day.

"Of course, no one wins without great players. But good players don't always win. Don't beat yourself. Be a good enough teacher so the kids know what to do. There isn't a player on the squad who won't try to do his job if he knows his job.

"In all sports, when you talk to a loser, they complain about mistakes, turnovers, interceptions, mental errors, bad breaks. We tried to teach and coach well enough to eliminate those mistakes."

Today, Reade looks back to his roots, to his early coaching days in Iowa, 51 years ago, when he was an assistant on the only unbeaten team in school history. The experience helped him to form a philosophy that he carried throughout his career. In 16 years at Augustana, for example, only one player who played four years failed to graduate.

"We didn't know any more football than anyone else but our kids wanted to play and do what we asked," he said. "Today, it means more than Xs and Os and weight rooms and summer programs. You've got to make a kid aware that you care, that he will get good grades and become a good citizen.

"So many kids don't have structured home lives like they did in the 1950s. You must be interested in him as a person, not just his 40-yard dash time and his bench press or what he can do for you. That will get him to work hard and perform up to his ability. At Geneseo, we tried to emphasize what the kids were doing now was most important, especially in the classroom."

Gordie Gillespie:
Carrying a Big Stick

Old-timers at Joliet Catholic refer to it as "the stick." Today, it rests in the school's trophy case, a three-foot-long dowel or painter's rod that Coach Gordie Gillespie used to signal plays to his quarterback during the 1975 season. It triggered the beginning of a dynasty that has produced 13 state championships.

"I was pulling out a bush in the ground and hurt my back," Gillespie recalled. "When we scrimmaged, I would stand in the offensive huddle and call plays. I didn't want to walk back and forth so I signaled plays in with a painter's rod.

"I had my hand on certain areas of the rod to determine if we wanted to run the ball inside. If I wiggled my fingers, it was a trap play. If I spread my hand, it gave location. For pass plays, I would touch various areas like a third-base coach giving signals in baseball.

"It wasn't rocket science. At the end of the 1975 season, a referee said it was against the rules to use a mechanical device to call plays. How would I signal in plays? But we were prepared for it. Paul Brown used to run guards into the game on every play. I used hand signals like in baseball. We were one of the first teams to use offensive signals."

Mark Parker quarterbacked the 1975 squad, which Gillespie said was the best he ever coached, the first of four straight state championship teams. He still remembers the first day that Gillespie brought the stick to practice.

"He was always thinking. You could always tell, he had a look on his face, he was thinking deeply," Parker said. "He painted spots on the stick. He had tape on it, too. He took our offense aside and said when he moved his hand on this spot or that spot, it meant this play or that play. He held the stick vertically for pass plays and horizontally for running plays. A lot of people tried to figure out what he was doing."

He only confused them. In 27 years, his teams were 222–54–6, a .798 winning percentage. He won five state titles. His four state champions from 1975 to 1978 lost only once in 52 games. His last five teams from 1981 to 1985 won 55 of 60 games.

His secret? Honesty, integrity, and hard work, he said. Gillespie played for some great coaches—Ray Meyer, Forddy Anderson, Doug Mills, Wally Roettger, and Phil Brownstein—and he understood how coaches could have a tremendous impact on their athletes. One of them, Dan Sharp, has coached Joliet Catholic to six state titles in the past nine years while winning 86 percent of his games.

"I told my parents that I wanted to go into teaching and hoped someday I could make a young man feel the way he makes me feel," Sharp said about Gillespie, his coach in 1972 and 1973. "He always saw the best in you and encouraged you. He truly cared about every kid he coached, star or not. He made you feel you could do anything if you put your mind to it."

Gillespie had a gentle, easygoing presence about him. Some say he had a "Vince Lombardi statuesque" appearance on the sideline with his ever-present long coat and hat à la Tom Landry. He didn't swear but he wasn't above grabbing a player by the facemask if he was unhappy with what he was doing. A player never dared to get caught being overconfident or cocky. He was all about perfection, execution, and fundamentals.

He studied the game. He learned a lot from Scooter McLean and Red McCarthy at Lewis. McCarthy picked up his blocking schemes from Ray Eliot at Illinois in the 1940s, the same schemes that Joliet Catholic employs today. And he learned cross-bucks and fullback traps from Eliot, the plays he ran against Ohio State in 1950, which remain the basis of Joliet Catholic's offense.

"I can't open up the hood of a car and tell you anything about it," Gillespie said, "but I did want to know more about whatever sport I was coaching. I didn't want to cheat my kids. The basis of good coaching is what goes on during the week, not on Friday night or Saturday afternoon."

"He saw the pool of talent, or lack of it, and made something out of it," said John Piazza, the starting linebacker on three state championship teams who now is the mayor of Lemont. "He made the best out of 5–7 and 5–8 kids who weighed 170 and 180 pounds and played defensive line. We knew if we listened to him and did what he taught us, we would be successful."

Parker, whose father coached basketball at Joliet Township in the 1950s and early 1960s, grew up in a basketball environment. People talked about Roger Powell and Jeff Hickman. Pat Mudron and Pat Lennon were well-known football players, two of the best players that Gillespie ever produced, but their reputations didn't rival Powell and Hickman. Beginning in 1975, however, Gillespie began to change the image.

"There was a godlike respect for a man who was so highly respected and thought of in the school and beyond," Parker said. "We went to practices and saw other people from other places watching. They were there for one man. And he talked to them all the time. He was one of those individuals that everyone can respond to, no matter who you are, the last person on the bench or the star of the team. He treated everyone as if they were important. He never, ever abused his position."

Gillespie was a workaholic. He made that point to his players: "No one will outwork us," he said. Joliet Catholic's tradition isn't laced with a lot of Tom Thayers or Mike Alstotts. Instead, the program is built on the backs of hardworking, average players, few of whom earned Division I scholarships.

"You have to pay attention to detail," he told Parker as they prepared for the 1975 season. "If you want to be as good as you want to be, you can't accept less than perfection in your preparation and execution. You can't be outworked."

"Kids have to put out and work if they are going to reach any goals in athletics," Gillespie said. "You have to be intelligent and be a student of the game. Kids need to be pushed. They want to be pushed. Twenty-five percent are self-starters. The others need to be pushed. Our job is to teach the game so well that we don't have to be there. That's when you are a good coach."

Gillespie was born and raised on the Northwest Side of Chicago. In the 1940s, Chicago public school students were permitted to participate in only one sport, football or basketball. Gillespie starred on Phil Brownstein's 23–2 Kelvyn Park basketball team that won the Public League title in 1943 before losing to eventual state champion Paris in the state quarterfinals.

From then on, his resume reads like a travelogue. He played basketball at Illinois and DePaul, spent two years in the Navy, then coached basketball and baseball at Joliet Catholic and Lewis University. He never had played or coached football but, in 1953, he became frosh-soph football coach at Joliet Catholic. In 1959, he became head coach. At the same time, he was a teacher and athletic director at Lewis, then in 1976 moved to nearby St. Francis as baseball and football coach and athletic director.

After retiring at Joliet Catholic in 1985, Gillespie talked to the Chicago Cubs about introducing a universal system of teaching in their minor league system. But when general manager Larry Himes was demoted, the job fell through. In 1995, Gillespie became baseball coach at Ripon College in Wisconsin. In 2005, at age 79, he was asked to return to St. Francis to coach the baseball program.

"I have no plans to retire," he said. "I don't play golf or hunt or fish. I wouldn't know what to do. I worked 60–70 hours each week. I rarely had free time. My only day off was Sunday to spend with my family.

"At 44, I was working at two schools and coaching three sports and making $10,000. But you can't buy the experience. I wouldn't change anything. I had seven children and never missed a meal. I never regretted the fact that I stayed in private education. I'd do it all over again, the same way."

Pat Cronin:
A Damon Runyon Character

Ray Jagielski, now a judge of the circuit court of Cook County, can recount dozens of stories that turned his old high school coach into a legend. But the best knee-slapper happened when newly hired Pat Cronin came to St. Rita to conduct his first team meeting and Jagielski wondered if he was as good as advertised.

"I was a junior and we had gone 0–9 the year before," said Jagielski, a 5–9, 152-pound guard. "We had heard what he had done at De La Salle in the Chicagoland Prep League, that he had won a few titles in a row. We also had heard he was a no-nonsense guy, stern. I was very nervous and apprehensive. We didn't know what to expect."

Cronin's first speech was a masterpiece of child psychology. A confirmed bachelor who loved his beer, loved to party, and—if you believe the testimony of his closest friends—loved to chase women, Cronin also knew how to coach and how to motivate high school athletes, whether they were third-stringers or future NFL players.

"I heard some of you young men like to go out and party. Some of you young men like the ladies," Cronin told Jagielski and his teammates. "Let me give you some advice: When it comes to partying, there will be none of that. You will commit yourself to this team and to this school.

"When it comes to the young ladies, if you had a chance to go out with Ann-Margret or have a St. Rita football workout, I want you to consider what you would do very, very carefully."

There was a long pause. Then Cronin continued.

"Don't be silly," he said. "Don't make a rash decision that you will regret the rest of your life. Go out with Ann-Margret, then explain to me why you were late for practice. I'll certainly understand and then you will have to work twice as hard."

Everybody broke up in laughter. It eased the tension in the room. Cronin had a thorough understanding of what made high school athletes tick. When he walked into a room, the tall Irishman commanded attention. He took a team that was 1–20 the previous three seasons, including 0–9 in 1968, went 5–4 in 1969, produced an 11–2 Prep Bowl champion in 1970, then masterminded a mythical state championship team in 1971.

"That started the Cronin legend, when the mystique began," Jagielski said.

Mark Zavagnin, the leader of Cronin's 1978 state championship team who later played at Notre Dame, also was spellbound by Cronin's magic. And dumbfounded, too. Just when you thought you were beginning to understand him, he would demonstrate that you really didn't know him at all. But Cronin always had a method to his madness. He always was seeking to make a point.

In 1978, St. Rita was ranked No. 1 in the Chicago area in the preseason and the Mustangs played up to the hype by storming to a 42–0 halftime lead and crushing Bloom 55–0 in the season opener in Chicago Heights. The team was sharpened to a razor, double sessions for 16 days without a day off. Three-and-a-half-hour practices. Cronin knew he had the makings of a great team and he wanted to be sure it played up to expectations.

"After the game, everybody was happy and hugging, the parents and the players and the students," Zavagnin said. "On the bus ride home, everyone was having a good time. You could talk on the bus because we had won. You couldn't talk if we lost."

But the atmosphere changed quickly after the players showered in the locker room at St. Rita. Cronin came in and slammed the door.

"Gentlemen, practice tomorrow morning at 7:30 A.M.," he announced.

"We all looked at each other," Zavagnin said. "This is a joke, right? We won 55–0. No one said anything. We knew we'd go out and have fun."

Fun was a three-hour practice in full pads on Sunday morning in Marquette Park. "It was the hardest practice we ever had. He ran us for 24 minutes of power drills. I never saw so many guys throw up. Some guys didn't come to school on Monday because they were so beat up from Saturday and Sunday," Zavagnin said.

Cronin delivered his message. "Let me tell you one thing," he told his players. "You're not that good. You could be good but you're not that good yet."

"That was the kind of guy he was," Zavagnin said. "He was never satisfied. He would find something wrong even if we won 55–0. To this day, I don't think I ever met a guy who worked so hard to make his team the very best. He tried to run me off the team as a freshman because I was a little runt (5–7, 135) and couldn't win a title for him. But he made me get better."

Cronin was a character out of a Damon Runyon novel. He wouldn't win any beauty pageants. He rarely wore anything but blue or gray polyester pants. He never wore a hat except a stocking cap if it got too cold. He had an apartment at 63rd and Lawndale, not far from the school. He didn't wash dishes for months at a time. He liked beer and Early Times whiskey, cigarettes, reading books, watching films, Italian food, and women, not necessarily in that order. He once forgot that he invited another woman to a party along with his date. He never took a vacation. He didn't hunt or fish or play golf. But he liked the horses.

Most of all, Maurice Patrick Cronin was dedicated to football and devoted to his players. He had a first-class staff that included Ed Miller, Pete Hester, Jack Lord, Jim Hoffman, Woody Urchak, Ray Jagielski, Bob Craig, Ray Bugal, Jim Angsten, Bob Glascott, Tom Sola, and Bill Brady. A Vince Lombardi fan, he would sit in a lawn chair at practice and run the 28 roll, a version of the Green Bay Packers' sweep, over and over until he was satisfied that his players got it right.

Ironically, he made his reputation as a basketball player. He grew up on the Northwest Side. His boyhood friend was Fr. John Smyth, later an All-American at Notre Dame. They attended St. Genevieve grammar school together. Then Cronin went to St. Patrick, where he graduated in 1952. Later, he was inducted to the school's Hall of Fame for his basketball skills. Smyth went to DePaul Academy. After graduation, Cronin went to Benedictine College in Kansas.

"He and I were very close. We had Irish backgrounds," Fr. Smyth said. "He was a hypochondriac. He always said he was sick. But never once did I ever hear him say anything bad about anyone. Honestly, I didn't think he'd be a good football coach. I thought he was too laid back and easygoing. Then I saw him at De La Salle and St. Rita. He did a fantastic job in demanding respect from his players. His good side and his talents came out. When you had him as a friend, he was always in the corner with you."

Cronin was dedicated to football and his players. But he thrived on organized confusion. It wasn't unlike him to come in on Thursday and scrap the game plan that the staff and team had been working on all week and install a new strategy for the offense and defense.

"He was big and loud and had something on his mind that he wanted done and you had to get there," said Billy Marek, who starred on the 1970 and 1971 teams and was Wisconsin's all-time leading rusher when he graduated in 1976. "He was all about the team. He always seemed to know what was on your mind and what you were thinking. You always felt he cared about you."

Bugal recalled how Cronin would do things for people that he didn't want any recognition for. "If there were kids in trouble, athletes or nonathletes, if they couldn't pay their tuition, he'd dig into his own pocket to help them. He'd write a check, no fanfare," said Bugal, who owned a bar that Cronin often frequented.

Dennis Lick, probably the best player ever to come out of St. Rita, remembered that Cronin was a master of motivation who would use any ploy or gimmick to inspire a player or the team. "He knew how to push the right buttons," said Lick, a 6–5, 280-pound lineman who went to Wisconsin with Marek and later played for seven years with the Chicago Bears.

"You didn't know when he was telling the truth and when he wasn't," Lick said. "At a practice on the day before a game with Leo, Coach Lord showed up with a black eye. Cronin said the Leo coach had said something bad about St. Rita and Lord got into a fight. That's what he said. Later, we found out it wasn't true. But it gave us a little extra incentive to go out and win."

In fact, Lick was the object of one of Cronin's most celebrated pregame pep talks. In 1976, before a game with Mount Carmel at Gately Stadium, Cronin stood in front of his squad while Lick, a massive figure in his new Bears jacket, witnessed the scene from the back of the room.

"Those Mount Carmel people say the old man can't coach anymore, that time has passed me by, that I'm over the hill, that we aren't as good as we used to be," Cronin said. "Is that right, Dennis? Can't I coach anymore? Has the game passed me by?"

"No, Coach, you still can coach," shouted Lick, jumping up and down like a young teenager who was hearing Cronin's inspiring words for the first time. The players stormed out of the locker room and crushed a Mount Carmel team that was coached by Cronin's former assistant, Jack Lord, 41–12.

When Jim Angsten joined his staff in 1978, Cronin had stopped drinking and going to bars. His beverage of choice was 7-Up. But years of booze had taken its toll. His health was slipping on and off. He had had heart problems for years. He died on Christmas Eve in 1984.

But Angsten still remembers one of his old coach's most memorable speeches. It was in 1982 and St. Rita needed to beat powerful St. Laurence by at least six points to qualify for the state playoff.

"He would pick his spots and pick his games," said Angsten, who was defensive coordinator at St. Rita for 20 years. "It was an unbelievable speech, about kids not having a chance to play with people who care about you, about the quality of being a St. Rita kid and being able to play with other good kids."

Trailing by seven points, St. Rita rallied to win 21–7.

"That was Cronin," Angsten summed up.

Bob Shannon:
The Tradition Continues

It doesn't seem likely, given the fact that East St. Louis' football program boasts one of the longest winning traditions in state history, but Bob Shannon followed a coaching legacy built by Wirt Downing and Fred Cameron only because two other candidates didn't want the job.

"I got hired at East St. Louis Lincoln in 1971," recalled Shannon. "I found out later that East St. Louis' enrollment had increased and they needed a coach. Lincoln said they wanted to send their worst coach to East St. Louis. So they sent me, the one with the least amount of seniority, the one who didn't hang out with the others."

After four years, Shannon told Coach Cornelius Perry that he was leaving to go to graduate school. But Perry said he was retiring and wanted Shannon to stay. East St. Louis officials wanted track coach Jimmy Lewis or Lincoln's defensive coordinator Joe Simmons to succeed Perry. But Lewis didn't want to coach football and Simmons wouldn't go to East St. Louis. So Shannon got the job by default.

"They didn't expect me to keep the job very long because Simmons was supposed to come the next year," Shannon said. "But we did well and kept doing well and they kept letting me come back. Then we won our first state championship in 1979 and Simmons came over as my defensive coordinator."

Shannon became one of the most successful coaches in state history. In 20 years, his teams posted a record of 202–34, a .856 winning percentage. They won six state championships, including three in a row from 1983 to 1985, and finished second twice. In a nine-year period from 1983 to 1991, the Flyers were 115–6.

"I was aware of the tradition before I got there," he said. "It is all about winning. People on the outside only accept winning. If we didn't make the state playoff or win the state title, it was a bad year.

"But I never looked at it that way. As long as the kids gave me what they had, as long as they overachieved and never underachieved but improved, it was satisfactory. I set my own standards. People said I was working too hard, that I would burn myself out. But it wasn't work for me. My hobby was coaching football, not playing golf."

If you were a football player, growing up in East St. Louis wasn't as bad as the economy. Sure, the city was in decline. People and businesses were moving out. Street gangs, alcohol, and drugs were plentiful. But youngsters were aware of Kellen Winslow, Cleveland Crosby, and the 1974 team that finished second in the state playoff. They recognized that football was a ticket out of town.

"Growing up wasn't hard. I didn't know I didn't have a lot," said Dana Howard, who later was an All-America linebacker at Illinois. "My mother and father cared for us. We didn't have a $200,000 household but we didn't know we were poor. It was a great environment to grow up in, it taught me valuable lessons. I figured if I could survive here, I could survive anywhere."

For players like Howard, Kerry Glenn, Ronnie Cameron, Arthur Sargent, Bryan Cox, Kerwin Price, Lavent Blaylock, Chris Moore, and Alvin Jones, football was a classroom and Shannon was the teacher. All of them received a thorough education that sent most of them to college and some of them to the NFL. Even today, if they had it to do all over again, they insist they wouldn't want to grow up under any other circumstances.

"Shannon did a great job of coaching me. No coach could ever be as hard as Shannon," said Glenn, who starred on the 1979 state championship team and later played at Minnesota and for eight years in the NFL. "We had some good players who didn't want to work hard and Shannon wouldn't tolerate it. Either you liked it or you didn't. I liked it because it prepared me for life and college and the pros."

Everything about Shannon and East St. Louis football was tough. Shannon thought about football for 24 hours a day. In the summer, he would bring players into his office to watch film. Practice was two or three hours a day in 100-degree heat. And they played their home games at Parsons Field, a surface of rocks and dirt that dated to the 1920s and never failed to intimidate opponents.

"There was a mystique about it," Howard said. "It was as close to hell as they were going to get."

Shannon was intimidating, too. All of his players were scared of his wooden paddle with holes in it. When a player flunked a course or skipped a class or didn't do what he was supposed to do, like get in a fight or disrespect a teacher, Shannon would gather everyone in a circle before practice, the player would get in a three-point stance and Shannon would apply the paddle to the youngster's behind.

"I got it once for skipping class to get a haircut the day before a game," Howard said. "It was the worst thing that could happen. You didn't want to do anything to jeopardize not playing in a game. In three years, no one missed a game for disciplinary reasons. Shannon always handled it and took control of any problem with his guys. We were all like his sons."

"He was the first male role model I had. He had a big influence on my life," said Cameron, who quarterbacked the 1983 and 1984 state championship teams. "He told me, 'Take care of your family, pay the bills, and take care of your responsibilities.' That was the best advice I ever received."

Shannon had strict rules. If you didn't have grades to qualify for college, you couldn't play. If you were disrespectful to anyone in school, teacher or coach, he'd bench you, no matter who you were. That's how Cameron got his job. A senior quarterback who was supposed to be the starter in 1983 stopped coming to practice in the summer. So Shannon went to Cameron's house with a playbook.

"Start learning these. You are the quarterback," Shannon said.

"I made sure I wasn't going to miss any practices," Cameron said.

Glenn said he wouldn't have gone as far as he has in football or life if not for Shannon. "He coached great talent but many kids only wanted to smoke weed or drink beer or hang out with girls. But he looked out for his kids. You can only respect a person who wants to make a difference with kids," he said.

Shannon grew up in a time when kids listened to older people who had experience and wisdom and wouldn't intentionally lead anyone astray. Born in Port Gibson, Mississippi, he was raised in Natchez, Mississippi. His father worked in a sawmill and his mother washed dishes in historic Stanton Hall in Natchez. The second oldest of 11 children, he was the only member of his family who went to high school.

In a time before Alabama and Ole Miss began to recruit black athletes, Shannon earned a football scholarship to Tennessee State to play with Claude Humphrey, Eldridge Dickey, and Vernon Holland. He played for John Merritt, who coached Robeson's Roy Curry at Jackson State. He was drafted by the Washington Redskins and Coach Vince Lombardi but didn't make the team. Soon afterward, he heard about a job opening in East St. Louis.

"Discipline and toughness was the trademark of my program," he said. "Lombardi said you can take five plays out of any game and change the outcome. We didn't want those five plays to happen to us.

"Good athletes had to be disciplined because they came from undisciplined environments. Lincoln always got the best pure athletes. I got the second and third guy who was willing to work and wanted to prove something. Kids went to Lincoln because they could do what they wanted to do and didn't have to deal with Shannon.

"I wouldn't deal with thugs, bad kids. A kid tried to beat out Ronnie Cameron and didn't. So he turned over my car. He said I made a mistake. Later, he was sentenced to 30 years for murder. The other kids didn't want him on the team, either."

John O'Boyle:
The Seven-Degrees Solution

When John O'Boyle showed up in Stockton in the fall of 1959, all he wanted to do was coach and teach science and driver's education. Born and raised in Sturgeon Bay, Wisconsin, he saw a notice about a teacher's vacancy in Stockton and was aware that teachers in Illinois were paid more than in Wisconsin.

"It was a friendly little town, a farming community, very sports minded, very supportive of the athletic program," he recalled. "They had a good program when I came in. We had good numbers, a good work ethic. And we had a great weight-training program, tough farm boys baling hay in the summer."

There were other unique things about Stockton. Located on Route 20, it had a reputation of being a speed trap for tourists driving from Chicago to Galena. The first pound of Kraft cheese was made in Stockton in the early 1900s. McDonald's didn't arrive until a few years ago. The first football game was played in 1919. The football field, now named after O'Boyle, was built on a seven-degree incline from west to east.

"There always was a mystique that we would get into the fourth quarter going downhill," said Tim Finn, who played on two teams that finished second in the state playoff. "We'd kick off into the wind and go uphill in the third quarter so we would be going downhill in the fourth quarter. We felt it made a difference a time or two."

O'Boyle had a mystique, too. And he made a big difference. He coached for 35 years, from 1963 to 1997, and won 79 percent of his games (279–74–1). When he retired, he was the winningest coach in state history. He won state championships in 1978 and 1991 and finished second in 1975 and 1977. In a 13-year period, he lost only 13 games.

He put Stockton on the map by guiding his 1969 team to a 9–0 record in the pre-playoff era. In a showdown with powerful conference rival Dakota, Stockton rallied to win 13–7 in Week 7. The team was led by quarterbacks Joe Morgan and Jim Vanderheyden, guard/linebacker Mike Toepfer, and guard Charlie Krahmer.

"It is hard to imagine that any team would feature two offensive guards," said John Vanderheyden, a second-string guard on the 1969 powerhouse who played on teams that went 48–2 in three seasons. "But O'Boyle was a big Vince Lombardi fan. He patterned some offensive plays around the Green Bay Packers sweep, which used guards so much. The offensive guards, Toepfer and Krahmer, were a very important part of O'Boyle's scheme, pulling and trapping on nearly every play."

O'Boyle came from the Lombardi school. He didn't produce a lot of scholarship athletes but he had the ability to take average talent and get more out of them than anyone else. He never raised his voice or cursed or chastised his players. His summer program amounted to running the streets of Stockton. His best advice to his players? "Play hard, play clean, play smart," he said.

He had more superstitions than pass plays in his playbook. He wore a 1963 letter jacket to every game, a pair of penny loafers, and the same socks, shirt, and pants. Before every game, he would go to a diner on Main Street and get a cup of coffee and a candy bar and the owner would give him a stick of gum before he left. He always chewed gum on the sideline. He never tolerated profanity or poor sportsmanship from his players.

"The players joked about how difficult it was for the media to interview him while he was coaching," John Vanderheyden said. "They would ask, 'How good is your team? How does your backfield look this year?' He would say, 'I have a blond, brunette, and redhead.' He had a target on his back so he really tried not to say anything that could be used by another coach or community against him."

Jeff Eastlick, who starred on Stockton's 1978 state championship team, recalled that O'Boyle had a "professional presence" that the players bought into. He wasn't Coach or John. He always was Mr. O'Boyle, even to this day. Except when he was referred to as Big Sam.

"We used to do things in seventh and eighth grade that we shouldn't have been doing," Eastlick said. "We had a code word when someone was coming. To knock it off, we'd say Sam. But when O'Boyle came around, it was Big Sam. You could be in school or goofing around in the summer but that was the code to knock it off."

O'Boyle was all about preparation. He choreographed each play, spelling out the way things had to be done. If a player couldn't do it his way, O'Boyle would find someone who could. One year, a running back fumbled several times in the first two games and never played in the backfield for the rest of the year.

"He put marks on the field where he wanted you to put your feet," said Eastlick, who carried the ball 13 times in a row and scored the clinching touchdown in a 9–0 victory over Carlinville for the 1978 state title. "We went over it and over it. It was drudgery but what made it bearable on Friday night was he would holler the play from the sideline and the opponent knew what was coming but they couldn't stop it because we ran it so perfectly."

O'Boyle picked up the wing-T offense and 5–2 defense from his predecessor, Emery Munson, and never skipped a beat. He employed two running backs, a wingback, and a tight end. If he wanted to get fancy, he split the tight end out wide. His game plan was all about toughness, execution, precision, and discipline. He believed in grinding the clock and running the ball, not throwing it.

O'Boyle had only one assistant, Hank Ezel, who was his line coach for 22 years. They coached in an era before game films. His teams never looked at a game film. Instead, he relied on scouting reports provided by parents or friends or alumni who were assigned to scout opponents. It wasn't a perfect science but it worked.

"Looking back, we didn't realize at the time what we were accomplishing," Toepfer said. "He was the type of coach who made you better than you were. The scouts would have diagrams of plays that other teams ran. And they'd give us their tendencies. On Thursday before a game, the second team would run through the offense. He knew what to expect and he prepared us so well."

O'Boyle had a simple philosophy: score more points than the other team. He has seen the game evolve from the wing-T to the shotgun or spread offense but he preferred his style of ball control. He looked for quick kids who could block and ball carriers who didn't fumble or make mistakes. And he shunned summer and youth development programs, which are so popular today.

"A lot of times when kids start young, they are labeled a success or a failure," O'Boyle said. "But kids develop at different rates. Sometimes they are good as freshmen and not so good as seniors. Or they become better athletes as seniors. Sometimes a more mature kid levels off."

The best way to develop young players, O'Boyle insists, is to put helmets and pads on junior high school kids in the spring and teach them offense and fundamentals. "Teach the game and generate interest and enthusiasm and trigger a desire to play football. Then you don't have to worry about burnout at a young age," he said.

"I didn't think I would coach for 35 years. But I took it one year at a time and I enjoyed it. I enjoyed the challenge on Friday nights, the preparation. I enjoyed the relationship with fellow coaches and players. I never felt any pressure from parents. If it was there, I didn't feel it. The biggest pressure was self-generated by myself, to see if the kids could match the success of the kids who came before them."

Gary Korhonen: Setting a Precedent

When he was a freshman at Richards High School in Oak Lawn, Ron Pratl's football team was 2–6–1 and lost to Thornridge 62–0. It was Gary Korhonen's second season as Richards' varsity coach. It took a while—Korhonen was 28–26 in his first six years—but it was apparent that things were changing and the program was headed in a new direction.

"He scared the crap out of me when I first met him," Pratl said. "He was a disciplinarian. He had a rule. Richards didn't have lights at the time so we played on Saturday afternoon. You had to be in your house by 10 o'clock on Friday night. To be sure, he'd call your house. He wouldn't listen to anyone else. You had to get on the phone.

"On one Friday, three friends and I went to Burger King in Oak Lawn. On the way back, we got stopped by a freight train. We parked the car in the Elks Club parking lot, went through the stopped train, and ran a mile-and-a-half to be sure we would be home. I walked in my house at five minutes to 10. If you weren't home, you wouldn't dress for the game, no matter who you were."

Korhonen didn't grow up eating eggs Benedict for breakfast. He was raised on Chicago's North Side, in the Uptown neighborhood, graduated from Amundsen in 1958, and earned a football scholarship to Upper Iowa. He coached at Elkader, Iowa, for two years before landing a job at Richards when the school opened in 1965.

"My philosophy is to get up early and work hard and outwork my opponents. I'm not as smart as they are but I can try to outwork them," Korhonen said. "I did a lot of looking around and I realized that one of the most important things in coaching was to hire a staff that believes in what you believe in."

So Korhonen hired Frank Salvatori, John Rutkowski, and Bill Porter and built a dynasty in an area where everybody said it couldn't be done. When he became head coach in 1972, the program was 11–49–1 and had never had a winning season. The first thing he did was establish a weightlifting program, which was unique for that era. Some athletes ran the stairs at the old Palos Toboggan Slide and pushed cars around the school parking lot. He was convinced that strength was the name of the game, one of its most overlooked aspects.

"I have the head coaching title but it isn't all about me but about my coaching staff. Without them, I would be nothing. Nobody works for me, we all work for each other," Korhonen said. "The toughest thing to do was change the mental approach, thinking you can win every game and not just do a good job and hold the score down."

Korhonen retired after the 2007 season as the winningest coach in state history. He won 77 percent (306–91) of his games in 36 years. In his last 30 years, he had only one losing season. Since 1985, he won 10 or more games in 16 seasons. From 1985 to 1992, his teams were 87–12, including two 14–0 state championships in 1988 and 1989. From 1994 to 1998, he was 52–8. He also finished second in 2001. In 2008, he was named the National High School Coach of the Year.

To be successful, Korhonen also had to learn to recruit, a hush-hush word in the Illinois High School Association and public school systems but a reality in the Chicago area. He lost All-State fullback Kevin King to St. Laurence, which lured dozens of outstanding athletes away from Richards in the 1970s.

"I had to sell my program in the community," he said. "I saw Richards growing from 1972 to 1973 with split shifts. One of the best things that happened to us was when Shepard opened in 1975. They took half of our kids and made us concentrate on the remaining areas in our district—Oak Lawn, Chicago Ridge, and Robbins.

"It was a big step forward. It made us get into the grade schools and see more grammar school games and recruit kids who might go to Brother Rice, Marist, Mount Carmel, St. Rita, St. Laurence, or Leo. We didn't win all the battles but we got on the map and showed people what we had."

Korhonen attracted blue-collar kids, the lunch-bucket crowd, hard-nosed, hard-scrabble kids who came from Calumet Park rather than Hinsdale. They rolled up their sleeves and said "yes, sir" and "no, sir." They were rough on the edges but they were honest and willing to work hard. "They lacked finesse but please don't invite them to an alley fight," Korhonen said.

He is proud to say that he developed nearly 300 college football players, including five who reached the NFL—Joe Montgomery, Dwayne Goodrich, Jim Jones, Demetrius Smith, and Mike Jones.

Montgomery probably was Korhonen's greatest achievement. And Montgomery, who wasn't allowed to play football until he was 16 and didn't play as a freshman, never fails to credit Korhonen for helping to turn his life around and teaching him how to be successful after football.

"You have to have a work ethic," said Montgomery, who started only one game at Ohio State but played for four years in the NFL before retiring in 2006. "There is a difference between having talent and work ethic. Talent will take you only so far. What happens after sports is over? You have to have a work ethic to still make things happen, to find a way to get it done. Korhonen finds the way. No matter what field you are involved in, you have to work hard."

Montgomery came from a drug-infested society. Five of his uncles are in jail. One is a rapist, another is on Death Row. Both of his parents were teenagers. He beat the odds. He was told that he had only a 3 percent chance of getting out of Robbins. One who did was NBA star Dwyane Wade. Most kids in his neighborhood befriended the local drug dealer for false love and support. Montgomery was determined to succeed. Instead of a drug dealer, he befriended Korhonen.

"I was intimidated by him. He humbles you, like [former Ohio State coach] Woody Hayes," Montgomery said. "He told me, 'Keep your confidence.' He was relentless, a workaholic. He worked on my work ethic. When I was having trouble passing the ACT, he would help me instead of having lunch. He listed me at 6–1 and 218 pounds to impress college recruiters because if they knew I was 5–10 or 5–11, they wouldn't be interested."

He was listed at 5–11 and 235 pounds at the NFL combine when he ran 4.38, prompting the New York Giants to select him as the 49th player in the 1999 NFL draft.

"Korhonen would do everything he could to get you into college," Montgomery said. "He thought education was the base for success. He doesn't stop. That's why he is so successful. His work ethic rubs off on you. There is no way in the world I would say it was disappointing that we didn't win a state championship when I was at Richards. I have a Rose Bowl ring, a Sugar Bowl ring, and an NFC championship ring. So I'm not disappointed in the least. God is good."

Matt Senffner:
Know Your Capabilities

It took Providence's Matt Senffner a few years to learn how to become a winning football coach. But once he got the hang of it, he never let go. And Robert Cruz, who quarterbacked two 14–0 state championship teams, sensed there was something special—maybe even a little eerie—about the way Senffner went about it.

"When I was a junior, during double sessions, it was a rainy day," Cruz recalled. "We all saw this man [Senffner] walk outside and stare at the sky. Five minutes later, he told us to go outside—and it's sunny. Once we got off the field, it started to rain again.

"When he had a feeling, you went with it. In close games, he'd say 'Run this' when the traditional thinking would be 'Why would we run this?' Against Richards in the state semifinals in 1995, with seven minutes left in the third quarter, it's third-and-seven. I wanted to throw a pass. He said to run the middle trap to the fullback and we broke it for a 60-yard touchdown. It told me he could foresee things. He had a great feeling for the game. When a big decision had to be made, he made the right one."

Senffner, who attended Joliet Catholic and played football for legendary coach Gordie Gillespie, was hired at Providence Catholic in New Lenox in 1966, when the school was only five years old. He was 2–21 in his first three years and didn't produce a winning team in his first seven seasons.

"When I came, the function of football was to try to get more kids enrolled," he said. "I learned patience and perseverance. If you want to be successful, you better become a good teacher. I felt I was a good teacher in the classroom. After my first three years, the light went on. Football is all about teaching. I had to do a better job of preparing myself."

Senffner started to attend clinics. He bought a lot of books on football. He copied things that Gillespie, his old mentor, did. Later, he added some new tricks and completed his offensive philosophy by studying Illinois coach Mike White's passing game. As offensive line coach, he taught his players to be more athletic.

"You have to find yourself. You have to know exactly what your capabilities are and what your strong suits are and live with them as a coach," he said. "You also have to fill your coaching staff with good people and not be afraid to learn from them. Give them responsibilities and share information. I have learned so much football from my assistants.

"But sometimes you can get too filled with clinic talk. You have to know your personnel and learn to work with what you have. We always talk about putting our kids in position to be successful on offense and defense, not to dig holes that you can't get out of. Once we started to go toe-to-toe with everyone and our linemen developed good feet and hands and athletic skills, we could be competitive with anyone."

Competitive? How about dominate? In an 11-year period from 1994 to 2004, Senffner's teams won 139 of 151 games. From 1987 to 2004, he produced nine state championship teams, including four in a row from 1994 to 1997, and also finished second on two occasions. During one span in the 1990s, Providence won 50 games in a row. When he closed his 38-year career in 2004, he was the winningest coach in state history with a 300–114–1 record, a .724 winning percentage.

"At first, I was surprised by our success," he admitted. "You wonder if maybe it was a fluke. After we won our first state title in 1987, we didn't do anything until 1991. Then from 1994 on—well, that's when I as a coach started to realize that I could get a sense about a team. We started 14 juniors. I told the kids they can be something special. I could say it and not be cocky. The kids began to believe in themselves. That was the first of three 14–0 teams and we went on to win 50 games in a row."

Pete Bercich, a sophomore linebacker on the 1987 team, said Senffner prepared him physically and mentally to go on to Notre Dame and to play for Lou Holtz. From there, he went on to a seven-year career with the Minnesota Vikings in the NFL.

"Like Holtz, he had a way of doing things. If you didn't do it his way, it was unacceptable," Bercich said. "If guys aren't doing things right, it's either because they are coached poorly or it is allowed. Matt made it clear that not doing it right wasn't allowed. Perfection was expected. You feared the reaper. You didn't want to be the guy who got him mad or screwed up.

"He didn't pull punches or hold hands. He didn't run the kind of program where kids were allowed to be prima donnas. He wasn't interested in being your friend. He was an authority figure. He had a system, a philosophy, and a standard. And he stuck to it. He was as simple as it gets, Football 101, old Joe Paterno. He didn't want to beat you with smoking mirrors, the option, or the spread. He was just interested in imposing his will on his team. And you wanted to please him. You wanted to be one of his tough guys."

He made it clear to one and all what was expected. There was no gray area. His temper tantrums at practice were stuff of legend. He always wore a blue and white St. Mary's Nativity hat with a furry ball on top. It doesn't match the tan pants and green jacket he wears to all games. He swears a lot but tries not to. And he won't permit his players to curse. He always delivered the same pregame speech—"Pop 'em in the mouth," he said. Then he'd slam his fist into his other hand and say it again.

"He knew which buttons to push on each kid, who he could jump on and who he couldn't, who he could yell at and who he couldn't," said Patrick Doyle, who played on the 2004 state championship team with his twin brother, Ryan. "He would tell us,

'I have seven [state championship] rings. This is your team. If you want a ring, you have to work for it. If you want one, I'll coach and help you win one."

"He didn't have to grab us and take us to the weight room," said Eric Steinbach, who played on two state championship teams and currently is an All-NFL lineman with the Cleveland Browns. "We followed the older guys. We knew what we had to do to keep up the tradition. We didn't want to be on a team that didn't win. To us, winning 50 games in a row wasn't good enough."

Players also recalled that Senffner had a habit of not remembering names very well. "Hey, fuzznuts," he would say to a player whose name he had forgotten. They knew they had to do something outstanding for him to remember.

"He liked to play golf a lot. When he went golfing and had a good day, it was a good day for practice," Patrick Doyle said. "But it was a bad day for practice if he had a bad day on the golf course. He bragged that he was a pretty good golfer. How good? 'I shot 102 today,' he would say. 'Good job, coach,' we would say."

Dan Sharp: Six Titles in Nine Years

Dan Sharp was a backup end on Joliet Catholic's 1973 football team and didn't play in college. He joked that he played three positions in high school—guard, tackle, and end of the bench. Most of the time, he said, he stood next to Coach Gordie Gillespie on the sideline. Talk about a learning experience.

"That's where I got my passion to coach," Sharp recalled. "I tried to learn everything about the game from him, the mental aspect and preparation. He is unbelievable in how well he prepares his teams and staff for games and the season. I learned how to study, how to prepare my team no matter what the talent level, to put them in a position to win. He always reminded me that it is much harder to win and stay on top than it is to lose."

Since he succeeded Bob Stone in 1997, Sharp has experienced very little except winning. In 12 years, he has won 130 of 153 games, a staggering .850 winning percentage, one of the highest in state history. His teams have won six state championships. Gillespie said Sharp's 1999 and 2007 winners were as good as any of his five state champions.

"Coach Sharp models himself after Coach Gillespie, how he deals with kids on and off the field," said Mike Goolsby, an All-State linebacker on the 1999 state championship team who later played at Notre Dame. "He genuinely cares about the kids. I've played football at the highest level and sometimes coaches let their egos get in the way. But Coach Sharp truly believes in what Joliet Catholic stands for."

The oldest of five boys, Sharp played football and basketball in grade school and participated in Gillespie's "Stars for Tomorrow" park district baseball program. But he wasn't a star. He enjoyed going to football games and admiring Pat Mudron, Pat Ward, Larry McKeon, and the great Joliet Catholic teams of the 1960s.

"As a young kid, I hung around the football field. It always felt like a special brotherhood to be part of Joliet Catholic," he said. "Unless you experienced it, it is difficult to describe. The Carmelite fathers would challenge you in the classroom and help prepare you for the rest of your life.

"I'd see the Victory Tower on top of the school and I would get chills. When you walk into the gym, there is a picture of Pat Mudron, the school's only state wrestling champion. There are old trophies and pictures of the unbeaten teams of the 1960s and the state championship teams of the 1970s.

"There was great spirit. The pep rallies were a mini-version of Notre Dame. Kids would sing the fight song between classes. You knew you were someplace special, especially when they lit up the tower after winning a game and you could see the light shining over the entire downtown area. On the trip back to the school, as the bus crossed the bridge on I-80, you'd see the light and you'd have a great feeling of pride."

After graduating from Illinois Benedictine in 1978, he taught and coached at Lemont for one year, then was hired at Joliet Catholic to teach math and coach freshman football and basketball. Gillespie brought him up to the varsity in 1983. When Gillespie retired in 1985, he brought Sharp with him to College of St. Francis as his offensive coordinator.

In 1985, Sharp applied for the Joliet Catholic job with Bob Stone and Jim Boyter, who was hired and produced a state championship team in 1987. Sharp was disheartened. Young and ambitious, he thought he deserved to be head coach. But he learned that he wasn't ready. He spent seven years with his mentor, Gillespie, learning Xs and Os and how to manage a program.

"It was a blessing that I didn't get the job in 1985," Sharp said. "I had seven years to prepare and mature in my profession. After the 1992 season, I went to Minooka to see if I had it in me to be a head coach. I tried it on my own for four years. We won our first playoff game in school history with a win over Morris and got to the semifinals."

After Bob Stone resigned at Joliet Catholic in 1996—he had won 81 percent (80–19) in eight years and won a state title in 1990—Sharp didn't apply for the vacancy. But the school called. They recruited him. He was hired as head football coach and athletic director. This time, he was ready.

"He came in with his double-wing offense and tweaked it based on his personnel," Goolsby said. "He fit in perfectly with what Joliet Catholic always has done. He knows his Xs and Os. He is a football historian. He has a wealth of football knowledge."

Chris Jeske, an All-State linebacker on the 2003 and 2004 state championship teams who was the *Chicago Sun-Times* Player of the Year in 2004, said he could write a book on the lessons that Sharp taught him.

"Even as much as he strives for perfection for his team and for his kids to be successful on the field, he wants them to be even more successful in life," said Jeske, who played football at Northwestern. "To him, football is a means to a better education and a better set of values of character, discipline, teamwork, and camaraderie.

"I saw his passion every day, how he enjoyed coaching. He told me that it's tough when you face adversity but if you stay strong and lead the way, you can be an example and show what type of man you are. Man, he said, is defined by how he acts in time of adversity."

Sharp surrounded himself with a loyal and hardworking staff that believed in the same system and values that he did. Cory McLaughlin has assisted for 30 years, Dave Douglas for 25. Sharp even brought back his old boss, Gillespie, to serve as a consultant—sort of like Roy Williams bringing back Dean Smith or Bill Self bringing back Phog Allen or Nick Saban bringing back Bear Bryant or Charlie Weis bringing back Knute Rockne.

Most of all, he wanted to teach the tradition of Joliet Catholic. "It is very important that they stand on the shoulders of people who came before them. I want them to realize the responsibility of what they represent when they take the field," Sharp said.

In 1997, before he began his remarkable run of state championships, he tweaked his double-wing offense, flexing his ends to create 10 gaps for the defense to defend instead of eight. He describes it as more of a stretch offense than a spread. It features a unique combination of power, passing, option, and misdirection that utilizes all of the personnel. How effective is it? Last season, the Hilltoppers set an all-time state record by amassing 6,651 yards of total offense in 14 games.

"We're getting better at it," Sharp said, "but we still haven't played our best game yet."

Sharp said he has only two superstitions—he doesn't eat on game day and he always wears his game day hat, which was presented to him by the principal when he was hired. He admits it has begun to get a bit dingy and might have to be replaced.

But he is big on discipline. Don't do anything that will embarrass yourself, your family, the school, or the program. No drinking. No drugs. Be on time for practice, be in the weight room, and keep your grades up. He monitors grades once a week and is proud that his 2007 squad averaged 3.4 on a 4.0 scale.

"When someone did something wrong, Gordie would say, 'I'll trade you for a dog and shoot the dog.' Me? I will punch you in the Adam's apple."

"So much of my success I attribute to him. I would take a bullet for him," said Goolsby, now a corporate stockbroker in Chicago. "When someone messed up, he would put his hands on his hips, close his eyes, cock his head back, and draw a big breath. But he never swore. He got upset with kids who swore on the field. I can still see him counting to 10 to calm himself down while thinking how to handle a mistake."

Frank Lenti: The General

Simeon Rice, who played on two state championship teams at Mount Carmel, was a two-time All-American at Illinois, was a four-time All-Pro selection, and earned one Super Bowl ring during an 11-year NFL career, never will forget the first time he met Frank Lenti.

"My first reaction to him was he is a military-minded and task-oriented and very disciplined person," Rice said. "When I saw him as a freshman, he had a big stick and wore sunglasses. 'There is no way I can play for him,' I said to myself.

"He was very intimidating. Nothing but manhood came from his mouth. He was like a captain in the army, very military. But he was fair. I bought into the drill, the work ethic, the discipline, the commitment, being the best.

"I knew I wanted to be great so I bought into the passion of football that they were selling. They gave me direction. I think the reason that he is so successful is that he is able to communicate to kids in such a way that they buy into it."

Rice and others who played for Lenti, including Mike McGrew, Bart Newman, Matt Cushing, Ed Stewart, and Tony Mazurkiewicz, understood that he preached a blue-collar mentality—"us versus the world," they said—and he taught his players to play with their hearts, that size wasn't an excuse or a handicap, that winning and losing came down to skill and passion—and outworking your opponent.

Lenti, the oldest of six children, is a creature of habit. He doesn't like to change things. He consumes the same postgame meal, fried chicken, always Popeye's or KFC. He drinks a lot of milk and folds his socks the same way. He clings to the same routine year after year, team after team, practice after practice. He has run the split back veer offense for 24 years, since he picked it up from former Houston coach Bill Yeoman, the inventor of the veer, former Notre Dame coach Lou Holtz, and former NFL coach Homer Rice.

"The way we practiced in 1988 and the way they practice now is one and the same," said Newman, a lineman on the 1988 state championship team who played four years at Yale. "Coach Lenti said it doesn't matter what we do, the same offense, option right, option left, between the guards, the mind-set was if we execute, it doesn't matter if they know what is coming."

The philosophy has worked. Lenti is arguably the most successful coach in state history. In 25 years, his teams have posted a record of 284–47, a .858 winning percentage. He has won nine state championships and finished second on four occasions. During a 17-year period from 1986 to 2002, he was 209–22. In the 1990s, his teams were 122–12 with five state titles.

"If you are going to play Mount Carmel, you better bring your lunch," Lenti said. "Our kids will play hard, smart, and together. Other coaches say we generally are a hard team to beat because we are well coached and don't beat ourselves. Good self-discipline is what you do when nobody is watching.

"We set a standard. We're always raising the bar. Why have we been successful for so long? Because we are never satisfied. We want all of our kids to walk out the door saying he did the best he could."

When Lenti talks about his team being well coached, he isn't talking about himself. He is referring to a staff of well-heeled and knowledgeable assistants that has included his younger brother David, who has been his defensive coordinator since 1989; Pete Kammholz, a 24-year veteran; Tom Sulo, a 22-year veteran; Bill Nolan; and Mark Antonietti. He once had four head coaches on his staff—John Potocki, Bob Padjen, Mark Carmen, and Don Sebestyen.

"It is important to have stability on your staff," he said. "It allows for consistency. Kids feel comfortable with guys who are educating them in the classroom and on the field. They aren't assistant coaches, they are my co-coaches, my friends."

Lenti was born on Chicago's South Side and raised on 87th and Stony Island. Baseball was his sport growing up. He played third base and captained Mount Carmel's baseball team as a senior. He didn't play football. He went out as a freshman but was dubbed too small at 5 feet, 110 pounds, and was cut.

He never gave up on football, however. After graduating from Mount Carmel in 1969, he played for two years at Loyola University before the sport was dropped. He earned a bachelor's degree in history and social studies and a master's degree in the teaching of reading from Chicago State.

He coached sophomore football at St. Francis de Sales for two years, started a program for fifth and sixth graders at St. Barnabas in Beverly, served as defensive coordinator to Coach Frank Esposito at Thornton for five years, was a grad assistant to Lou Holtz at Arkansas in 1981, became Bill Barz' defensive coordinator at Mount Carmel, and then became head coach in 1984.

He once toyed with the idea of coaching in college and he has had some offers to coach at other high schools. He talked to Holtz about going to Notre Dame in 1990 and 1991. He once looked into the job at Thornridge. And he was offered the job at Evanston. But he said the time wasn't right.

"I have the job I want—great kids, great administration, great faculty, great facilities," he said. "There is no reason to be anywhere else than Mount Carmel."

A voracious reader, Lenti has a collection of more than 8,000 books. All of them aren't football-related but all are nonfiction, including many biographies. Most deal with teaching and coaching philosophies by great coaches such as Bear Bryant, Bill Walsh, and Bo Schembechler.

"Looking back, I felt I was so well prepared for college by the type of program we had at Mount Carmel—the structure of the practices, the expectations, the way coaches took us through drills, film watching, the amount of time in preparation," said Ed Stewart, who played on two state championship teams, played on two national championship teams at Nebraska, and currently is the Big 12 Conference's assistant commissioner for football and student services.

"There is a mystique that surrounds great programs, like Nebraska or Notre Dame or Michigan. At Mount Carmel, you grow up knowing there is something special there. You find out a lot when you get there. You learn what the expectations are. Coach

Lenti had high expectations for us as players but had equally high expectations for himself and his staff. Everyone felt they were working as hard if not harder than they were asking us to work."

Mike McGrew, who quarterbacked the state championship teams of 1990 and 1991, was looking for a father figure at a critical time in his life—his parents were going through a divorce—and he found him in Lenti. Born and raised in Chicago Heights, he traveled 45 minutes each morning to attend school. He emerged as one of the most successful student-athletes to come out of Mount Carmel. His backup was Donovan McNabb.

"If not for Coach Lenti, I don't know how things could have turned out," said McGrew, who later played at Northwestern, obtained a master's degree in integrated marketing communications, and currently is regional communications director for W. W. Granger Inc., an industrial supply distributor based in Lake Forest, Illinois.

"I could have ended up like some friends who ran with street gangs or got involved with drugs or dropped out of sports. I stayed focused on sports. And I was in the upper 10 percent of my class. I learned a lot about what a leader should look like. Coach Lenti comes across as a tough disciplinarian but he has a heart of gold. He really cares about his players."

Lenti has been preaching the same philosophy as long as he has been teaching the split back veer.

"What we try to teach our kids is to be responsible young adults, be the best person you can be, be the best student you can be, then be the best athlete you can be," he said.

In his acknowledgments in his 2004 book, *Rush To Judgment—The Simeon Rice Story*, Rice wrote, "To the Mount Carmel community, thanks for keeping your promise that you come to Carmel as a boy and leave as a man. That phrase could not be truer."

Frank Lenti couldn't ask for anything more.

Mount Carmel coach Frank Lenti is the most successful coach in Illinois in the past three decades. In 25 years, he has won 86 percent (284–47) of his games and produced nine state championship teams. Photo courtesy of the Illinois High School Association.

Donald "Deek" Pollard coached Pittsfield to six consecutive winning seasons from 1966 to 1971. The 1972 team also was unbeaten, establishing a state-record 64–game winning streak. Photo courtesy of Deek Pollard.

Evanston coach Murney Lazier (right) built one of the winningest programs in state history. In 18 years, he lost only 17 games. He produced six unbeaten teams, and his 1971 squad, quarterbacked by his son Shaun (left), was regarded as one of the best in state history. Photo courtesy of Shaun Lazier.

Stockton coach John O'Boyle (left) with assistants Jim Sullivan and Brad Fox as the Blackhawks beat Arcola 32–6 to win the Class 1A championship in 1991. Photo courtesy of the Illinois High School Association.

Gordie Gillespie (left) and Dan Sharp have formed one of the most successful coaching tandems in state history. Gillespie won four state titles in a row in the 1970s and added another in 1981. Sharp, his former assistant, later succeeded his old boss and has won six state titles in the past 10 years. Photo courtesy of the Illinois High School Association.

Providence's Matt Senffner retired after the 2005 season as the winningest football coach in state history. He had a 38-year record of 300–114–1, a .729 winning percentage. And he had accumulated nine state championships. Photo courtesy of the Illinois High School Association.

St. Rita coach Pat Cronin orchestrated and choreographed one of the strongest programs in the state in the 1970s. His 1970 and 1971 teams won back-to-back Prep Bowls and his 1978 squad won the state championship. His staff was deep and talented. (left to right) Tom Sola, Bob Craig, Tom Berry, Ray Jagielski, Cronin, Woody Urchak, Ray Bugal, John Pergi, and Bill Brady. Earlier, Jack Lord and Jim Hoffman also were on the staff. Photo courtesy of Ray Bugal.

East St. Louis coach Bob Shannon is hoisted on the shoulders of his players after winning the 1979 state championship. It was the first of six titles that Shannon won during his 20–year career at East St. Louis. He posted a record of 202–34, a .856 winning percentage. Photo courtesy of Bob Shannon.

Chicago Sun-Times high school sports reporter Joe Goddard presents the Team of the Year trophy to Hinsdale Central coach Harvey Dickinson and his team leaders after the 1967 season. Left to right, Ken Koranda, Bruce Elliott, Goddard, Herb Briick, Dickinson, Ken Braid, Skip Korty, and Paul Frederickson. Dickinson retired from coaching after his team completed an 8–0 season. Photo courtesy of Hinsdale Historical Society.

Gary Korhonen of Richards retired after the 2007 season as the winningest football coach in state history. He won 315 games and produced state championship teams in 1988 and 1989. Photo courtesy of Gary Korhonen.

Only Illinois High School teams to win
4 State Championships in a school year.
Watson-Swimming   Kramer-Tennis
          Dickinson-Athletic Director
Krupicka-Gymnastics   Ohl-Soccer
1975-76

Hinsdale Central football coach Harvey Dickinson produced four unbeaten teams from 1960 to 1967, including three in a row. As athletic director, he hired coaches who produced an unprecedented four state championships in 1975–1976. Left to right, Don Watson (swimming), Jay Kramer (tennis), Dickinson, Neil Krupicka (gymnastics), and Dick Ohl (soccer). Dickinson was named National Athletic Director of the Year in 1977. Photo courtesy of Diane "Dede" Dickinson Barnard.

3
The Teams

Mount Carmel 1950:
Best Team of Its Era

Tom Carey recalls how he prepared to become the quarterback of Mount Carmel's 1950 football team, acknowledged in a *Chicago Sun-Times* poll as the best in state history.

Bob McBride was the coach when Carey, an undersized but eager freshman, showed up for the first team meeting at the South Side Catholic school. McBride said the 11 toughest kids in the room would start.

"Football is a tough, physical sport," McBride told them, "but if you do the things I tell you to do, I will assure you that you won't get hurt if you get in shape and keep in shape."

Carey got the message. He joined the wrestling team to get in shape, to prove he was one of the 11 toughest kids in school. He weighed 117 pounds as a freshman and won the novice championship in the Central AAU competition. As a senior, he was 5–7 and weighed 135, even though he was listed on the football program at 175.

McBride left after two years and Mount Carmel called Terry Brennan, a 1949 Notre Dame graduate who had become a national celebrity by returning a kickoff for a touchdown against Army in 1948, but hadn't applied for the job and had no coaching experience. He was 36–6 in four years, and then was hired to serve on Frank Leahy's staff at Notre Dame as a 25-year-old.

Brennan's first team finished 5–4, losing to Johnny Lattner and Fenwick, Leo, Loyola, and Aquinas, N.Y., 40–0 in the season finale. But everybody returned in 1950. The Caravan finished 11–0, smashed DePaul 51–14 for the Catholic League championship and Public League kingpin Lane Tech 45–20 in the Prep Bowl. They scored 464 points, allowed 121, and played five games in Soldier Field.

Seven players were named All-Catholic, four were named All-State, three were named All-America, and five went to Notre Dame. Carey passed for 793 yards and 14 touchdowns, and Tim McHugh rushed for 1,198 yards, averaged 10 yards per carry, and scored 18 touchdowns. The team still holds the school single-game total offense record with 589 yards against DePaul.

"It wasn't a big team but they had very good team speed. They were strong and smart and tough," Brennan said. "Some people thought I was nuts to have Tom Carey at quarterback on offense and linebacker on defense. But he was the undefeated middleweight wrestling champion in the city and I felt sorry for his opponents. I never enjoyed four years more than my time at Mount Carmel."

The line averaged 160–165 pounds. Ted Cachey later played and was team captain at Michigan as a 175-pound offensive lineman. Fullback Dan Shannon was the biggest of all at 195 pounds. They were one of the first high school teams to adopt the revolutionary split-T offense, which Brennan picked up from Oklahoma coach Bud Wilkinson. At Brennan's suggestion, Carey spent 10 days at Oklahoma's spring practice to learn the system.

"The first thing I learned was how to read defenses, what plays worked against which defenses," Carey said. "We perfected it in 1950. The key to running it was when you break out of the huddle, set yourself, then read the defense. If you called dive in the huddle and they bring their linebackers up to form a nine-man line, how do you deal with it? We'd change the play, fake the dive, and pitch out."

"Pitch out" meant the ball was going to McHugh, arguably the greatest player in school history. As a junior, he ran behind center Dick Frasor, guards Cachey and Van Snyder, tackles Bill Walsh and Bob Dunklau, and ends Paul Matz and Paul Leoni. He left after the season because he had so many scholarship offers, was named a freshman All-American at Illinois by *Collier's* magazine, then walked off the 1952 Rose Bowl team after a disagreement and was described in a *Chicago Tribune* article as "the strangest athlete in history."

"I had a hard head. I was big on my way or the highway. I've always been that way," McHugh admitted. "But I loved my time at Mount Carmel. Terry Brennan was the best coach I ever played under and I played under George Halas, Paddy Driscoll, and Ray Eliot. I thought I was special and everybody else was just there. But after becoming involved with them, I came to realize how good the others were."

They outscored an outstanding St. George team coached by Max Burnell and led by running back Dick Fitzgerald 35–27 in Week 4. But they didn't fully begin to realize that they were something special until they smashed Leo 27–0 in Week 7 at Soldier Field. Leo was the acknowledged power on the South Side. The Lions had lost to Mount Carmel only twice in the previous 16 years. "We arrived when we beat Leo," Carey said.

Mount Carmel swept the Catholic League's South Division but the North ended up in a three-way tie and had to conduct a playoff. Faced with a two-week layoff, Brennan called Austin coach Bill Heiland, whose team had lost a coin flip to play for the Public League title. They met at Hanson Stadium and the Caravan raced to a 32–7 lead before settling for a 32–21 victory.

"Austin was unbeaten and they said they were the biggest and best team in the city," Carey said. "Brennan didn't want to win the city title with some other team saying they could have beaten us. We asked, 'What happens if we lose a practice game, then win city?' Brennan said, 'That's why we are going to play them because we don't want anyone saying we were lucky that we didn't play them.' He really loved the game."

Brennan was smart, a motivator, a technician, a strategist. Even though he was only two or three years older than his players, he was always called Coach, never Terry. He didn't socialize with his players and never invited them to his home. Some thought he was caught up in his own celebrity but he was respected by one and all.

"If you swore or did anything wrong, he would take you to Bunker Hill, a mound of dirt on the practice field, and you had to go one-on-one with him," Shannon said. "He was a boxer. You didn't fool around with him. We were so well prepared going into games, we never thought we weren't ready for an opponent."

Shannon learned discipline the hard way. One day at practice, Brennan asked Shannon to block him.

"I was a smart aleck and my elbow got high and I hit him in the side of his face," Shannon recalled.

"Do it one more time," Brennan told him.

"He whopped me and knocked me on my fanny," Shannon said. "I never, ever did that again. It was always 'Yes, sir.' There was no sass after that."

Was it the best team ever?

"Take the era into consideration. In our era, yes," Brennan said. "We didn't have 200-pound running backs or 300-pound linemen. Now kids are bigger, stronger, and faster. Could we win today? No. We didn't have a guy who weighed 200 pounds. Today, they would overpower us."

"With our will to win and our determination? Yes, we could win today," Cachey said. "We had great chemistry. We jelled, played together, and Brennan was able to bring out the best in us. But if you had all of that with 330-pound linemen—well, physically, it's hard to see how we could be competitive today. But in that era, we were the best there was."

Jack "Junior" Stephens, a defensive back on the 1950 team who went to Notre Dame on a basketball scholarship, graduated as the leading scorer in school history and also played football for Frank Leahy, said the differences go deeper than that.

"Today, people make a lot of comparisons between now and then," he said. "We grew up in World War II and the Depression. We had a lot of responsibility and not a lot was handed to us. Today, kids get too much handed to them.

"The difference between our team and now is television. We played sports. Now they play video games. They don't have the same desire as we did. Kids aren't as hungry today to play sports. Today, it's all about I, I, I rather than team, team, team."

Fenwick 1962: The Jim DiLullo Show

The Chicago Catholic League was so competitive that every school sought to gain an edge. There were no rules, just results. It was reported that one school clipped the scoring plays from its game film. Schools dispatched spies to film the practices of upcoming opponents. They even hid in the belfry at the old priory at Harlem and Division in Oak Park to observe Fenwick's workouts.

Coach John Jardine was ahead of his time. He inserted radio sets in his players' helmets. Jardine had a Dick Tracy-like wristwatch that enabled him to talk directly to quarterback John Gorman. During one game, Weber, aware of Jardine's communication to his players, installed a technological bug on the sideline in an attempt to pick up his conversation.

But nothing could stop Fenwick's 1962 team.

"It was one of the best teams I've ever been around," said Rudy Gaddini, who played under legendary Fenwick coach Tony Lawless and assisted Jardine on the 1962 squad. "Any team that goes unbeaten, no matter what level, has to be good. They were good on offense and defense."

So why aren't the Friars, who gained national attention by playing before 91,328 in the Prep Bowl in Soldier Field, ranked with St. Rita 1963 and 1971 and Evanston 1971 and Joliet Catholic 1975 and East St. Louis 1985 among the best teams in state history?

"They dominated games but even though they sent six players to Division I schools [four to Notre Dame], not as many shined in college," Gaddini said. "But they had a lot of good high school players. Only one player [246-pound lineman Jim Gatziolis] had a shot at the pros and an injury kept him out."

When Lawless retired after the 1956 season, Ralph Peterson coached for two years, leaving after Fenwick lost to Austin 20–7 in the 1958 Prep Bowl. He was succeeded by Jardine, whose 1959 team lost to Lane Tech 19–0 in the Prep Bowl. But Jardine went on to post a five-year record of 45–6–1 (a .875 winning percentage) before resigning to join Jack Mollenkopf's staff at Purdue. Later, he assisted Tommy Prothro at UCLA, then was head coach at Wisconsin from 1970 to 1977.

"Jardine was a similar make of Tony Lawless but with a lot more humor. There was levity in his discipline," said Dick Caldarazzo, a 1966 graduate who played next to Dan Dierdorf at Michigan. "Jardine probably was one of the greatest pep-talk guys I have heard. If you had a game against a weak team, he still found something about the game that would get you in tears and inspire you to tear them apart."

In 1961, Fenwick lost to Weber in the Catholic League championship game and Weber went on to beat Lane Tech in the Prep Bowl. But the Friars had plenty of talent and experience returning. They were ranked No. 1 in the state in the *Chicago Sun-Times*' preseason poll. Nobody argued the point.

"I've got the horses so I'll let them run," Jardine said.

Led by *Chicago Sun-Times* Player of the Year Jim DiLullo, Tim Wengierski, and Dan Dinello, Fenwick averaged 31.7 points and 311 yards per game. In a 10–0 season, the Friars shut out six opponents, the first five in a row, allowed only 32 points, and capped it off with a resounding 40–0 rout of Schurz in the Prep Bowl. Their closest game was a 16–0 decision over Weber in Week 3. After the season, one poll ranked Fenwick No. 6 in the nation.

There were high expectations. They trailed St. Philip 14–12 at halftime in Week 6, then rallied to win 38–14.

"We didn't go into the locker room at halftime because people were throwing bottles at us," Gatziolis recalled. "So we went into the bus and Jardine inspired us. I still get emotional today just thinking about it. We really wanted to play for Jardine and Gaddini."

DiLullo averaged 9.3 yards per carry, Wengierski 6.2, and Dinello 8.7 running behind Gatziolis, Mike Barry, Jim Selke, and Joe Marsico. In the Prep Bowl, DiLullo recorded the most spectacular performance in the history of the All-City event. The 6–1, 196-pound senior rushed 12 times for 224 yards and scored five touchdowns on runs of 4, 14, 6, 97, and 70 yards. He finished the season with 130 points.

"He was a great runner," Gaddini said. "He could have played in college [at Notre Dame]. But he had bad shoulders and he got caught in a changeover of coaches. He was a big kid who was quick and could run."

"The key to our team was you couldn't key on DiLullo," Gatziolis said. "Dinello and Wengierski could bust a long one on any play."

Gatziolis didn't want to go to Fenwick. All of his friends were going to Austin, which had beaten Fenwick in the 1959 Prep Bowl. He was too big—he weighed 177 pounds in sixth grade—to play CYO (Catholic Youth Organization) football. And he couldn't play as a freshman because he had to undergo an operation to remove a fatty tumor on his side.

Why did he choose Fenwick over Austin? His mother insisted because her son had been expelled from Resurrection grammar school twice for fighting in seventh and eighth grades. She wanted him to get more discipline. So he enrolled at Fenwick.

He hardly played football at all until his senior season. After missing his freshman year because of surgery, he missed his sophomore season because he suffered a knee injury in a collision with an automobile while playing football on the street. As a junior, he suffered an ankle injury in Week 3 and was sidelined for the remainder of the season.

He finally got his chance—and stayed healthy—as a senior. Longtime sportswriter Tommy Kouzmanoff of *Chicago's American* said Gatziolis was "one of the best offensive linemen to come out of Chicago in a long time." Jardine said Gatziolis was his most pleasant surprise.

The 6–1, 255-pound offensive tackle/middle guard impressed enough college coaches to land 45 scholarship offers. He went to Wisconsin, then transferred to Nebraska. He played briefly in the NFL, signing free-agent contracts with the Cardinals and Bears. After a series of injuries, he retired in 1973.

Jardine's staff, which included Gaddini and line coach Jack Lewis, who later coached at Immaculate Conception, drilled his players on fundamentals, as Lawless had done, and added some offensive innovations to take pressure off his running game. He taught the science of the game, not just Xs and Os.

While DiLullo, Wengierski, Dinello, and the running game earned most of the headlines, the passing game with Gorman throwing to George Vrechek, Matt Hayes, and Joe Cirrincione couldn't be overlooked. Neither could the defense, which didn't permit an opponent to penetrate its 10-yard-line in the first five games and allowed only 96.6 yards per game during the season. Gatziolis, Marsico, Gorman, and Wengierski were standouts.

"Why isn't Fenwick's 1962 team rated among the best of all time?" Gatziolis said. "Back then, they didn't dissect teams like they do today. There were no recruiting services, no Internet. I was the only one who had a shot to go to the pros and an injury kept me out. Four guys went to Notre Dame. DiLullo got hurt. The others didn't play much. Gorman was a second-stringer on Michigan State's national championship team. People measure teams by what players did after high school."

But Dan O'Brien, the legendary Fenwick coach who observed Catholic League football for seven decades, said the 1962 team was one of the best ever to come out of Chicago.

"That's a pretty good endorsement," Gatziolis said. "Imagine, if I had gone to Austin, none of this would have happened to me."

Metamora 1968: Stromberger's Gadget Play

One of Coach Marty Stromberger's hobbies was to draw up different plays and formations. He called them "gadget plays" and he often inserted them during practice sessions as a form of entertainment for his players. He rarely used them in game situations and if he did, they usually didn't work.

"One of my strengths was being innovative with Xs and Os," he said. "I was the first guy to run the inside belly series in central Illinois. Nobody could find the ball. It took a long time for the defenses to catch up with what we were doing."

As it turned out, one of Stromberger's gadget plays made a difference in the most important game of the 1968 season. It triggered Metamora's 46–34 victory over Chillicothe and propelled the Redbirds to an unbeaten season, their second in three years. Stromberger said it was the best team he ever coached. Old-timers claim it was the best team in school history, better than 1964 or 1973 or 1975 or 2007.

Metamora had lost only four games in 1963, 1964, and 1965—three of them to archrival Chillicothe. Stromberger and Chillicothe coach George Taylor were good friends. "But he was my nemesis," Stromberger said. Going into Week 5, both teams were unbeaten. Everyone agreed it was the biggest game of the year.

Chillicothe was led by 6–1, 218-pound fullback Mason Minnes, who later played at Illinois. He was named to the *Chicago Daily News'* Little All-State team that included quarterback Don Stanhouse of Du Quoin and lineman John Ruzich of Pittsfield.

"I hit Minnes as hard as I could and I just bounced off him," recalled Dick Krumholz. "I knew then that this wasn't to be like any other game."

"It was the pinnacle of the season. Everything else was a buildup," said Dick Schertz, who scored five touchdowns in the game. "The crowd was screaming constantly. People surrounded the field, three and four deep. It was the biggest crowd I saw in my high school career."

Metamora fell behind 14–0. It was the only time during the season that the defense couldn't stop an opponent. Chillicothe still led 26–24 with 30 seconds left in the first half. Stromberger decided to pull a gadget play out of his bag of tricks. It was called the double reverse pass.

"I figured we had nothing to lose at that point. We might as well do it," Stromberger said. "We ran the play and it worked and we went ahead. It put momentum on our side of the field for the first time. And we never lost it."

Quarterback Rick Hodel saw it coming. Stromberger called time-out to explain his strategy. "Let's try this," he said. The players had messed around with the play during practice but nobody thought it would be called in a critical situation against Chillicothe. It was the last play before halftime and Hodel took the snap at his own 30.

Hodel handed off to wingback Brad Belsly, who went on a sweep to his left. Krumholz lined up on the left side, faked a block, ran down the middle of the field, then angled to his right. Hodel drifted to the right. Belsly stopped and threw back to Hodel, who wound up and threw the ball as far as he could in Krumholz' direction. Krumholz caught it and ran untouched into the end zone to score the go-ahead touchdown.

"It turned the game around," Hodel said. "We took control in the second half."

"That play defined the game," Krumholz said. "We never trailed after that. Some said it was the greatest high school game they ever saw. In those days, it was all about winning the conference and going undefeated. It would have been interesting to see how far we would have gone in a state playoff."

The 1968 team came from different communities and different backgrounds. "They were very good kids but they were characters. They liked to have a good time. I was a disciplinarian. I didn't like nonsense. If you are going to get in trouble, I told them, you'll be in trouble with me," Stromberger said.

Linemen Mike Schmitt and Mike Rudolph came from Spring Bay, on the Illinois River. They were known as "the river rats." They got into so much trouble, nothing serious, that they had to be placed in different classrooms. They were two of the four starters who were caught at a drinking party prior to the 1968 season. Stromberger suspended all of them from playing in the opening game.

Rudolph was 6 feet tall and weighed 240 pounds. Schmitt was 6–0 and 225. Neither played football in college. Rudolph still limps from a bum knee. He never opted for surgery. Everybody worked. Schmitt sold vegetables, pumpkins, and Christmas trees at an open market. Others worked on farms, baling hay and tasseling corn. Some stocked groceries or worked in gas stations. They never heard of a weight room.

Rudolph and Schmitt were the hub of a defensive line that included Gordon Hahn and Jack Geick. As the offensive tackles, Rudolph and Schmitt would get upset if the running backs didn't run through the hole correctly. Schertz and Phil Blyler, the only juniors in the starting lineup, backed up the line. Later, Stromberger said Schertz was the best athlete he ever coached.

Most agreed that the key to the team's success was the coaching genius of Stromberger, Bob Lillie, and Ron Scheiber, the scouting of Chuck Leonard, and the offensive line of Schmitt, Hahn, and Rudolph at tackle, Blyler and Ken Belsly at guard, center Pat Hogan, and ends Jim Schoonover and Steve Deatherage.

"It was a team of wild horses with a bridle on them but it was all you could do to hold them," Schertz said. "Lillie came up with a team blocking scheme and no one had a good handle on it. We felt we were better prepared than anyone else and we couldn't help but think we had size and strength over everyone else in the conference."

The 1968 squad set school records by averaging 35.4 points per game and recording the widest victory margin (26.1). The Redbirds crushed Tremont 74–6 and Farmington 51–14. Only one opponent, Chillicothe, scored more than two touchdowns. They played only eight games because they couldn't find an opponent to fill an open date. Nobody wanted to make a trip to Metamora.

"After our last game in 1967 (a 20–7 loss to Normal University High), we told Stromberger that we wouldn't lose in 1968 and we didn't," Hodel said. "We were pretty confident in what we could do. We had balance on offense and an experienced line. We knew we had the makings of being really good."

The first-game suspensions sent a message that Stromberger meant business and the team had enough talent to win without four starters. The Chillicothe victory told them that, even if the defense didn't play up to its norm, the offense had enough punch to beat a good opponent. They were so good that some second-stringers received votes for All-Conference recognition because they saw more playing time than the starters.

Interestingly, not a single player earned a scholarship to a Division I college. Schertz later was inducted into Illinois State's Hall of Fame as a defensive end. The team was inducted into the Peoria Hall of Fame in 2007.

"There is a lot of talk about which team was better, the best team ever to play at Metamora," Schertz said. "Our 1968 team was the best because of Hodel's ability at quarterback, his ability to pass, and our big offensive line. That set us apart. We set the tone for what was to follow."

Schmitt, who said he didn't remember the trick play in the Chillicothe game because he was too busy blocking somebody, said after 40 years what comes to mind about the 1968 season "is hearing steel cleats on the concrete coming out of the gym, the smell of fresh-cut grass, and the noise of the crowd and the butterflies in your stomach that felt so terrible until you make the first hit and it all goes away."

St. Rita 1971: The Difference between Great and Super

How tough was Billy Marek?

Well, the 5–8, 195-pound running back with 4.7 speed who some coaches said was too short and not fast enough to play in the Big Ten played his entire junior year with a broken leg.

Marek broke a fibula during an August scrimmage but Dr. Bob Hamilton, who was characterized as "the healer" by the hundreds of high school athletes who sought his help over the years, said the injury "will hurt but won't get any worse."

He was sidelined early in the season. He reinjured his leg in a game against Mendel. And he missed the Catholic League championship game against Loyola. But he returned for the Prep Bowl and rushed 28 times for 128 yards in a 12–8 victory over Lane Tech.

He did it with a broken leg and despite the fact that Lane Tech scouts had discovered a flaw in Marek's running style.

"He tips every play," said Lane Tech assistant Pete Hester, a one-time assistant at St. Rita. "If you watch him line up, if he is running straight, his feet are staggered. If he is going to run wide, his feet are parallel. We keyed on him. We had an extra guy filling the hole when he changed his stance. But he still gained 128 yards against us."

"He is still the kid with the grin on his face," said Jim Hoffman, who was the offensive coordinator for the 1970 and 1971 Prep Bowl champions. "I never saw a better high school running back. His feet hardly ever left the ground. He had great vision."

"He was the best running back ever to play in the Catholic League," said Bob Glascott, who was the offensive line coach. "He made the difference between a great team and a super team."

Marek, by his own admission, thought football every day of the year. He endured 30 days of spring football, double and triple sessions, even during Easter break. And the team went to camp at St. Joseph's College in Rensselaer, Indiana, every year. The Chicago Bears were on one side of the room and St. Rita on the other side. They ate in the same cafeteria.

"I busted my leg in a scrimmage and (Coach Pat) Cronin said, 'You got two weeks. If you're not back, someone else will take your place.' Two weeks later, I went out there with a pad on my cast and played. It hurt like hell. Cronin would jump in front of me to see if I could make a cut. But I wanted to prove that a 5–8 kid with 4.7 speed could still get it done. I still enjoy a challenge," Marek said.

St. Rita finished with a 10–2–1 record in 1970, quite a turnabout from the 0–9 finish of 1968. Quarterback Neil Sullivan, the Prep Bowl MVP who passed for 113 yards and one touchdown and set up the other, graduated. But Marek, tackles Dennis Lick and John Rock, guards Ray Jagielski and John Killeen, halfback Sherwin Hunt, end John Hannigan, defensive back Bob Jilek, and middle guard Bob Eppenstein would return to form the nucleus of the 1971 powerhouse.

By all accounts, Coach Pat Cronin's 1971 team was one of the best of all time in Illinois. How good? Evanston coach Murney Lazier rated his 1971 squad as the best he ever produced, the best of his six unbeaten teams. But it only ranked No. 2 behind St. Rita throughout the season.

"I still get an argument from Emery Moorehead. 'We would have beat you,' he always tells me," said Lick about Moorehead, a starter on Lazier's 1971 team and a former teammate of Lick's on the Bears' 1985 Super Bowl championship team.

"Coming off our Prep Bowl victory over Lane Tech, we were ranked No. 1 from the start of the 1971 season. We had everybody back. It would have been disappointing to lose. But after we beat Morgan Park (18–12) in the Prep Bowl to finish with a 13–0 record, there was no celebrating. In fact, almost everyone was crying. We didn't play as well as we should have. Cronin said, 'You won, be happy.' But we expected perfection and we didn't perform. We were disappointed in our game."

The 1971 team featured four All-Staters—Marek, Lick, Rock, and defensive tackle Joe Norwick. Marek, Lick, and Norwick earned scholarships to Wisconsin. Others were recruited, too. Ohio State coach Woody Hayes came to see them play.

As it turned out, Lick, a massive 6–5, 275-pound tackle, was the best prospect of all. He played for seven years in the NFL. Dick Butkus, hoping to persuade him to attend Illinois, took him out to dinner. But Wisconsin had an edge because Assistant Coach Chuck McBride, a South Sider, recruited Lick for two years. Instead of staying at a hotel, he slept in a spare bedroom in the Lick house. He and Lick's father often went out for drinks. When Michigan coach Bo Schembechler came to visit, McBride opened the door.

"Lick had something you can't describe," Hoffman said. "He could put his mind into gear. He'd run the steps at St. Rita Stadium in the off-season but he never lifted weights. For such a big lineman, things were so easy for him. He was a case of mind over matter. His attitude was 'I'm better than they are. I can play in the NFL on one leg.' The Catholic League never saw a better offensive lineman."

But 1971 wasn't a piece of cake. The Catholic League was in its prime—great teams, great coaches, great players. Leo and Loyola had beaten St. Rita in 1970 and were seeking to repeat. Mendel was a powerhouse. St. Laurence was a budding power. Mount Carmel, Gordon Tech, Brother Rice, and Fenwick couldn't be taken lightly.

"We felt we had the best team," Marek said. "We didn't blow anybody away but we felt we should win the games. There was more pressure on us. People thought we should win by bigger margins. But nobody in the league gave us an inch. We struggled a lot of times. The league was tough."

The Mustangs edged Loyola 14–13 in an early season game. St. Laurence was in position to register a big upset but quarterback Bruce Strimel executed a screen pass on a fourth-and-12 play and St. Rita went on to score the winning touchdown.

In the Catholic League playoff against Mendel, Marek was injured late in the game and Mendel led 21–20 with four minutes to play. But Hoffman called for eight straight lead rushes and Marek came back to score the winning touchdown. In a rematch with Loyola, Marek couldn't play but backup Sherwin Hunt rushed for 200 yards and St. Rita won 26–8.

Then there was the "middle screen," which St. Rita employed effectively in the Morgan Park game and then executed to perfection as Marek streaked 85 yards behind a convoy of blockers to give the Mustangs an 18–6 lead with 1:15 to play. Marek also rushed 22 times for 178 yards and one touchdown. In three years, he rushed for more than 3,000 yards. As a senior, he scored 27 touchdowns.

"How talented they were. How lucky we were to coach such talent," Glascott said. "Cronin said they were so good that the staff had to be careful not to screw them up. They were the best ever. The only other team that compares to it was Mount Carmel's 1950 team."

Evanston 1971:
Even without Howard Jones

Even today, Coach Murney Lazier and the members of his unbeaten 1971 team speculate how much better they could have been if Howard Jones hadn't broken his arm in a Labor Day scrimmage and was forced to miss the entire season.

"He was the best football player I ever coached," Lazier said. "I first saw him playing eighth-grade football on a field in Evanston. He ran so fast you couldn't see him. We have film of him breaking the hole, seeing defensive backs reaching for him, and him running past them. When you see speed and talent like that, you don't see it very often."

Jones has to be included in any conversation about the best athlete in state high school history. In football, he was an All-State running back as a sophomore and senior, even though he played only 11 games. He also was a three-time state champion in the 100- and 220-yard dashes and ran on two gold-medal-winning 880-yard relay teams.

"In his first game against Hinsdale Central in 1970, he gets smacked in the face and comes out bleeding. He said to me, 'When can I get back in?' I knew I had a player," Lazier said. "He was timed in the 40-yard dash in a full football suit in 4.4 seconds and it looked like he was loafing. He ran the 220-yard dash with a bad hamstring in 20.8 seconds. He weighed 210 pounds and ran 9.5 for 100 yards and 4.35 for 40, the fastest we ever timed."

It was obvious the 1971 team was going to be very good, with or without Jones. Lazier later said it was the best team he ever coached. The Wildkits were coming off a 7–1 season in which they had lost to Hinsdale Central 28–12 in the opener. A record 14 players were named to the All-Suburban League team. Six players, including fullback Steve Greene, wingback Emery Moorehead, offensive tackle Keith Bruns, and quarterback Shawn Lazier, the coach's son, earned Division I scholarships.

After Jones' injury, Lazier shifted Kevin Keith from wingback to Jones' halfback position and moved Moorehead from end to Keith's wingback spot. The Wildkits never lost a beat. In an 8–0 season, they averaged 41.8 points while allowing 38 and registering five shutouts, the last four in a row. Most important, they avenged their earlier loss to Hinsdale Central, winning 45–24 in the opener. The pattern for the season was set.

The team, a unanimous choice of coaches and athletic directors as the best in the history of the Suburban League (1913 to 1975), and one of the two best teams in state history (with St. Rita's 1971 team), also averaged 419 yards per game and 10.7 yards per rush. All four offensive backs averaged 100 yards rushing per game. And the first-team defense was not scored upon in the last seven games.

Emery Moorehead couldn't wait to be a part of it. He grew up a block-and-a-half from the football field and would sneak under a fence to watch the varsity games on Saturday afternoon. He didn't play football until he got to high school. "I couldn't wait for the day I could play at Evanston," he said. "I remember the great players—Carlos Matthews, Kit Basler, Toby Wilt, Cornell Champion. Farrel Jones, one of the stars of the 1968 state championship basketball team, was a tight end. Howard Jones was the first player to come up to the varsity as a sophomore.

"Every year, they were undefeated. If you lost one game, you couldn't be considered a great Evanston team. There was a lot of tradition, a lot of great players and teams going back to Paddy Driscoll. When you walked through the Hall of Fame in the athletic department, there were so many legendary players. You wanted to be part of it."

Moorehead described Lazier as the best teacher he ever had. "The remarkable thing about him was he could take a 160-pound kid and put him at nose or tackle and make him think he could handle the 220-pound he was going against. He would have him psyched up and ready to play. He was a great motivator," Moorehead said.

Lazier didn't have to do much motivating in 1971. The players still recalled how the Hinsdale Central players lined up after the 1970 game and chanted, "We're No. 1, we're No. 1!" as they filed back to the locker room. And Lazier stoked their fires by pasting stories from a Hinsdale newspaper describing the Wildkits as "pot bellied, sloppy, with no hitters" to their lockers.

"We never had time to think that we had lost our best running back," said Moorehead, who later played at Colorado and on the Bears' 1985 Super Bowl championship team. "I averaged 9.8 yards per carry, Greene averaged 9.9, and Keith 6.9. I ran 65 yards on my first carry against Waukegan and never got touched.

"One of the things that Lazier did that some people didn't do was break down film and give scouting reports. He knew the tendencies of what the opposing offense and defense would do in certain situations. He knew what to expect. He called audibles, something Colorado didn't even do when I got there. He was so innovative.

"One of the biggest lessons I learned was I wasn't the best player on that team—it probably was Keith or Greene—but I learned that when you are on a great team, a lot of people get pulled along and get noticed. It was the same way in Colorado. I never was All-Big Eight but I played in the NFL for 12 years, the last 8 with the Bears."

In fact, Shawn Lazier insists the loss of Jones made Evanston an ever better team in 1971 because it forced his father to make personnel decisions that made the Wildkits multidimensional. They didn't rely on one star. They had four backs running behind a huge offensive line led by Bruns, Joe Pieper, and Gary Stajduhar.

Murney Lazier was determined to avenge the loss to Hinsdale Central. He was particularly incensed when a Hinsdale newspaper article mentioned how the Evanston quarterback lined up behind a guard on one play. Instead of preparing for the Suburban League season as he usually did, Lazier planned for the Hinsdale Central opener of 1971 as if it were Michigan–Ohio State or Oklahoma–Texas or Notre Dame–USC.

"The Friday before each game, Coach Lazier always played fight songs. He would spend Thursday night after practice decorating the locker room," said defensive end

George Bridgeforth. "He had the articles from the 1970 loss on the bulletin board. Moreover, each player had an article about Hinsdale Central and a handwritten note placed in his locker. My article featured a picture and a note about Hinsdale's outstanding halfback, Bob Hartig. I did not know the guy but I hated him so much that if I met him today, I would probably rip his head off. Murney made it clear that they did not respect us."

If that wasn't enough, Lazier installed Hinsdale Central's wishbone offense in his playbook. It was a spectacular offensive show. Hinsdale's Pete Bylsma caught nine passes for 317 yards, including touchdown receptions of 74, 88, and 59 yards. It remains the most single-game receiving yardage in state history.

But it wasn't nearly enough to thwart Evanston's attack. The Wildkits amassed 404 yards, 315 rushing. Greene scored on bursts of 39 and 42 yards. Keith scored on a 55-yard punt return and on runs of 18 and 6 yards. Moorehead scored on a 20-yarder. They built a 25–0 lead midway in the second quarter and never looked back.

"Back then, we played smash-mouth football. Cross-body blocks were legal and I was a headhunter," Bridgeforth said. "On their opening punt, it was fielded by Kevin Keith. I cross-body blocked two Hinsdale players and rolled into a third and Kevin took it in for a touchdown. But the play was called back because of a penalty. When they punted on the next play, I cross-body blocked the same three guys and Kevin took it back for a touchdown. I usually did not talk trash. But as I looked up, I said, 'Welcome to Evanston.' A lot of us didn't care if we went 0–15 as long as we beat Hinsdale."

Decatur St. Teresa, 1972: 404–6

Terry Howley knows as much about football at St. Teresa High School in Decatur as anyone you can imagine. A 1965 graduate, he served as an assistant coach for 14 years under head coaches Dick Munn, Ed Boehm, and Ralph McQuiggan. He coached on four unbeaten teams and three state champions in the 1970s.

So which St. Teresa team was the best?

Howley, Munn, Boehm, McQuiggan, current coach Scott Davis, and players of that glorious decade in the school's history agree that Munn's 1972 and 1973 pre-playoff teams were bigger, more talented, more skillful, and had more depth than Boehm's 1974 and 1975 state champions.

"I wasn't aware that the state playoff was coming [in 1974]," Munn said. "I wish we would have had a playoff in 1972 and 1973. Our 1970 [7–1–1] and 1971 [8–1] teams could have won small-school titles. And our 1972 and 1973 teams were good enough to win at a higher level in the state playoff.

"Our edge was a combination of size and speed and mystique. We weren't going to be beaten. The way we approached the game sounds cocky. Maybe we were brash and said too much. But back then, 35 years ago. I was pretty cocky. My attitude rubbed off on the kids. We changed things around from what had happened in the past. We were not going to be beaten."

But which was better, 1972 or 1973?

Munn picks 1972. They scored 404 points and allowed only 6. To this day, Munn recalls the name of the Tolono Unity player who returned a kickoff for the lone touchdown, David Hardin. And Jackie Jackson still reminds Munn that it was his fault that Hardin broke loose and prevented St. Teresa from recording an unscored-upon season.

The team boasted a trio of gifted running backs in Mark Bushell, Mike O'Connell, and Jim Ferriozi. They ran behind a massive offensive line led by tight end Jack Haskell (6–5, 230), tackle John Chizevesky (6–4, 210), and guards Dan Doyle (6–2, 225), who played at Missouri, and Bobby Norton (6–2, 220), who played at Illinois.

Munn concedes that most people, including Howley, favor 1973. It also was unstoppable, scoring 435 points while permitting only 27. Once again, Bushell, O'Connell, and Ferriozi were in the backfield. Other standouts were quarterback Mark Feldman, tight end Rick Forbes (6–3, 210), and guards Jerry Dawson (6–2, 230) and Mike Doyle, Dan's brother. Dawson, O'Connell, and Mike Doyle played at Southern Illinois.

"I say 1972 had the edge only because the 1973 team was sitting on the bench," Munn said. "When I left, 23 kids from St. Teresa were playing football in college, some at Missouri, Illinois, Air Force, Illinois State, and Southern Illinois. What set them apart was their size and speed."

Howley, who served as mayor of Decatur from 1995 to 2003, recalls that St. Teresa was so dominant in 1972 and 1973 that rivals in the Okaw Valley wanted to toss them out of the conference. Because Munn didn't want to run up the score, the second-stringers had more playing time than the starters. In the final game of the 1973 season, with St. Teresa beating Mount Zion 70–0 in the fourth quarter, Munn put linemen in the backfield and running backs in the line—and they still scored a touchdown.

"In those days, you had to play so many quarters to letter on the varsity," Howley recalled. "Munn was told that no senior had played enough time to letter in the first nine games because they had sat out the second half. So he would have to make an exception that year."

The 1973 team didn't produce any Division I players but boasted four high school All-Americans. And it played an extra game, beating larger-city rival Decatur Eisenhower 25–7 at Pickett Field in the season opener. Scott Davis was a two-way starter on the Eisenhower team.

"I knew about the St. Teresa program growing up," Davis said. "I had friends in junior high school who went to St. Teresa while I went to Eisenhower. The best teams that St. Teresa ever had were my friends in 1971, 1972, and 1973. Unfortunately, there was no state playoff at that time."

Craig Bundy, now the football coach at Bradley-Bourbonnais, started on the 1972 and 1973 teams and he claims that, while neither team was ever tested, the 1972 team was more dominating. Opponents rarely crossed midfield. They beat Tolono

Unity 55–6, the only touchdown they allowed in nine games, and Bundy, a free safety, had four interceptions in a 32–0 victory over Decatur Lakeview. The Lakeview quarterback was Gary Schultz, a three-time national punt, pass, and kick champion who had converted a field goal in every game.

Bundy didn't play football until his junior year at St. Teresa. He preferred basketball and baseball. He had grown up going to Decatur High School basketball games at historic Kintner Gym. Bundy's father went to Decatur but his mother steered him to St. Teresa. There was no debate over the issue.

"All my friends were football players. When I was a freshman, we turned the corner in football and got real good," Bundy said. "So I went out as a junior. Munn was my freshman and junior varsity basketball coach so I knew what I was getting into. It looked like fun. I played on two unbeaten teams."

So did Mark Bushell, who described Munn as "a Bob Knight kind of guy, a brilliant strategist." And he said the 1972 team was "the best collection of guys I played with." Mike Boyd was the quarterback, O'Connell was the leading rusher and three-time city scoring leader, while Bushell was the leading receiver from his running back position.

"In 1973, we didn't have as many outstanding athletes as 1972 and we weren't as big, as strong, or as fast," Bushell said. "The feeling was we wished we could play more games and see how good we were, maybe schedule a team from Chicago. But the season was what it was. We didn't think about a state playoff. My brother Marty played on some great teams with great athletes. But were they as good as we were? It makes for good conversation."

"You'd have a hard time finding a better team than 1972," O'Connell said. "People said we were like a college team playing against high school teams. No one came close to us. We won 60–0 and 77–0. Our offensive line was huge and everyone was fast. Everyone lived for Friday nights, crowds of 6,500, and the school enrollment was under 400. I felt the 1972 team could play in any class."

Joliet Catholic 1975: Gordie's Best Team

Tom Thayer, an All-State lineman who played on two state championship teams at Joliet Catholic and later played at Notre Dame and on the Chicago Bears' 1985 Super Bowl championship team, remembers when he wasn't even the best player in his own house.

"As a sophomore, every major college coach in the country was in our living room because my brother Rick, who was two years older than me, was the star of the 1975 and 1976 teams. Everybody was recruiting him," Tom said.

Rick Thayer, a fullback, decided to attend Miami University in Florida. After one season, however, he transferred to Hillsdale, Michigan. As a junior in high school, Rick had been described as "the next Larry Csonka," a comparison to the Buffalo Bills' All-Pro fullback. But it didn't work out. Nobody was more disappointed than his younger brother.

"I had more of a chance to succeed after seeing what my brother went through," Tom said. "It was disappointing for me, given his high school success. But I learned from his experience. The whole experience of being a running back and being away from home created a different experience for him. Notre Dame gave me an opportunity to succeed."

So did Joliet Catholic. In those days, kids wanted to play football for Coach Gordie Gillespie and play in Joliet Memorial Stadium. "As a kid in grade school and as a freshman, my goal was to play under the lights on Friday night in front of a big crowd," Tom said.

Under Gillespie's guidance, Joliet Catholic was becoming a dynasty. He produced several outstanding teams and players in the pre-playoff era. He had unbeaten teams in 1965 and 1967. He lost only once in 1966, 1972, and 1973. The teams featured Larry McKeon, now head coach at Naperville North, Jim Warsaw, Rich Hucek, Tom Gullickson, Bob Barney, Bob Steinke, and Mike Condon.

But the Hilltoppers climbed to the top of the mountain in 1975. Led by fullback Rick Thayer, quarterback Mark Parker, running backs Chris Rink and Dave Benigni, linebacker Roger Hewlett, offensive linemen Tony Tomich, Jim Trizna, and Bill Draznik, and defensive linemen Jeff Simon and Mike Carberry, they swept through a 13-game schedule and crushed Springfield Griffin 34–14 for the school's first state football championship.

Joliet Catholic scored 434 points while allowing only 80. In the nine-game regular season, the defense permitted only five touchdowns and no opponent got closer than 20 points. The offensive line averaged 220 pounds, big for that time. Benigni rushed for 1,026 yards, Thayer ran for 903, and Parker passed for 1,237.

"It was my best team," said Gillespie, who was to produce four more state championship teams in the next six years. "We had size, a great quarterback in Parker, an outstanding offense, and a defense that was just as good. We had no weaknesses."

With the introduction of the state playoff in 1974, traditionally strong high school programs from Joliet Catholic to East St. Louis to Geneseo to Mount Carmel had an opportunity to demonstrate how good they were against the best competition in the state.

"One of the things that is difficult for people to understand is that it was difficult to go beyond a successful season before the playoff system came into being," Parker said. "They had successful teams at Joliet Catholic in the 1950s and 1960s but they never had a chance to play for a state title. Now we did. It was a magical time, so new to us."

Gillespie's 1974 squad had started 0–3, then won seven in a row before losing to Barrington 28–20 in the quarterfinals of the first state playoff. With so many returning lettermen, however, there were great expectations for 1975. Even so, the playoff format was so new—only conference champions qualified at the time—that there were no guarantees and everybody just kept their fingers crossed.

"You didn't know if you had a chance to do something," Parker said. "We just hoped to make the playoff. I didn't think we could win. I asked myself, 'Are we good enough?' We didn't have great speed on offense or defense. But we were looking forward to finally playing together as seniors."

A strike of Joliet's public school teachers was settled before Joliet Catholic trounced Joliet Central 34–0 in the season opener. Even after one-sided victories over Bolingbrook (36–8), Joliet East (44–0), Joliet West (40–6), Romeoville (52–0), and Argo (48–6), the Hilltoppers weren't sure how good they were—until they smashed Marian Catholic and star running back Greg Damiani 38–8 in Week 7.

"We felt good about things after that," Parker said.

In their last regular-season game, they fell behind Lockport when Kip Carmen scored on a 47-yard run. But they rallied to win 28–8.

In the quarterfinals, top-ranked Joliet Catholic was pitted against second-rated Hillcrest. It wasn't settled until the last play of the game. Joliet Catholic led 20–14 and Hillcrest fumbled on fourth down at the goal line. Joliet Catholic took a safety in the last 20 seconds to win 20–16.

The state final wasn't taxing. Springfield Griffin led early 7–0 but Joliet Catholic scored 34 points in a row—three on touchdowns by Rick Thayer. The Hilltoppers controlled the game, amassing 337 yards to Griffin's 128 and 24 first downs to 11. Benigni rushed for 72 yards, Thayer 65. Parker passed for 72.

Leading 18–7 at halftime, Joliet Catholic seized momentum in the third quarter as Trizna kicked off and Ben Mutz recovered a loose ball on Griffin's 32. Five plays later, Thayer scored, Parker passed for a two-point conversion, and Griffin never recovered.

"They are the greatest and deserve to be called the greatest," Gillespie said of his team afterward.

Springfield Griffin coach George Fleischli didn't argue the point. "This is the best football team we have met by far. Their movement didn't hurt us. They just overpowered us. We were outmanned," he said.

Gillespie, always the historian, related the experience to his basketball-playing days at Kelvyn Park in 1943, when his team won the Chicago Public League championship in Chicago Stadium before a huge crowd and qualified for the Sweet Sixteen.

"A city team had never won a game Downstate," he said. "We won a game [Kewanee 45–30], then drew Paris, which went on to win the state title. The game was tied with four minutes to go but our two best players fouled out. I couldn't dribble down the floor. They pressured us and we lost by 11.

"That's the same kind of feeling I had in 1975. Pinch me. What am I doing here? It was the same feeling I had when DePaul played Kentucky's Wonder Five in Chicago Stadium and I was guarding Wah Wah Jones. You don't ever forget experiences like that—the awe of playing for a state championship, great athletes. Gee, we won. It was so hard to imagine."

Geneseo 1976: The Green Machine

Trying to determine which Geneseo football team was best of all is tantamount to asking UCLA coach John Wooden to single out his best basketball team or Joe Paterno to pick the best of his Penn State football teams. To avoid any controversy, when asked to pick his best team, Bob Reade said, "I haven't coached it yet and probably never will."

"I never compared teams or players," said Reade, who produced eight unbeaten teams and three state champions in his 17-year career. "All of them played different schedules against different teams. It isn't fair to compare. Some teams would have had trouble being undefeated in another year. There were some teams that nobody could have touched. It's too bad some people couldn't see the Penney/Pearson teams of the 1960s, before the state playoff began."

From 1966 to 1970, Reade coached five straight unbeaten teams that fashioned a 52-game unbeaten streak. The only blemish was a 7–7 tie with Princeton in 1968. He also produced an 8–0–2 team in 1973, the year before the state playoff was introduced. His 1974 team lost 3–0 in the second round to a West Chicago team that went on to win the state championship.

"When the playoff began, I set a goal that we would be state champion early," Reade said. "I owed it to the teams of the past to be state champion. They would have won if they had a playoff. And I wanted to prove that our streak wasn't a fluke."

Football has been king in Geneseo since anyone can remember. Coach Henry Bogue produced an unbeaten, unscored-upon team in 1928. Fritz Humbert was the star of the team, a town legend who later played at Illinois and with the Chicago Bears.

Ted Lawrence coached an unbeaten conference champion in 1959. Old-timers remember playing against Mendota's Bill Brown. Steve Penney and Barry Pearson starred on the 1966 and 1967 unbeaten teams. In 1967, they were tagged as the "touchdown twins" as Penney scored 21 touchdowns, Pearson 20.

But what about the 1969 team with Bob Orsi, Rick Penney, and Vic Boblett? Or the 1970 powerhouse that featured Rick Penney, Doug Arnold, Jerry Hart, Tommy Nelson, Jim Gray, and Steve Klemmer? In their big game against Ottawa, which attracted a crowd of 13,000, the Green Machine prevailed 42–6. Both teams were ranked No. 1 in their classes by the *Illinois Prep Sports Special* newspaper.

"It was the era of the Green Machine," said Pearson, who later played at Northwestern and spent five years in the NFL. "The game is different now. We had mythical state champions, no playoff. You think you are pretty damn good but you'd like to test yourself. We would have liked to play bigger schools like Moline or Rock Island, like we did in basketball. It would have meant something to see if we were that good. We thought so. We felt we were invincible."

But Reade's 1976 team accomplished things that no other did. Even Reade said it was special because it went 13–0 and won the school's first state championship. Running back Wayne Strader, perhaps the best player in school history, was the leader. And the Maple Leafs beat Metamora, another traditional power, 20–12 for the state title. Metamora was the defending state champion, was ranked No. 1 in the state, and had won 30 games in a row and 42 of its last 44. Geneseo had lost only 19 games in the previous 15 years.

"We focused on it. We promised ourselves and the team, 'We're going to be state champions,'" Reade said. "I challenged the seniors. 'This is your last chance,' I said in 1974, when we got to the quarterfinals. Then we got to the semifinals in 1975. But 1976 was their time."

Strader, who was born in Summersville, West Virginia, where his father and grandfather worked in the coal mines, moved to Geneseo in 1968, and settled in a farmhouse about 15 miles outside of town. He rode an old 10-speed bicycle to work out in the summer. Dirt poor, the closest house was a mile and a half down the road. He played youth football for three years and quickly realized that football was his calling.

"I went to my first game in 1968 and I was hooked," he said. "There was an electricity about the football program, a lot of community support. People looked up to the football players. I wanted to be one of them with a G on the side of my helmet. I wanted to try to do something to make the community proud of what I was doing."

In 1976, Strader made everybody proud. He had rushed for 1,404 yards in 1975 as Geneseo finished 10–2, losing to Geneva in the state semifinals. Strader and Ed Ryan were the only returnees with much experience. They had high expectations but others picked Geneseo to finish third in the conference behind Rochelle and Princeton.

"We were as good as we were because senior Jon Peterson stepped up at quarterback and safety, played those positions as well as they had been played, and also ran the wing-T," Strader said. "As a junior, Peterson didn't play. Four guys tried out for quarterback and Peterson elevated his game. He couldn't get the ball to me fast enough so he developed a hop step to get to the outside belly."

Geneseo registered four shutouts in the regular season and allowed only two touchdowns in three other games. They won two shootouts, 35–32 over Macomb in Week 3 and 35–22 over Kewanee in Week 9. In the state playoff, the Green Machine overpowered Providence 34–6, Lisle 35–6, and Sycamore 25–6 before meeting Metamora in the final.

Macomb was led by Phil Bradley, who later played at Missouri. They surprised Geneseo with a shotgun offense in the second half and led 32–28 with 1:30 to play. Strader scored with 40 seconds remaining. Bradley threw a pass into the end zone on the last play but the ball was knocked away to preserve the victory.

"Too much was made of what I did," said Strader, who rushed for 1,055 yards as a sophomore, 1,404 as a junior, and 2,013 yards and 33 touchdowns as a senior. In the state playoff, he set an all-time record by rushing for 861 yards in four games, including 188 in the final game.

To Strader, it was memorable for several reasons. On the opening kickoff, he thought he had broken away but a defender hooked a finger in Strader's jersey. He broke away on a punt return but Ryan got in his way and he was run down from behind at the 12. He attempted to pass on an option play, fumbled, and Metamora's Doug Neff recovered and ran 72 yards to score.

In the second quarter, the 6–3, 205-pound Strader was hit in the chest, fumbled, had the wind knocked out of him, and was forced to sit out the rest of the first half. Cold, he took a hot shower and trainers put blankets over him. At halftime, someone suggested he should be taken to a hospital but his father said his son wasn't going anywhere.

In the second half, Strader returned and rushed 23 times for 161 yards and two touchdowns, a 36-yarder in the third quarter to force a tie at 12 and a two-yard plunge with 1:05 left for the game-winner. In the last two periods, Geneseo rushed 28 times for 180 yards.

Geneseo drove 89 yards in 13 plays only to see Strader fumble at Metamora's 11 with 4:18 to play. But on fourth-and-seven from its 24, a bad snap on a punt was fumbled and recovered by Brian Westemeyer at the 8. Strader scored three plays later.

Geneseo's defense was keyed by 221-pound tackle Dennis Brooks, Westemeyer, Shawn Hart, Strader, Ryan, and Chris Ford.

"I remember thinking as we walked on the field in street clothes before the game and talking about the guys who came before us, that we were playing for guys who wore green and gold before us," Strader said. "We were pretty stinking good and had salty dogs up front who would get after you. It was a great thing to finally bring home an official state title and validate what had been said about Geneseo in the past.

"I was a football hero. I dated the homecoming queen and the prom queen. No kid ever had a better life in high school than I did."

East St. Louis 1985: Shannon's Best Team

In 1978, after East St. Louis was overwhelmed by eventual state champion St. Rita 48–12 in the quarterfinals of the Class 5A playoff, Flyer coach Bob Shannon was asked what he had learned.

"What good was," he said.

Shannon returned to East St. Louis and vowed never to repeat that humbling and embarrassing experience.

"We got ready to play against those kinds of teams," he said. "We weren't strong enough or tough enough to play against them."

The following year, Shannon guided his team to its first state championship. In 1983, his team shut out nine opponents in 13 games en route to another state title. The Flyers won again in 1984 but the 1985 squad was the best of all, the best of Shannon's six state champions, one of the best teams in state history. Shannon's teams won 44 games in a row from 1983 to 1986.

"The rap on inner-city teams over the years is they have a lot of talent and speed but they underachieve," Shannon said. "We always wanted our opponents to be surprised by how well disciplined we were, how hard we played, how well we executed, how well we played."

It all came together in 1985. East St. Louis capped its third unbeaten season in a row with a 46–0 rout of Brother Rice, which had defeated two Chicago Catholic League rivals to reach the final. Along the way, the Flyers crushed Danville 44–0, Lockport 58–12, Sandburg 13–0, and Buffalo Grove 33–7 to dominate the Class 6A playoff and earn *USA Today*'s rating as the No. 1 high school team in the nation.

"We played them tough until the last three minutes of the first half and trailed 19–0 at halftime. Then they got away from us," Brother Rice coach Tom Mitchell said. "After scouting them and watching them on film, we never told our kids how good they were."

Curiously, in his 1992 book on Shannon, *The Right Kind of Heroes*, Kevin Horrigan, former sports editor of the *St. Louis Post-Dispatch*, dwells on the 1990 and 1991 seasons but fails to mention the 1985 team.

Ronnie Cameron, who quarterbacked East St. Louis to the 1983 and 1984 state titles, had graduated. But Kerwin Price stepped in and the high-powered offense, which included running backs Michael Cox and Marvin Lampkin and wide receivers Arthur Sargent and Cortez Robinson, never skipped a beat. On defense, Sargent, Bryan Cox, Antonio King, Greg Lockhart, and Anthony Buckner stood out.

The 1985 state final was one of the most one-sided games in playoff history. East St. Louis was so dominant. The Flyers rushed for 338 yards and passed for 175. Michael Cox rushed for 194 yards and one touchdown, Kerwin Price threw four touchdown passes and Cortez Robinson caught four passes for 109 yards and one TD.

Shannon said Sargent, a 6–2, 195-pounder who scored the first two touchdowns of the 1985 state final on a 33-yard pass reception and a 70-yard interception return, was the best player he ever coached. An outstanding athlete, Sargent set a national record in the 330-meter low hurdles. He played split end for the first time as a senior and scored 20 touchdowns.

Lampkin was a rarity, a sophomore starter at a three-year school. His mother instilled discipline in her son at an early age and prevented him from being influenced by crime and drugs and the gangs that had begun to infiltrate the community, the Vice Lords and the Black Gangster Disciples. He followed his junior high school coach to East St. Louis Lincoln, but left for East St. Louis after only one practice.

"I grew up with East St. Louis. I knew I wanted to be a Flyer," he said. "I knew about the tradition—Fred Cameron, Cornelius Perry, Alvin Jones, Victor Scott, Kellen Winslow. My idol was Terry Hill, who played on the 1978 team. He wore No. 22, the only jersey ever retired at East St. Louis.

"People talked about the 1974 team that started the dynasty and set the stage for what was to come. East Side was like a pro team. I'd go to Parsons Field and I was in awe when I watched them warm up. They were always a well-disciplined team in the midst of a city that had a lot of crime. You never heard anything about football players getting into trouble. There was always a sense of how we would win, not if we would win."

In 1985, Lampkin was so young he wasn't sure what he was getting into. He knew the team had great talent but didn't realize the magnitude of the talent until two weeks into two-a-days. By then, it was obvious.

"The talent level was awesome at every position. And the team leadership stood out. Bryan Cox wouldn't tolerate anyone messing around," Lampkin said. "Everybody was committed to the four Ps—planning, preparation, practice, performance. The team executed at the highest level in all four areas. In the state final [46–0 over Brother Rice], we put it all together and showed how talented the team was."

Shannon expected to field a strong team in 1985—and it could have been even better. James Harris, who later played for the Los Angeles Rams, was supposed to be the junior quarterback on the 1985 squad. At 6–4 and 210 pounds, Harris was a superior athlete with a bazooka-like arm.

"But he listened to kids on the street," Shannon said. "I told him, 'James, you have to show up for weight training.' But he didn't come. In the summer, I told him that he could be our tight end but not our quarterback. I didn't know who the quarterback would be at the time but I knew it wouldn't be him because he had denied me."

In the end, Harris enrolled at East St. Louis Lincoln and played on a state championship basketball team with LaPhonso Ellis as a senior in 1987. Shannon moved Kerwin Price, the team's leading rusher in 1984, from running back to quarterback. In his first game, he threw four touchdown passes as East St. Louis smashed Lincoln 61–7. The Flyers intercepted Harris four times and chased him all over Parsons Field.

"Harris could have been the best athlete I ever coached," Shannon said. "But he thought the rules didn't apply to him. He was the kind of guy you never want to be forced to use because he will cause a breakdown in your discipline."

Today, Harris admits he made a mistake. However, he claims he transferred to Lincoln because Shannon insisted that he remove an earring that he always wore. Harris refused to comply with Shannon's demand.

"When I got to college, it became clearer to me," Harris told a *Chicago Sun-Times* reporter. "He was right about the earring. I don't have any animosity toward Coach Shannon. In fact, I regret having to transfer. I think I could have done a lot better if I had stayed at East St. Louis. I would have acquired better quarterbacking skills. At Lincoln, I became a basketball player, which wasn't my first love. I always wanted to be a quarterback. But my pride got in my way."

Even without Harris, the 1985 team was so good that it punted only 10 times in 14 games. The Flyers scored 671 points in 14 games, averaging 47.9 per game. Lampkin, who rushed for 1,000 yards, went to Iowa. Bryan Cox, who later played in the NFL, was the defensive leader. The secondary, led by Sargent, had a stable of 4.5 runners. In one playoff game, the Flyers intercepted the first two passes and returned them for touchdowns.

Bryan Cox said Shannon had a dramatic effect on everybody who came through his program. "He is one of the most honest people I've ever met. Sometimes he would be too honest and it could hurt your feelings. But that honesty was what helped a lot of people in his program to go on and be successful," he told *Sports Illustrated*.

"The key was knowing how to deal with good players, not being afraid to discipline your stars. You can't just praise them," Shannon said. "I want them to be a leader in college and the NFL and the city. You can't come back and be high and tell kids what you did when you were here. I want them to come back and be a role model. I expressed tough love to them and it worked well."

Mount Carmel 1988: "No Super Stars"

It isn't accurate to say that Mount Carmel's football tradition began when Bart Newman arrived in 1985. But it is reasonable to acknowledge that Newman had everything to do with the emergence of the Frank Lenti era at the South Side school. Not a bad label for a kid who wasn't into sports and admitted he chose to enroll as an afterthought.

Born and raised in Oak Forest, Newman planned to follow most of his close friends who were going to Marist, where his older brother went. He played football for the Oak Forest Raiders but didn't take sports very seriously. He was into academics. But after one visit to Mount Carmel, he said he was hooked.

"I decided to check it out," Newman said. "I talked to Lenti. I was really impressed. He talked about football for five minutes, then the rest of the time he talked academics. What appealed to me, even though it was an all-boys school, I was meeting a lot of different people from different suburbs and parts of the city."

Newman got into football. He grew two inches between his sophomore and junior years and became a 6–1, 230-pound guard and the leader of the 1988 state championship team. It was Lenti's first state champion and, in his view, the best of his nine state championship teams. It triggered a string of four state champions in a row that won 53 of 56 games.

"When I got there, Lenti was a young coach who was taking over for Bill Barz, who had won a state title in 1980," Newman said. "We talked about 1980 and talked about building the tradition and winning consistently. We knew early that we had a special class, that we could do something. The rallying cry was to build it [tradition] back up."

It was a work in progress. The 1986 team won 13 in a row before losing to Wheaton North and *Chicago Sun-Times* Player of the Year Kent Graham 34–14 in the state final. The 1987 team went 10–3, losing to East St. Louis 21–7 in the semifinals.

But 1988 had a different feel to it. There weren't any superstars on the roster, no one who attracted so much as an invitation to visit a major Division I school. The team was filled with Bart Newmans and Dan Millers and Nairobi Allens and Warren Cushingberrys and Steve Rauschs—smart, quick, aggressive, relentless, unflappable.

"I did think they were a team that could win a state title," Lenti said. "There were no egos. All they cared about was being successful together. They had great chemistry. It was a great bunch to coach. One of our mottos was: It isn't how big you are, it's how big you play. Only one team in the state playoff was smaller than us."

But Newman said there were high expectations among the players. "I vividly remember our disappointing loss to East St. Louis. After classes on Monday, a corps of juniors got together in the weight room. We started to work out for the next season. We knew with what was coming back that we had a good team. We knew we were good enough to be state champion," he said.

The 1988 squad scored 341 points and allowed only 79. The Caravan permitted more than one touchdown in only one game. In the last three games of the state playoff, they eliminated three unbeaten teams—Homewood-Flossmoor (H-F, 13–12), St. Rita (18–7), and East St. Louis (21–7). All four were ranked nationally by *USA Today*, the first time Illinois had so many teams represented.

H-F was the key game. At the time, H-F was rated No. 1 in the state and Mount Carmel was No. 2. It was a cold, rainy day in November and Mount Carmel trailed 12–0 at halftime before a crowd of 10,000 at Gately Stadium.

"But nobody panicked," Newman recalled. "They punted with three minutes to play. We got the ball at our eight. Ten seniors and one junior looked around in the huddle. There was calmness. We knew what we had to do. Even on the drive, we had a 15-yard penalty that we had to overcome."

Mount Carmel drove to H-F's two. Then Lenti called time-out with 20 seconds remaining. He called two plays. On the first, Nairobi Allen attempted to leap over the defensive line and was stopped at the half-yard line. With two seconds left, Dan Miller took a snap on an option run/pass play and flipped a pass to flanker Mike Griffin. A defender tipped the ball into the air but tight end Mark Norville slipped underneath it and caught the ball while lying on his back for the game-winner.

The offensive leaders were Miller, who completed 101 of 174 passes for 1,452 yards and 7 touchdowns; Allen, who rushed for 894 yards and scored 14 touchdowns; and Norville, who caught 44 passes for 731 yards and 7 touchdowns. Defensively, linebacker Matt Yeager was the leading tackler with 101.

Newman and Norville were All-State selections and joined tackles Lloyd Acklin, Allen, Miller, strong safety Mike Pippin, center Steve Rausch, running back Ed Stewart, Yeager, and tackle Tom Zoretic on the All-Catholic team.

In the final against East St. Louis, which had won three consecutive state titles in 1983, 1984, and 1985 and was runner-up in 1987, Mount Carmel prevailed 21–7. The offense, sparked by Allen and Miller, amassed 418 yards to East St. Louis' 268. The defense limited the Flyers to 102 yards rushing.

When it was over, Newman had started more games in a varsity jersey (41) than anyone in school history. He considered walking on at Purdue. But he conceded he was too short for big-time football. He visited four Ivy League schools. Having graduated 20th in a class of 250 with an ACT score of 29, he knew he could attend any one of them. He chose Yale, becoming the ninth Mount Carmel football player to choose the prestigious school. He played football for four years. Today, he is an independent financial adviser and owns his own company on the trading floor of the Chicago Board of Trade.

"Looking back, I take a lot of pride, our class and the classes around us, that we helped to be a part of a group that got the ball rolling again," Newman said. "In the 1990s, winning was expected. But not in the 1980s. Now I feel a small part of what has happened—the new campus, new buildings, the revitalized neighborhood, the new science building, baseball field, athletic building. The school has survived and now it is thriving."

Wheaton Warrenville South 1998: Best Offense Ever?

When asked to choose the best team he coached in his 22-year career at Wheaton Warrenville South, John Thorne found himself between a rock and a hard place.

"The team that should have been ranked best was 1992, which was ranked No. 7 in the nation. The 1998 team was ranked No. 13 in the nation and wasn't even ranked No. 1 in the Chicago area because Mount Carmel was rated No. 1," Thorne said.

"We had three dynamite teams that didn't win state titles. And we had some teams that won state titles that were great overachievers. One team I will remember more is my first team in 1980 that was 5–4. Every team had something special about it. The opportunity to coach your own son [Jeff in 1988 and 1989] is something every father should be able to do."

But 1998 gets the nod. It was perhaps the most prolific offensive team in state history. The Tigers swept through a 14–0 season by averaging 43.9 points per game, capping it off with a 42–14 rout of Barrington for the Class 6A championship. They had a running clock in seven games. The defense recorded four shutouts and permitted only two opponents to score more than two touchdowns.

The individual statistics were mind-boggling. Quarterback Jon Beutjer passed for 3,946 yards and set a national record with 60 touchdowns. In the state final, he passed for 490 yards and six touchdowns. Wide receiver Jon Schweighardt caught 94 passes for 1,572 yards and 26 touchdowns. Wide receiver Eric McGoey caught 60 for 1,274 yards and 21 touchdowns. Running back Corrice Burns rushed for 1,354 yards and 18 touchdowns.

Offensively and defensively, it was the most productive team in state history—43.9 points per game, 85 touchdowns, 5,892 total yards, 615 first downs, 56 takeaways. Beutjer completed 65 percent of his passes and had an incomprehensible quarterback rating of 210.7. Nick Duffy was credited with 131 tackles.

It all began after the 1997 season, after Wheaton Warrenville South had lost to Lockport in the first round of the playoff. Thorne cited a lack of senior leadership and off-the-field problems for the disappointing 6–4 finish.

He called Beutjer, Schweighardt, Duffy, and linebacker Brendan Ferrari to a meeting. He told the four juniors that they probably would be his captains for 1998. To a man, they promised Thorne that he would have no problems with the senior class. With that assurance, Thorne knew it would be a special group.

"It was the first time I ever heard that from a group of high school kids," said Ron Muhitch, then the defensive coordinator.

During the summer, Thorne decided to switch to a spread offense with a single running back. Why? His team had done well running the option, but now he had a 6–5, 180-pound quarterback who was getting beat up on option plays and didn't read the option very well but was a great thrower. He also realized he had some great receivers.

At a clinic, Thorne heard a coach from Northern Arizona explain why a single back and four receiver offense was the best in football. It caught his attention. He discussed the offense with his staff and began toying with the idea. "Do we have the right personnel to do it?" he wondered.

He tested his plan during 7-on-7 games in the summer. Normally, they'd play 23 games. But Thorne scheduled 42. After 22 games, he felt the offense wouldn't work. "We were terrible," he said. Then, after about 25 games, the players began to grasp the concept. It began to make sense to them. The receivers learned how to find green grass and Beutjer was finding different receivers. All the pieces of the puzzle began to fit together.

"I didn't dream we would be able to do so many things," Thorne said. "Our linemen had great feet. They weren't big but they were able to block and protect Beutjer. We put in 1-, 2-, and 3-step passes. We also went to the shotgun. The defense got the ball back so many times. The game that was most impressive was when we beat Naperville North 42–6. They had three NFL players. And we had a running clock."

Beutjer never knew anything except winning. As a ball boy for Wheaton Central teams from fifth to eighth grades, he was on the field for the state championship games in 1990, 1991, 1992, 1995, and 1996. He saw a lot of good teams and great players. All he could dream about was being the starting quarterback and leading his team to the state title. "I never knew the program when it was struggling," he said.

Thorne's new spread offense, which featured four or five receivers on every snap, gave Beutjer the freedom to change the play on the field at any time. His job was to get the ball in the hands of his receivers—Schweighardt, McGoey, Jerome Collins, or Brian Whitkanack.

"It's a quarterback's dream to change a play at any time," Beutjer said. "I always had the freedom to do it. It was one of the reasons we were so successful. If the defense had double or single coverage, we would make them pay for playing that defense."

Beutjer loved to call the fade pass, a vertical route in which he threw to the sideline. He and Schweighardt, who grew up a block away from each other, practiced it for hours in Beutjer's front yard while they were growing up.

"We always pretended that we had to throw the fade to win the state championship game," Beutjer said. "We did it twice in the state final against Barrington. It's a route you want to run when the defensive back is in press coverage, in the receiver's face. The receiver wants to get by him and go vertical. You want to throw the ball to the sideline so he runs away from the defender. It's hard to intercept. You throw it high and to the area and trust the receiver to separate himself from the defensive back and go after it."

Schweighardt, who was a state champion in the intermediate hurdles, turned 89-fade into a defensive coordinator's nightmare. "Schweighardt is the best receiver who ever came out of this school. He did more at the end of a Beutjer pass than anyone. He could take a slant pattern and turn it into an 80-yard touchdown run. He also could lay out and dive for a ball like he had done it forever," Muhitch said.

The defense, anchored by Duffy, Ferrari, Pat Crosby, and Erik Aister, was effective but overshadowed by the offense. And despite the success of the passing game, the outcome of any game rarely came down to a big catch or a big play. In fact, perhaps the most competitive game of the season was decided by the running game.

"We were behind 26–14 in the first half against Naperville Central in the state quarterfinals. It was the only time we had a serious thought that we might lose," Schweighardt said.

"I still recall how Thorne adjusted at halftime. They had a three-man front and dropped eight players into pass coverage. There were no open lanes, nowhere to throw the ball against a four-deep zone. Everything was covered. So we started to run the ball with Burns and beat them 40–26. We shut them out in the second half."

Later, Schweighardt played on a Big Ten championship team at Northwestern and went to the Rose Bowl. But it wasn't the same as it was in 1998 at Wheaton Warrenville South.

"I have more memories with the high school kids I grew up with," Schweighardt said. "They were closer relationships. It was the same with Coach Thorne. You don't have a close, fatherly relationship with your college coach. Coach Thorne started a tradition. He wanted you to be part of something. People wanted to belong to it. They wanted to wear that jersey on Friday. They were proud to wear it."

Joliet Catholic 1999: "They Had It All"

When you've won six state championships in nine years, how do you determine which one was best? The one that set a state record for total offense? The one that sent seven players to Division I schools? The one that had three 1,000-yard rushers? The one that was compared to Gordie Gillespie's 1975 powerhouse?

"You could debate which Joliet Catholic team was best, 1975 or 1999 or 2004 or 2007," said Nick Clancy, the leader of the 2007 squad. "But we had a chip on our shoulder. We hadn't won a state title since 2004. We lost to Mount Carmel in the opener, then dominated the rest of the season. We set a total offense record. We weren't cocky or arrogant. We wanted our play to do our talking, not our mouths. We knew what we had as a team."

But Dan Sharp singles out his 1999 squad, his first state champion. They had a lot to prove. In 1998, they had been humiliated by Marmion Military 13–7 in the second round and came back to beat Hubbard in the Prep Bowl to complete a 10–4 season. In the season opener, the Hilltoppers scored a 10–7 upset at Gately Stadium over a Mount Carmel team that was ranked among the top 10 in the nation.

"When we beat Mount Carmel, we knew we had something special," said Mike Goolsby, who keyed the defense with Mike Maloney and Pat McShane. "We got the ball rolling again. We put the school and the program back where it should have been. It was our first state championship since 1990. Our class and that team put Joliet Catholic back on the map in football in this state. We revitalized the program."

The 1999 Hilltoppers went 14–0 and scored 596 points while allowing 164. They rushed for 300 yards per game. They ousted traditional powers Morris and Geneseo in the state quarterfinals and semifinals, then crushed another traditional power, Metamora, 48–13 for the championship. Joe Van Tassel rushed for 1,481 yards, averaged eight yards per carry, and scored 26 touchdowns and 227 points.

"They had it all, offense and defense," Sharp said. "It was my first championship and that's always special. We had only 28 freshmen when I got there and they were the seniors on the 1999 team. They stuck together and worked hard. You could see the progression. They set a standard for other teams to follow."

Goolsby, an All-State linebacker who later played at Notre Dame, said there were several players on the team who really stepped up their games from their junior to senior years. They were the remnants of a program that had lost four in a row to Mount Carmel, including 45–0 in 1997 and 21–10 in 1998.

For example, Ryan Ruettiger didn't play at all as a junior and emerged as an All-Conference cornerback in 1999. Guard Matt Troha also didn't play as a junior. Joe Van Tassel had a breakout season at running back, eclipsing some of Mike Alstott's school records.

It also marked the varsity debut of Jeremy Russell "J. R." Zwierzynski, whom Sharp singled out as the best player he has coached. He was brought up to the varsity for the playoffs as a freshman and he scored a touchdown in the Prep Bowl victory over Hubbard. As a sophomore, he split time with Justin Kinsella. They alternated every other series and Zwierzynski finished with 13 touchdowns and 539 yards, Kinsella 12 touchdowns and 577 yards.

"It was a fun year," Zwierzynski said. "It was a good learning experience for me. It gave me leadership skills. I got eased into it rather than being tossed into the fire. There wasn't as much pressure on me. I wasn't the go-to guy. Joe Van Tassel was the go-to guy. I was being groomed for the following year."

In 2000, Zwierzynski was the conference MVP while rushing for 2,073 yards and scoring 29 touchdowns as Joliet Catholic beat Metamora for the state title for the second year in a row to complete a 14–0 season. His signature play was a spectacular

78-yard scoring run with a minute to play that lifted the Hilltoppers past Pontiac 28–20 in the semifinals.

"When we won state in 1999, I won with older guys that I didn't hang around with much," J. R. said. "But 2000 was with my good friends. It made it more special. Me and Chris Gruber in the backfield, Mike Kolodziej at tight end, guys I played with as freshmen on the sophomore team. We hung out a lot at the bowling alley on Jefferson."

In 2001, he repeated as conference MVP, rushed for 2,340 yards, averaged 9.7 yards per carry, scored 39 touchdowns, and scored 260 points as Joliet Catholic filled some holes in the offensive line, recovered from an opening loss to Mount Carmel, and went on to win a third state title in a row by holding off Morris 27–20.

But the season was best remembered for the Hilltoppers' dramatic 56–50 victory over Riverside-Brookfield (R-B) in the quarterfinals. Zwierzynski carried 42 times for 312 yards and five touchdowns and Joliet Catholic rushed for 538 yards and 34 first downs. But R-B quarterback Tim Brasic, running Coach Otto Zeman's exciting five-wide-and-let-it-fly spread offense, completed 24 of 49 passes for 575 yards and seven touchdowns.

"We ran every down and they passed every down. It was a shootout," Zwierzynski recalled. "They were on our two-yard line at the end and going for the lead. But Chris Minarich knocked down a pass on fourth-and-goal to win the game for us. It was the most intense game we ever played. It all came down to one play."

Unfortunately, J. R.'s post–high school career wasn't as successful. He finished with 89 touchdowns and 5,070 yards rushing in his career. He surpassed all of Mike Alstott's school records. The target of a whirlwind recruiting campaign, he chose Penn State. He was swept off his feet by the aura of legendary coach Joe Paterno. But his love affair didn't last very long.

"I was red-shirted as a freshman and switched to linebacker as a sophomore," he said. "I struggled with the changeover from offense to defense. I was there for three years on special teams. I got stuck behind two All-Americans. I felt Coach Paterno lost confidence in me. I struggled to regain confidence in myself."

In his fourth year, he got a chance to earn a starting spot as a running back when the starter was injured. But he tweaked his knee. All of a sudden, he was a backup. The younger players began to see more playing time. Zwierzynski was lost in the shuffle. He graduated with a degree in business management, then decided to transfer to Western Illinois, where he was named offensive newcomer of the year in the Gateway Conference as a tight end in his fifth year.

"I felt bad for J. R. There were a lot of places he could have played where he would have fit in," Sharp said. "He just didn't get an opportunity. I would have loved to have him stay on the offensive side of the ball. He could have been a good fullback in the Big Ten, like Mike Alstott."

"Those three years at Joliet Catholic were the best years of my life so far," Zwierzynski said. "You don't have as much responsibility in high school, you just played football. There weren't as much politics as there were in college. It was more fun. It was great fun to play with your friends, people you grew up with and live with and stay in contact with for the rest of your life. Me and Gruber, Minarich, Kolodziej, and Jake Jaworski are still close. We go out on most weekends."

Providence 2001:
Senffner's Best Handiwork

Perhaps it was fate that drew them all together. They took different paths but they all ended up at Providence Catholic in New Lenox. Coach Matt Senffner had produced six state championship teams from 1987 to 1997. But when they enrolled in the fall of 1998, they had no idea that as seniors they would emerge as the best team in school history.

Mike Budde and Jim Berthold grew up in Homer Glen and played for the Homer Stallions. All of their friends, including Kevin Parker and Mike Howlett, played with the Stallions. They wanted to keep playing football together. Providence coaches came to see them play. They were drawn to the school for many reasons.

Berthold's cousin, Scott Peters, played on the 1996 and 1997 state championship teams. He had nothing but good things to say about the school. They got sideline passes for the games and met players in the locker room. Eric Steinbach, now an NFL standout, was a 6–7, 235-pound lineman who towered over everyone. He was bigger than life. They were awestruck in his presence.

Budde came to Providence as a wide receiver. But when he tossed a ball to freshman quarterback coach Mike Uremovich, the coach immediately recommended the youngster to Dave Ernst, the offensive coordinator on the varsity level. Truth be told, Budde really enrolled at Providence to play baseball. Later, he earned a baseball scholarship to Eastern Illinois.

Mike Mentz grew up in Oak Forest and played for the Oak Forest Raiders. He thought about attending Mount Carmel. But after going to an open house at the school on Chicago's South Side, he determined it was too far away. He felt Joliet Catholic, another option, also was too far away. After one year at Oak Forest, he transferred to Providence.

"I had been interested in going to Providence in eighth grade," Mentz said. "I knew they had a good football program and I knew they had good running backs. 'You can be the next Justin Ruggio or Louis Medina,' I said to myself. 'Why can't I help bring a state championship to Providence like they did?' I wanted to be a part of it."

It wasn't an easy transition. As an eighth grader, Mentz' team had gone 10–0 and beaten the Homer Stallions, New Lenox Mustangs, and Mokena Burros, all feeder programs for Providence. Budde, Berthold, and their friends didn't like getting their butts kicked by an outsider from Oak Forest. When Mentz arrived as a sophomore, he wondered if he would be accepted.

"I had an adjustment to make," he said. "I knew they had a starting running back [Howlett]. I knew I had to stake my claim in trying to win a starting spot. I wanted my play to speak for myself. I didn't want to talk trash. It was like starting a new job, trying to get acclimated to new surroundings and new teammates. I just had to go out there and prove that I could play."

Mentz was just what the doctor ordered. As freshmen, the class of 2001 started slowly. They were 4–5 and, according to Berthold, not that good. They lost to St. Rita 40–6. And they lost to Mount Carmel.

"We didn't play as a team, even in practice," Berthold said. "There were a lot of cliques, kids who played for the Stallions, Hornets, Mustangs, and Pioneers. Kids wore their old team jackets. It was like separate teams. The coaches said that was enough. We knew we had talent but we didn't play as a team. And we knew we couldn't win if we didn't start to play as a team."

All of that began to change in their sophomore year. Mentz fit right in. In his first game against Bishop McNamara, he stiff-armed a defender and broke away on a 40-yard touchdown run. They went 8–1 and started to feel good about themselves.

As juniors, Mentz, linebackers Rory Steinbach and Mike Eggert, and offensive lineman Brian Lydigsen made an immediate impact in 2000. Budde was backup quarterback. Berthold backed up Mentz and at fullback. Matt Rogers, a 6–5, 267-pound offensive lineman who would become the only Division I recruit in the class, also was a backup.

One thing didn't change, however. Providence lost to Mount Carmel 38–12 for the state championship. It marked the fifth time in the past three years that Providence had lost to Mount Carmel, dating to the 28–3 loss to the Caravan in the 1998 state final that snapped Providence's string of four state championships in a row.

The loss to Mount Carmel was especially painful to Mentz, who was stuffed at the line of scrimmage in his first carry, then broke a 67-yarder but was caught from behind by Chad Dickinson. He grabbed Mentz' left ankle and landed on Mentz' right ankle, resulting in a sprain that forced Mentz to watch the remainder of the game from the sideline.

"Remember this game for next year," Budde said.

"We had gone to Providence with hopes of winning at least one state title, if not more," Mentz said. "We knew they had won four in a row in the 1990s. Rory Steinbach's brother had three championship rings. We didn't want to be the class that graduated with no state titles and not beat Mount Carmel while we were there."

Joliet Catholic, with J. R. Zwierzynski, was the preseason favorite in 2001, on its way to a third state title in a row. In the annual Green-and-White scrimmage, the defense shut out the offense 3–0. "I don't know if we have a really good defense or a really bad offense," said Senffner, who handpicked Steinbach, Eggert, Lydigsen, and defensive lineman Chris Markelz as the team leaders.

The Celtics opened on a bittersweet note. They looked sluggish in a 23–8 victory over Leo and doubts arose about how good they were. In Week 2, however, after Budde was injured and replaced by Nick Stanton, Mentz rushed 37 times for 252 yards and three touchdowns in a 21–7 victory over a Bolingbrook team that reached the state semifinals.

"When you talk about 2001, the game that comes to mind above all others is St. Rita in Week 4. We won 28–7. It was the game after 9/11, a very emotional game," Berthold said. "I recall saying a prayer with the team before the game. One of my best friends, Mike Sisti, who was injured and couldn't play, gave me an American flag bandana to wear under my helmet. I wore it for every game afterward."

But the game everyone remembers was Week 7—Providence 10, Mount Carmel 7. The Caravan, which had soundly beaten Joliet Catholic 35–21 in Week 2, was ranked No. 1 in the state and No. 5 in the nation, according to *USA Today*. It was the biggest game of the year, played in front of television cameras and an overflow crowd at Gately Stadium.

Senffner installed an unorthodox spread offense for the game. In the last three minutes of the first half, Matt Gross kicked a 30-yard field goal and Budde threw a 50-yard pass to Bobby Peplowski, setting up Howlett's 10-yard touchdown run with 13 seconds left to give Providence a 10–0 lead.

In the fourth quarter, Providence was nursing a three-point lead when Budde was intercepted. With one second to play, Mount Carmel's Kelly Karlen, who had missed a 33-yard field goal earlier, missed a 30-yarder wide left. Budde couldn't bear to look.

"It was the hardest hitting game I ever played in," Berthold said. "Niall Campbell, Mount Carmel's middle linebacker, was a headhunter. Mentz and I had a hard time finding holes. We played every play like it was our last. Nothing happened until Budde hit that pass to Peplowski. That was the biggest play of the game, the game-turner."

The victory moved Providence to No. 2 in the state and a berth among the top 20 in the national poll. The Celtics claimed the No. 1 spot when Naperville Central lost to Downers Grove South in the Class 8A final, a few hours after Providence trounced Richards 41–0 for the Class 6A crown.

But first the Celtics had to get past Loyola in Week 9. Both teams were 8–0 and the Catholic League Blue title was at stake. Loyola had beaten Mount Carmel the week after Providence. The Celtics prevailed 23–20 as Loyola missed a tying field goal in the closing seconds, as Mount Carmel had done earlier. The difference was Gross' field goal with one second left in the first half. It was set up by Budde's 33-yard screen pass to Mentz to the three.

Providence was tested only once in the playoff, outlasting Decatur MacArthur 34–28 in the second round. Mentz and Berthold each scored twice but MacArthur tied at 28 with five minutes to play. Berthold busted a 65-yarder to the 10 and Howlett scored from the 2 for the game-winner.

In the final, Providence scored three times in the second quarter, stormed to a 27–0 halftime lead, and coasted to a 41–0 victory as Mentz rushed for 135 yards and two touchdowns and Berthold rushed for 109 yards and two touchdowns.

Mentz finished with 1,972 yards and 24 touchdowns, Berthold rushed for 802 yards, Budde passed for 1,289 yards and 16 touchdowns, and Peplowski caught 34 passes for 776 yards and eight touchdowns. Senffner said the defense, anchored by

Steinbach, Eggert, Markelz, lineman Derrick Knapczyk, and backs Mark Reiter and Matt Gannon was "hands down" the best he ever had.

"We were a good team. But were we the best? I never heard that Coach Senffner said we were the best," Berthold said. "That means something. It sends shivers down my spine, even today. We played against teams that had a lot of Division I players. But we didn't play like they were the only ones there. I didn't have a problem throwing my 6–2, 185-pound body into a 370-pound lineman to make room for Mentz."

It's all smiles after the 1998 Class 6A championship game as (left to right) wide receiver Jon Schweighardt, quarterback Jon Beutjer, and Coach John Thorne celebrate Wheaton Warrenville South's 42–14 victory over Barrington. Photo courtesy of the Illinois High School Association.

Providence running back Mike Mentz (left) and quarterback Mike Budde are all smiles after leading the Celtics past Bloomington 33–7 in the semifinals of the Class 6A playoff in 2001. Described as "the best team I ever coached" by Matt Senffner, they went on to trounce Richards 41–0 for the state title. Photo courtesy of Mike Mentz.

Running back Michael Cox was one reason why East St. Louis coach Bob Shannon described his 1985 state championship team as the best he ever produced—and one of the best in state history. Photo courtesy of the Illinois High School Association.

4
The Games

Glenbrook North 19,
East St. Louis 13 (OT): 1974

To this day, there are confusing twists to Glenbrook North's dramatic 19–13 overtime victory over East St. Louis in the championship game of the 1974 Class 5A playoff that haven't been explained to everybody's satisfaction and continue to leave others shaking their heads in disbelief.

For example, even players who were there wonder if the Western Union telegram that Glenbrook North coach Harold Samorian read during halftime really was sent by Chicago mayor Richard J. Daley. Or was it just another inspirational ploy by Coach Sam?

"All Chicagoland is pulling for you to bring home the state championship. Ignore the underdog rating. In our book you are the best. Borrow from West Point their slogan 'When the going gets tough, the tough get going.' Good luck. Richard J. Daley, Mayor."

Jack Moller, the Spartans' All-State linebacker, wasn't sure it was for real. "I thought it was a hoax, a gimmick he was using to jack us up. I never saw the telegram until a few years later when it appeared in a newspaper article. I guess it really was for real," he said.

Even the very last play of the game was fodder for debate. The official play-by-play reported that Glenbrook North's Rick Voight intercepted East St. Louis quarterback Maurice Tolson's fourth-down pass at the goal line. But the intended receiver, Kellen Winslow, thought Moller had "stuck his hand in and tipped the ball."

In fact, defensive back Brian Edwards picked it off. It was the same Brian Edwards who had charged up from his deep position in the secondary to tackle Evanston's Brian Rosinski short of the goal line on a two-point conversion attempt, preserving Glenbrook North's 7–6 victory in the playoff opener.

"On fourth down, East St. Louis had a great wide receiver in Eugene Byrd, who went to Michigan State. He was the primary target," Edwards recalled. "Barry Marks and Steve Potysman were covering him. I looked in my area. I could see [Tolson] was looking for Winslow. When he threw it, I went for the ball. I hit it with my right hand and it went straight up in the air. All I could think of was Winslow was 6–5 and I was 5–10. I caught it and Winslow fell on top of me.

"The game was over. I couldn't believe it just happened. It went from 'Oh my God, where is my receiver?' to 'Catch the ball' to 'I can't believe we have won.' Someone grabbed the ball. I don't have it. I would love to know where it is. It was on the ground and I went to get it but we started to celebrate and someone took it and ran off with it. It's probably on eBay right now."

It was the most improbable and stereotypical game of all, a state championship between all-white Glenbrook North and all-black East St. Louis, the rich kids from the North Shore pitted against the poor, hardscrabble ruffians who lived by the Big Muddy.

Some said the fate of the Illinois High School Association's newest postseason event was at stake. If so, they agreed, the outcome saved the state playoff.

Samorian evaluated East St. Louis' talent, examined the scouting reports, and determined that the Flyers "should have been 50 points better than us." East St. Louis sent three players to the NFL. Glenbrook North sent three players to Harvard. East St. Louis crushed Naperville Central 35–0 in the quarterfinals and Chicago Catholic League power Gordon Tech 46–0 in the semifinals. When the *Chicago Tribune* listed pre-playoff favorites, Glenbrook North wasn't one of them.

Glenbrook North was coming off a 7–2 season, having lost to Deerfield in the final game for the conference title. There were high expectations for 1974. Samorian determined he had good team speed, very intelligent players, and a good defense headed by Moller, an All-State candidate at middle linebacker. He brought up sophomore running back Greg Woodsum, shifted Bill Rogan from fullback to guard to team with Gary Rockoff, and installed Don Broadbridge at quarterback. Broadbridge had started as a third-stringer on the freshman B squad.

"We knew the state playoff was coming. That provided motivation," Samorian said. "That was the year we had to play three conference teams twice. We knew only the conference champion would go to state. We broke down the season into three sections—preseason, conference, and state playoff. We can't get in unless we win the conference. The kids bought into it."

"We were thinking playoff but we didn't think we could be state champion," Moller said. "Schools like St. Laurence were dominant, quite a bit better than us. East St. Louis and Evanston had an aura. Year in and year out, they were the best. At the time, the Suburban League was the dominant conference. We were in the Central Suburban, which wasn't thought of as one of the strongest leagues."

But Glenbrook North never fell behind an opponent in the regular season. The victory over Evanston in the playoff opener—it was legendary coach Murney Lazier's last game—was a big confidence-booster. Then the Spartans dispatched East Leyden 13–0 and Willowbrook 26–7. All of a sudden, critics and skeptics conceded Glenbrook North was for real. But could they beat East St. Louis? Hardly anyone outside of Northbrook thought so.

Samorian received a good scouting report from Gordon Tech coach Tom Winiecki, who suggested that the only way to contend with East St. Louis' speedy and high-powered offense was to keep it on the bench.

"They had better personnel. I would have hated to play them 10 times. They would beat us 8 of 10 times," Samorian said. "The big thing we tried to impress on our kids was keep the ball away from them. We tried to control the game with our ground game. If they got an easy score, we told our kids not to worry about it. We felt we could score on them because we had scored on everybody else."

On its second possession, Glenbrook North took advantage of a 25-yard punt and drove 39 yards in seven plays to score on Pete Bohr's 3-yard run. But the extra point attempt was botched when the center snap sailed over kicker Sam Poulos' head and his desperation pass fell incomplete.

In the second quarter, Broadbridge's fumble was recovered by Ron McGruder on Glenbrook North's 7 and Fred Ford scored two plays later. Cecil Griffin's kick gave East St. Louis a 7–6 edge at halftime.

East St. Louis extended its lead to 13–6 in the third period, driving 59 yards in 14 plays to score on Brian Leonard's six-yard run with 2:36 left. But Griffin's kick was wide.

On the fourth play of the fourth quarter, Broadbridge stunned East St. Louis by throwing a 50-yard touchdown pass to Poulos. It was only one of four passes that Broadbridge attempted in the game. Poulos' conversion forced a tie at 13.

Glenbrook North had a chance to win in regulation time. On the next series, Voight intercepted Tolson's pass at East St. Louis' 30. After a clipping penalty, the Spartans drove to the Flyers' 12. But Poulos' 29-yard field goal attempt was blocked.

East St. Louis had a chance to win, too. With two minutes to play, Mike Kiepura's halfback pass was intercepted by Ken Jones, who returned 40 yards to Glenbrook North's 29. On fourth-and-four at the 13, Tolson passed to Byrd, who was tackled by Marks for an eight-yard loss.

In the overtime, a delay of game penalty against East St. Louis gave Glenbrook North a second-and-goal situation at the four. Samorian scrapped his pass play and called for fullback Greg Van Schaack to run off tackle. On fourth down from the one, he scored. Once again, however, the extra point snap sailed high and Broadbridge, the holder, threw a pass to Moller that fell incomplete.

Edwards came up big on East St. Louis' possession. On first down, Leonard took a pitch and attempted to sweep around right end but Edwards tackled him for a four-yard loss. After Darnell Heavens gained three yards, Tolson threw two passes that were intended for Winslow. Both fell incomplete. The future Pro Football and College Hall of Famer never caught a pass in the game.

Glenbrook North did what it had to do to win. The Spartans accumulated 11 first downs and 228 yards to East St. Louis' nine first downs and 171 yards. Woodsum rushed 23 times for 112 yards. The defense, anchored by Moller (18 tackles), Potysman (12), Rockoff, Steve Berger, Marks, and Voight, stymied the Flyers' big-play attack.

"It was a magical year," said Edwards, who didn't become a starter until the second game of the state playoff. "When we first learned there would be a state playoff in 1974, Moller said, 'We will win it.' There was confidence among us. Someone always stepped up and made a big play. Samorian made us believe we would win any game, that the opponent put their pants on the same way, one leg at a time, the same as us.

"It taught a lot of valuable lessons, that there is a reward for hard work. After watching film, defensive coordinator Chuck Hanson would come on Monday with a booklet and give us a scouting report, a lot of pages, a lot of information. We played a lot of defenses—5–3 or 4–4 or 5–2. We were a very bright team. If you are prepared and organized, like in your job, you will have success. Maybe we could beat East St. Louis only once in 10 games or only once in 100, but we were prepared to beat them that day."

St. Laurence 22,
Glenbard West 21 (OT): 1976

The Class 5A championship game in 1976 came down to a goal line stand in overtime and Bill Hinsberger came awfully close to not being there at all.

"Hinsberger wouldn't have been on the team," said Ray Konrath, who was Coach Tom Kavanagh's defensive coordinator. "In triple sessions in August, I didn't have depth at nose guard behind Bill Baier. I put Hinsberger at nose one day. He didn't want to be there. He threw his helmet on the ground and walked to the locker room."

But Hinsberger came to his senses. He returned for the second session and apologized to Konrath. "Are you ready to play football like I want you to?" Konrath asked. "Yes, sir," Hinsberger replied.

Hinsberger, Baier, Jerry Barnicle, Mike Topps, Rich Antonacci, and Pete Stanisch collapsed on running back John Odom at the goal line to stifle Glenbard West's two-point conversion attempt in overtime, setting the stage for Ernie Wulff's game-tying seven-yard run. Matt Oskielunas converted the extra point to cap one of the most exciting games in state history.

Ironically, Wulff wasn't supposed to be there, either. Dave Hickey was a bone-jarring fullback in St. Laurence's wishbone offense. But he was injured in the final regular-season game against Brother Rice, and Wulff, a seldom-used but promising junior, made his first start against Glenbrook North in the opening round of the state playoff.

"The only time I played before Hickey went down was when I got to play in the second half at homecoming," Wulff recalled. "I was crapping in my pants when Hickey went down. I was scared. I hadn't practiced with the first string all year until after the Brother Rice game."

Wulff, a 5–11, 190-pounder, was well prepared. He had been practicing against St. Laurence's first-string defense all year. The Vikings shut out nine opponents during their 13–0 season, including the first four, six of the first seven, and Glenbrook North 9–0, Willowbrook 22–0, and New Trier East 21–0 in the first three rounds of the playoff.

The driving force was Kavanagh, who had seen his most talented team lose to Brother Rice in Week 9 of the 1974 season and fail to qualify for the first state playoff. He was determined that wasn't going to happen again. His 1976 squad returned only one starter, defensive back Neal Rourke, who was shifted to play quarterback. But the pieces were there. He only had to put them all together.

"There were no high expectations," Rourke said. "But you could tell throughout the summer that no one on the team was arrogant so the seniors jelled with the juniors. We became a team. I was there when they lost to Brother Rice in 1974. They were reading too much of their press clippings. We never had that. It played into our favor."

"Each game, we got better and better," said defensive end Kevin Basic. "We were riding a big wave. We feared no one. Losing wasn't something that came into our minds. When someone scored on us, we got harassed like we had lost the game. Even teachers got on us. My dad came to summer practice and said, 'If you win three games, you'll be lucky.' But we grew together and bonded."

After losing to eventual state champion Deerfield in the second round of the 1975 playoff, Glenbard West had high expectations for 1976. The Hilltoppers were ranked No. 1 in the Chicago area until they lost to Downers Grove North 6–0 in Week 9. After that, all they heard about was St. Laurence.

"We went into that season expecting to be Class 5A state champions, no question," said team captain Steve Pals. "St. Laurence had a rock solid defense. They had given up only five touchdowns all year. We had six shutouts. Defense was our trademark but we also had a strong offensive line and talented backs in Odom and Pat Kelleher."

Glenbard West scored on its first possession but the touchdown was nullified by a motion penalty and Chuck Burau kicked a 23-yard field goal. On its second drive, Glenbard West had another touchdown called back but quarterback Keith Jaske scored on a draw play. But Mark Ingold's two-point conversion run failed, so Glenbard West had to settle for a 9–0 lead.

St. Laurence got its wishbone untracked in the second quarter. Basic recovered a fumble in the end zone for one touchdown and scatback John Ewald scored on a one-yard run with 33 seconds left in the first half to give the Vikings a 15–9 advantage.

In the third quarter, Glenbard West tied as Pals and Chris Karalis tackled Rourke, forcing a fumble. Burau picked it up and ran 67 yards to score. Phil Smith's extra point attempt hit the crossbar and bounced back.

In the overtime, Glenbard West had first possession. Odom gained eight yards on first down, then was held for no gain, then ran over his left side for a touchdown.

Now what to do? Kick or go for two? Burau had suffered a sprained ankle in an earlier game and it was determined that Burau would kick field goals and Smith would kick extra points. Coach Bill Duchon opted to go for two. Odom was stacked up at the goal line.

"What I remember vividly is someone asked me before the game about how I thought the game would be decided and I said I hoped it doesn't come down to the kicking game because my two best kickers are hurt. And it hurt us," said Duchon, who was coaching his last game.

"Hats off to St. Laurence's defensive front," said Odom, who was limited to 52 yards in 21 carries, his lowest total of the season. "They were something special. We hadn't run up against anything like that all year. They were used to me breaking a big play. But that front was in my face so quick, I barely had time to react. My longest run was 12 yards."

Although memories of runs and tackles may have blurred with time, everybody remembers the brutal weather conditions. Glenbard West lineman Andy Cvengros said it was so cold, he couldn't feel his fingers or toes. "It was like I had jumped into a freezing lake," he said. Playing on Hancock Stadium's Astroturf surface was like playing on a parking lot. "I was so cold I didn't want to come out for the second half," said Glenbard West lineman Marty Detmer. The bands couldn't perform at halftime because the instruments had frozen.

To this day, Konrath recalls three things about the game:

1. It rained all day the day before the game. On game day, the wind chill factor was minus 15 degrees below zero. The field was so slippery, there was no traction. Players exchanged their cleats for tennis shoes worn by St. Laurence students. Hinsberger, who wore size 12, wore Konrath's coaching shoes that were painted gold.

2. Glenbard West kicked off. St. Laurence ran three plays and punted. Center Pete Grogan snapped the ball over punter Tom Brya's head and Glenbard West gained possession on the 20. When Grogan came off the field, he said, "Coach, I have no feeling in my fingers."

3. In overtime, Kavanagh pulled Konrath aside: "Ray, talk to the players. Give them the overtime rules." The next day, the local newspaper published a picture of Konrath talking to the players. "It was important at that time that the kids knew what the overtime rules were," Konrath said. Bob Fabrizio called the plays from the press box.

"We knew Kavanagh was an epileptic," Hinsberger said. "I think he had a seizure on the sideline in the state final. Ray Konrath took over in the overtime. Kavanagh didn't say a word. He was shaking off to the side. Something definitely happened."

Konrath admits his recollections of the closing minutes of the 1976 game are hazy. Of course, he was aware of Kavanagh's epilepsy. But he insists he wasn't aware of any seizure at the time, only that he had his job to do and he assumed Kavanagh was doing his job. Kavanagh retired after the 1977 season. He died in 1985 when he suffered an epileptic seizure and drowned after driving his car into a man-made lake.

St. Laurence was leading 15–9 and driving for what the Vikings thought would be a game-clinching touchdown in the third quarter when Kavanagh called a play that they had run only once before. It produced their only touchdown in the opening playoff victory over Glenbrook North. On Glenbard West's 30, Rourke attempted a quarterback sweep around left end. But Pals crashed, forced a fumble, and Burau picked it up and ran 67 yards to score.

"We didn't panic," Rourke said. "They scored in the overtime. That was a shock to us. Our defense hadn't given up a touchdown the whole game. But we stacked up their two-point conversion."

Then it was St. Laurence's turn.

On first down, Wulff gained three yards. Second down. In the huddle, there was silence. "Everybody knows what they have to do. Let's do it. Let's finish the game off," Rourke said. Rourke ran option left. He left the ball in Wulff's hands and he broke into the end zone. He finished with 104 yards in 25 carries.

"I was wide open, untouched," Wulff said.

"We were a family," said Basic, whom Kavanagh described as the best player he ever coached. "If someone got hurt on the field, we took it personally. The school never has had that closeness since. Everybody was a part of it. When we won the state title, it was like the whole school won, not just the football team."

Wheaton Warrenville South 40, Joliet Catholic 34 (2 OT): 1992

Coach John Thorne has many pleasant memories about his first state championship. He describes running back Phil Adler as "the heart and soul" of the team. Bobby Nelson was a swift ball-carrying threat. Linebacker Chris Olson anchored the defense. Doug MacLeod was an outstanding kicker.

"The smile is different when we see those players because they were the first ones to do it," he said. "It was a very special year. Beating Joliet Catholic and their tradition in the state final was special."

But Thorne also recalls Josh Zenner, who made a significant contribution to the 14–0 season but whose name was rarely, if ever, included in the postgame statistics.

"I saw him during the winter after the 1991 season," Thorne said. "I asked him, 'Where do you want to play next year?' He said, 'Coach, I'm not that big. I want to try really hard to make it on special teams. If you ever need someone to block, I'll be glad to be a blocking back.' He was the blocking back in front of Adler on the winning touchdown in the state championship game."

In 1992, Wheaton Warrenville South was coming off two state championship losses to Mount Carmel. Thorne knew he had some good players returning and he expected another good season—his last three teams had won 11, 12, and 11 games—but he never dreamed of 14–0. After all, he reasoned, he was running an option and asking a 140-pound receiver to block. "It doesn't sound like it should work but it did," he said.

Wheaton North was the power in Wheaton in the 1970s and 1980s. Phil Adler thought he was going to Wheaton North. His mother was going to move into North's district when her son was a sophomore. But he enrolled at Wheaton Central with his friends. As a senior, the school was renamed Wheaton Warrenville South (WW South) and the students moved to the new campus on Butterfield Road.

Jeff Thorne was the senior quarterback in 1988 and the program was turning around. The Tigers started 0–3 but rallied to win eight games in a row, beating Joliet Catholic 28–0 in the second round of the playoff before losing to Wheaton North 19–13.

"I saw that big things were happening," Adler said. "Marvel Scott was the best running back I ever saw. And I could be a part of it. They paved the road for everyone. As a freshman, I started off as a nose tackle [in eighth grade, he couldn't make the 150-pound limit] but by the end of double sessions, I was a running back. I looked like a lineman."

He got off to a shaky start. He was intimidated by Thorne. He was brought up to the varsity as a sophomore but he wondered if he was ready for the challenge. In a practice before his first start—he replaced Scott, who was hurt—he ran the wrong way on a sweep. He suffered a broken hand, played with the sophomores in a rubber cast, and was called upon for only three plays on the varsity.

After losing to Mount Carmel in the 1991 state final, Adler knew he and his classmates were on the threshold of something big. Thorne had introduced a two-platoon system. The roster was filled with talented athletes. They were overflowing with confidence. Before the 1992 season, they told Thorne that they would go 14–0.

"We knew instead of being a small school that was upsetting everyone, we could beat anyone," Adler said. "We learned each year that as we got closer, the more we listened to the coaches, our chances were good that we would win. All summer, we chanted, '14 and 0, 14 and 0.' We knew if we buckled down, got in shape, and listened to the coaches that we could beat anyone. We felt confident that we could dominate people."

They proved their point from the outset. In the opener, they beat traditional rival Glenbard West 27–10 in Glen Ellyn. "When we got on the bus to go to Glenbard West, we didn't know what we had. On the way back, we knew," Adler said.

In the playoff, they edged York 17–14 when the defense stopped the Dukes in a first-and-goal situation at the two in the fourth quarter. In the quarterfinals, the defense came up big again, forcing a fumble in the fourth quarter to preserve a 24–20 victory over Lake Forest. After eliminating Rockford Boylan 16–0 in the semifinals, they braced for a rematch with perennial power Joliet Catholic in the championship game. A year earlier, WW South had beaten Joliet Catholic and Mike Alstott 28–6 in the semifinals.

WW South broke out to a 14–0 lead in the first quarter on MacLeod's 19-yard run and Adler's 3-yard run. But Joliet Catholic closed to 14–13 as Matt Larsen ran for two touchdowns. MacLeod's 41-yard field goal gave the Tigers a 17–13 halftime edge.

Joliet Catholic went ahead in the third quarter on Mike Sopko's 20-yard run but WW South regained the lead on Nelson's 43-yard burst. Sopko's 51-yard run with 3:16 to play in the fourth quarter gave the Hilltoppers a 27–24 lead.

"I ran behind 6–6, 300-pound tackle Nick Ragusa," Sopko said. "After scoring with 3:16 to play, I felt we were in good shape with our solid defense. But they moved the ball downfield to kick the field goal with no time left. We were disappointed that our defense didn't stop them. Then they stopped us in the second overtime. They took momentum from us. They knocked the breath out of us. To be that close and not get there, it was disappointing."

"When we led 14–0, we felt real confident that we would win because our defense, the best part of our team, would hold them," Adler said. "But when Sopko scored on third-and-10 and broke that 51-yarder with 3:16 left—well, no one had done that on us all year. I thought, 'Here we go again, like last year.' We were behind and I didn't think we had enough time with our running game."

WW South got the ball on its 20 and quarterback Ben Klaas took charge. "He felt really confident. He made us feel it was like any other huddle," Adler recalled. On fourth-and-two at midfield, WW South called its last time-out.

"What do you want to run?" Thorne asked. "It's your season."

Adler said he wanted to run a sweep left. Nelson always ran sweeps so Joliet Catholic wouldn't expect it. Adler broke a 30-yarder to the 20 and Klaas threw a pass to Ken Sonnenberg to the 4, setting up MacLeod's tying field goal.

"We called a time-out before they kicked the field goal. We made a mistake, a coaching error. They didn't have any time-outs left. If we hadn't called time-out, the game would have been over. They had no time to kick it," Larsen said.

MacLeod converted the field goal but WW South was penalized because one offensive lineman forgot to go on the field. On the next snap, MacLeod kicked a 26-yarder to tie at 27.

In the first overtime, Adler scored on a five-yard run on second down. Joliet Catholic countered with a six-yard pass from Ray Chodorowski to Kevin Fittro.

In the second overtime, Tim Missavage recovered a fumble on first down to stifle Joliet Catholic's possession. Adler swept left and ran 10 yards on WW South's first snap to end one of the most exciting games in state history. He finished with 24 carries for 186 yards and three touchdowns.

"It might have been the national high school game of the year," Joliet Catholic coach Bob Stone summed up. "Both teams played a great game. Everybody realized they had been part of something special, back and forth, two heavyweight fighters slugging it out. It came down to a good player making big plays."

"You can't believe it's over. Then you see a pile of players on the field and you realize you just won state, what you have been trying to do for three years," Adler said. "When you put that much effort into something and you win, it's a great feeling.

"Personally, I had better games but nothing that exciting at the end. It was the most exciting game I ever played. For three years after it happened, I watched the tape all the time. I still talk about it with my friends and teammates. I can go over the whole game in my head. It's something you don't forget. Some say it's just high school but it's pretty neat."

Maine South 31, Mount Carmel 28: 1995

Brian Schmitz started his football career as a quarterback on Maine South's freshman B team, on a muddy 80-yard field behind the main grandstand. He had played soccer in his early years and had developed into a promising kicker. But he never wanted to be just a kicker. He always wanted to do more.

"I didn't want to tackle anyone but I wanted to catch it or throw it. I wanted to be an athlete who kicked," he said.

Schmitz emerged as one of the most gifted kickers in state history. He capped his high school career by converting one of the most dramatic field goals in the history of the state playoff, a 37-yarder with eight seconds to play that lifted Maine South to a 31–28 victory over favored Mount Carmel for the Class 5A championship.

"We had so much confidence in him. I never saw a better kicker," Maine South coach Phil Hopkins said. "We beat an established program like Mount Carmel. The conference was our goal in the past but now, I thought to myself, we want to win a state title every year. We can do this every year.

"We had such wonderful kids. Schmitz and [John] Schacke were playmakers. They were doing things on the field that I didn't even know what they were doing. They had taken over the offense."

Offensive coordinator Charlie Bliss, the architect of Maine South's four-wide-and-let-it-fly offense that produced two state championships and three seconds from 1995 to 2005, said Schacke set the tone for what was to follow.

"He is the quarterback that everyone is measured to," Bliss said. "He was on a 1–8 freshman team and a 5–3–1 sophomore team, sat on the bench as a junior, and won a state title as a senior with the team that turned the program around. We created our own monster. He never got rattled. He had a great sense of when guys would get open. He would make big plays in big games."

In the state final, he was intercepted twice in the first quarter. "Coach, I'm not playing very good, am I?" he said to Bliss. Then he proceeded to pass for a then-playoff-record 250 yards, including touchdown passes of 83, 44, and 22 yards, to spark one of the most dramatic upsets in state history.

Schacke was a three-sport athlete who thought baseball was his major sport and dreamed of playing for the Chicago Cubs. But he slowly gravitated to football because football was the most popular activity in the Park Ridge community—he started to play for the Falcons when he was in fifth grade—and he admired former Maine South quarterbacks such as Dan Ianno, Tom Fiddler, Gary Francis, and Bill Verbancik.

Then Schacke met Bliss. "He knows more about the quarterback position than anyone I've ever known. I had good people in college but Bliss knew more about the quarterback position in terms of fundamentals and technique than anyone. He could turn an average quarterback into a very good player," Schacke said.

His first experience with Bliss' teaching style was at a summer camp before his freshman year. He was one of 10 quarterbacks at the camp. Bliss unveiled a lot of drills that were as foreign to Schacke as the Chinese language—high release, using the lower body, following through, throwing over the goal post, footwork drills, working on drop backs, throwing 40 yards into a garbage can.

Then Schacke was introduced to Bliss' spread offense. He called it his "gangster offense." It featured the quarterback in a shotgun formation with one wideout on each side, one back and one tight end on each side. The back could go out for a normal pass or take a handoff from the quarterback, who also could run an option play. It was very effective in putting enormous pressure on opposing defenses.

"I went from a backup quarterback to an All-Stater," Schacke said. "For me, his teaching of technique and mechanics were keys. I had a decent arm but he got the most out of me."

It all came together in 1995. But it almost didn't. Schmitz suffered a broken leg in the opening game against York. He caught a pass and broke two tackles, then got rolled up on the goal line. He was sidelined for four weeks. Maine South started 2–2. The Hawks had rallied from a 21–3 halftime deficit to beat York 22–21 but had lost to Evanston and Waukegan. Nobody was too impressed.

"I was going to be the quarterback. But we had low expectations. Our senior class was 1–8 as freshmen. We didn't have many good players. We matured at a later age," Schacke said. "We had never been past the state quarterfinals. No one expected us to get there."

Hopkins wasn't sure which offense to use. He started with a wishbone formation with two tight ends. After falling behind York 21–3 in the opener, he inserted two and three wide receivers. After Schacke threw three touchdown passes to win the game, Hopkins realized his running and option offenses didn't fit his personnel. So he switched to two, three, and four wide receivers. His passing offense began to evolve.

Maine South went on a roll, winning its last five regular-season games, then beating Foreman 55–0, Danville 45–13, St. Rita 18–8, and Fenwick 24–21 in overtime in the playoff to set the stage for its matchup with Mount Carmel. The Caravan, led by quarterback John Welsh and running back Leondre Smith, had crushed perennial power East St. Louis 57–27 in the semifinals.

It wasn't so easy for Maine South. In the semifinal against Fenwick, on a muddy field at Oak Park Stadium, Schmitz kicked a 27-yard field goal on Maine South's first play after Fenwick had 14 snaps from the 10-yard-line but failed to score on its overtime possession.

Mount Carmel? "No one thought we had a chance. It was the aura of Mount Carmel. Even within our school, kids didn't think we had a chance. We even had two pep assemblies before the game," Schacke said.

"On top of that, we had our worst week of practice on offense. I had a very bad week of throwing the ball. They had a different defense, a cover three that we hadn't faced all year. They had deep coverage and we like to throw deep."

At halftime, Maine South trailed 21–14. The Hawks were beat up. Mount Carmel's physically tough defense had taken its toll. Schacke had a bag of ice on his knee. Wide receiver Rick Tosch was icing his sore ankle. They were happy that they were only one touchdown behind.

Hopkins, as always, remained calm under fire. He reminded his players that they were about to compete in their last two quarters of football in high school. A rah-rah speech wasn't necessary. Instead, he concentrated on assigning more blockers to counter Mount Carmel's blitzing tactics.

With better protection up front, Schacke had more time to throw. He threw for three touchdowns, an 83-yarder to Ben Wilson and 44 and 22-yarders to Schmitz, a 5–11, 135-pounder with 4.4 speed who was so athletic that he could dunk a basketball.

The Hawks, tied at 28 in the fourth quarter, regained possession at midfield with four minutes to play. On third-and-long, Schacke passed to Phil Rossi to the 40. On fourth down, Hopkins was going to call for a punt but defensive coordinator Carl Magsamen pleaded for a field goal. Schmitz attempted a 58-yard field goal—no one had ever kicked one farther than 53 yards—but it sailed wide right.

"In practice, I had made field goals from that distance many times," Schmitz said. "It was wide right but long enough. But I came through and took one step forward and got my leg taken out from under me. A flag was thrown right away. A roughing the kicker penalty. I've faked a lot of roughing the kicker penalties but this was legitimate."

After the 15-yard penalty was assessed, Maine South ran two plays, then Schmitz kicked a 37-yarder with eight seconds remaining to win the game.

"It was the biggest kick I ever made," said Schmitz, who was an All-America kicker at North Carolina. "I made it, a kick I knew I would make. I wouldn't miss two in a row to lose a championship. I made game-winners after that but never for a championship.

"I still have the ball on my parents' mantle in the basement. A kid at school who I didn't know gave me the ball that I kicked to win the Fenwick game. They are next to each other on the mantle. There's also a picture of me and Rick Tosch holding the ball before I am about to kick the winning field goal against Mount Carmel."

Driscoll 42, Mount Carmel 41 (2 OT): 2001

It came down to the last play in the second overtime period. It doesn't get any more dramatic than this. One play for the state championship.

Victor Arlis, known affectionately as "the pig" to his teammates, had plowed two yards for a touchdown and freshman Rick Albreski had converted the extra point to give Driscoll a 42–35 lead. But Downstate Mount Carmel responded, scoring on quarterback Luke Drone's third-down, 10-yard pass to Bryan Grant.

"At that time, I'm talking to my coaches. I want to go for it, I want to go for the two-point conversion and end it right there," said Mount Carmel coach Darren Peach. "I felt our team getting tired. Their offense had worn out our defense. They ran the ball effectively in the overtime."

Peach called time-out. "What do you want to do, go for it or kick the extra point?" he asked his players. They wanted to go for it. Peach called for a short-yardage set, a play that Driscoll's defense hadn't seen on tape. The Aces had used it to score on Drone's three-yard pass to Wayne Hammel in the first overtime.

"The play had three options," Peach explained. "We're lined up in a full T-formation. One tight end runs an out pattern. The other tight end runs a drag pattern. And one running back goes into the flat."

Anthony Gebhart, Driscoll's strong safety, became an outside linebacker as he moved up to the line of scrimmage in the Highlanders' goal line defense.

"Even though you have only a split-second to think about things after they break the huddle, the whole season goes through your eyes," Gebhart said. "It is a special moment in your career. You think of all the things you have done to get to that point. You realize you've put in too much time and effort to lose the game for your team.

"I had no idea what they were going to do but I wasn't going to let my guy beat me. I would do my job to help us win. Coach [Tim] Racki always said, 'Speed kills.' I wanted to play fast. They had been running a run with pulling linemen. They came out toward me and it looked like they were setting up to run. But the quarterback stopped and took a step back to pass. I just rushed him."

The quick-thinking 5–9, 165-pound junior applied pressure on Drone, forcing him to throw the ball before he wanted to. "He flipped the ball over my head when he saw me coming. I turned around and saw the ball was short," Gebhart said.

Pandemonium. The Driscoll players ran to the middle of the field, removed their helmets, and began to celebrate. Nick Gebhart, an assistant coach, ran onto the field and tackled his younger brother. "I have a picture of it in our basement," Anthony said.

"Look what we got started," said Peach, looking back on Driscoll's unprecedented string of seven state championships in a row.

"I wasn't thinking repeat," said Gebhart, who rushed for 128 yards and scored two touchdowns as Driscoll crushed Mount Carmel 42–0 in the 2002 state final. "Coach Racki always said it was about the journey, not the destination. It was a great ride, a special group of guys in a special moment where everything turned out right.

"We didn't play because it was our last game but because we loved playing with those guys. I always wanted to be a sparkplug, get the team going. When I go back to see the kids play, even though the coaches have changed, the kids still play the game the same. They are warriors on the field. Every game is like a street fight."

That's how Racki described his 2001 squad, a bunch of street fighters. "They were Ditka-esque that year. Football was a street fight for them. They weren't afraid of anybody," Racki said. He singled out Gebhart and Greg Turner, then a sophomore, as the best players he ever coached.

And, of course, there was "the pig." "That was the year of Victor Arlis," Racki said. The 6–1, 220-pound senior carried 303 times for 2,182 yards and 28 touchdowns. In the state final, he rushed 24 times for 135 yards and three touchdowns.

"He was heavier than 210 pounds," junior quarterback Matt Mahaney said. "He was a hard-nosed runner. He loved delivering a hit. He was quick into the hole and had power to run people over. He was our go-to guy. When the game was on the line, we'd give him the ball. He wanted it. Thirty-two lead was his call. He ran off guard and tackle on the right side."

Assistant Coach Mike Burzawa tagged Arlis with "the pig" label. He wasn't offended at the time. He still isn't. To this day, some coaches, teammates, and friends call him "Piggy." As a sophomore, he was a skinny 170-pounder. Then he gained some "chub" and, by his own admission, "looked sloppy chewing up the yards."

The program was at a low point when Arlis, linebackers Mike Freeman and Mike Tenuto, noseguard Kentin Lathrope, lineman Jim Vozzella, and defensive backs Jeremy Netzer, Paul Whetsel, and Mike Senese enrolled in the fall of 1998. Hardly anyone remembered that the Addison school had won a state championship in 1991.

Previous teams had finished 1–9 and 2–7. Only 20 freshmen came out for the team. But they advanced to the second round of the state playoff as sophomores, reached the quarterfinals as juniors, and, despite an 0–2 start as seniors, went on a 12-game winning streak that included a stunning 28–14 upset of heavily favored Pontiac in the quarterfinals and a 24–21 victory over Huntley in the semifinals in which they overcame a 21–3 halftime deficit.

They had dedicated the season to a former player, Ralphie La Brak, who had died of colon cancer. Each player wore a patch over his heart, a Superman symbol with a number 73, Ralphie's number, which was retired at the school. His brother Billy was a senior reserve on the 2001 team.

"We meshed well together, the seniors and juniors. My thoughts were, I didn't want my senior year to be like my brother's [2–7]," Arlis said. "The big turning point for us was beating Pontiac. It proved to a lot of people that we were going to be a tough team. We had no doubts. But after Pontiac, everybody knew."

"Everybody doubted that we could win, even the newspapers," said Lathrope, a 6–3, 270-pound noseman. "Pontiac was ranked No. 1. They had been favored in Class 5A but they came down to 4A for the playoff. They were the biggest team in 4A. They had a great team. Nobody wanted to play them."

They knew about Pontiac but they didn't know about Mount Carmel. The truth is most of the players and the rest of Driscoll community thought they were going to play Chicago Mount Carmel in the state final. They had never heard of Downstate Mount Carmel, the southeastern Illinois town on the Wabash River that had sent basketball star Archie Dees to Indiana.

Downstate Mount Carmel was a handful. The Aces had won state titles in 1974 and 1981 and had produced a long line of winning teams under Larry Davis, Larry Lockhart, and John Hart. In his first year, Peach had built a 12–1 team that had upset favored Mount Zion and Benton in the previous playoff games. Drone had passed for more than 1,500 yards and rushed for more than 800.

Mount Carmel led 21–18 at halftime and 28–18 with 5:48 left in the third quarter. Then Driscoll executed two long scoring drives, one for 90 yards and the other for 72 that was capped by Albreski's game-tying, 19-yard field goal with 10 seconds remaining to force overtime.

On the first drive, faced with a first-and-20 at its 10 following a penalty, Driscoll escaped as Mahaney threw a screen pass to Turner, who ran 53 yards to Mount Carmel's 37. Tenuto ran for 20 yards and, six plays later, Arlis scored from the 3.

"That was the turning point," Peach said. "They have first-and-20 at their 10. Then the screen pass to Turner, we miss a tackle, and they go to our 35. It was a big play. If we could have stopped them, we would have had great field position and win the state title."

In the fourth quarter, Mount Carmel drove 52 yards to Driscoll's 30, but Drone's fourth-and-three slant pass was intercepted by Gebhart at his 28 with 2:42 to play. Netzer ran 19 yards to trigger the march and Mahaney's 25-yard pass to Turner put the ball on Mount Carmel's 25. On fourth-and-three, Mahaney completed an 11-yard pass to Turner to the seven. Arlis reached the two before Albreski kicked the equalizer.

"Albreski showed great poise for a freshman," Arlis said. "There never was a point when I thought he wouldn't make a field goal or an extra point."

Freeman was credited with a state-record 19 tackles in the state final. Not a bad effort for a 6–2, 220-pounder who was hospitalized with a severe case of flu after arriving in Champaign on the night before the game and wasn't released until it was time to board the bus for the trip to Memorial Stadium.

"I have no idea how I played in the game," Freeman said. "I threw up during the game. I felt awful but there was no way I was going to miss the game. Coach Racki was getting other kids ready to play for me. He was the reason I made it. This was what I worked for my whole life. I didn't want a senior class ring, only a state championship ring."

Aledo 41, Carthage 40: 2002

The first thing that residents of Aledo are anxious to inform you about their small farming community in western Illinois is that it is the birthplace of country music singer Suzy Bogguss, a 1975 high school graduate and former homecoming queen.

The second thing is that Aledo is a football town.

Well, it wasn't always a football town. George Pratt produced several good teams in the late 1940s, 1950s, and early 1960s. But Aledo qualified for the state playoff only once from 1975 to 1988. Brian Applegate's team finished second in 1988, then fell to 0–9. Bill McCarty's teams won more than 70 percent of their games in the 1990s.

Then Cullen Welter, a 1992 graduate, succeeded McCarty in 1998. He won state championships in 1998 and 2001, and his 2002 squad was favored to repeat. The Green Dragons returned 10 starters, including quarterback Brett Lee, running backs

Chris Dixon and J. J. Dunn, and middle linebacker Matt Randall. They averaged 43 points per game, allowed fewer than 10, and played to a running clock five times.

"There were high expectations. We were preseason No. 1 in the state. We expected to repeat. It was all about going unbeaten. If we had lost, it would have been a failure," Lee said. "We didn't know if we were better than 1998 or 2001 but our goal was to do everything we could to go undefeated. We wanted to carry on the Aledo tradition and the best way was to go undefeated."

Although Welter later said he felt the 2001 team was his best, it didn't go unbeaten. The Green Dragons lost to Sherrard 36–24 in Week 7, then bounced back to outlast perennial power Carthage 48–36 in the first round of the state playoff, then beat Moweaqua A&M 27–24 for the Class 2A championship after trailing 21–14 at halftime. Lee's 35-yard touchdown pass to Troy Blaser with four minutes to play accounted for the winning margin.

"Everyone felt good but I didn't feel so good because I wasn't satisfied with one loss," Lee said. "When the clock ran out, I looked at Coach Welter. I said, 'Let's do it again and this time with no losses.' He shrugged me off and said to relax and try to enjoy it, that there is no guarantee what will happen next year. But all I could think about was that loss and 45 weeks until we could avenge that loss."

But Welter had to make some major adjustments. Blaser, who had caught 70 passes for more than 1,000 yards and was Lee's go-to guy in the offense, had graduated. So had two other receivers and middle linebacker Cody Hessman, the team's emotional leader. Welter knew he had elements of a good running game so he opted to throw the ball less and use Dixon and Dunn and Lee's running abilities on the option.

Aledo was an offensive machine. Dixon rushed for 1,606 yards and 30 touchdowns. Dunn rushed for 837 yards and scored 21 touchdowns. Lee, who passed for 2,800 yards and 24 touchdowns as a junior, threw for 1,755 yards and 19 touchdowns and rushed for 825 yards as a senior. Randall stepped in, led the conference in tackles, and became the team's emotional leader. Dixon and Dunn also stood out on defense.

No opponent came closer than 25 points until Week 9, when Aledo edged Macomb 21–14. In the playoff, they smashed Forreston 34–8, Amboy 40–0, North Boone 32–6, and Argenta-Oreana 28–7 to set the stage for its showdown with Carthage.

Carthage had won state titles in 1995, 1998, 1999, and 2000 under Coach Jim Unruh. The 2002 squad might have been just as good or better. The Blueboys averaged 48 points per game. In the state playoff, they crushed Cuba 54–14, Winchester 46–8, Sciota Northwestern 30–8, and Auburn 54–14 before meeting Aledo.

Ashton Gronewold averaged 11 yards per carry while rushing for 1,794 yards and 31 touchdowns. Cody Grotts rushed for 1,484 yards and 28 touchdowns.

Carthage built a 12–0 lead on quarterback Joe Reed's 54-yard pass to Blake Smith at the end of the first quarter and Gronewold's 59-yard run early in the second period. Later, a 32-yard scoring run by Gronewold and a 71-yard pass from Reed to Smith gave Carthage a commanding 34–16 advantage with 3:25 left in the third quarter.

"It was divine intervention," Welter said. "You tell your kids to play hard and never give up but Carthage was dominating the game. We were just playing for pride at that point."

"It was a freak accident," Lee said. "We had no business winning. But we kept plug-ging away and the ball kept bouncing our way."

Miraculously, Aledo scored three touchdowns in the last eight minutes to tie at 34 and force overtime. Lee provided the spark by throwing a 49-yard touchdown pass to Sam Salmon. Josh Bingham recovered a fumble at Carthage's nine, setting up Dunn's one-yard scoring plunge with 4:28 left. Brad Franks intercepted Reed's pass at Carthage's 41 and Lee threw for 11 and 16 yards before sneaking the last yard for the tying touchdown with 34 seconds to play. But Lee's two-point conversion run failed.

Amazingly, Carthage still had time to win in regulation. Gronewold ran for gains of 15, 19, and 17 yards to reach Aledo's 25. With two seconds left, Reed passed to Gronewold for an apparent touchdown—but it was nullified by an illegal block.

"I was celebrating with John Dickinson," Gronewold said. "Then I spotted the flag as we were jumping up and down in the end zone. When we lost, it was a horrible feeling, one of the lowest moments of my life. I still replay it. I still picture it after they scored, after the ball went through the uprights."

"I never felt comfortable with our lead," Unruh said. "We never really stopped them ourselves. They got momentum in the fourth quarter and we couldn't slow them down. I'm a pessimistic coach. I'm always looking for a flag. But we had opportuni-ties to win."

Gronewold, who rushed 25 times for 262 yards, ran 10 yards to score on the first play of the overtime session. But his two-point conversion run failed.

Dixon ran five yards and Dunn powered up the middle for four, then plunged over left guard for the touchdown. Bingham kicked the game-winning point.

"It was the most incredible game I've ever been a part of," Welter said.

Carthage amassed 493 yards, Aledo 406. Reed passed for 191 yards, Lee 175. But Carthage committed three turnovers that were critical in the outcome.

Aledo had rallied around Matt Simpson, the captain of the 2002 team who had been paralyzed in an automobile accident in January. "He was our emotional leader. He wore No. 81. We won the game 41–40. It adds up to 81, Simpson's number," Welter said.

"For us, it was gratification," Lee said. "We set a goal to win another state title and do it undefeated. It was almost euphoric that we had accomplished it but it was sad that we wouldn't be able to play Aledo football anymore. It meant so much to all of us."

Mount Carmel's Jonathan Boyd grabs onto the jersey of Maine South quarterback John Schacke during the 1995 Class 5A championship game. In one of the most dramatic of all state finals, Maine South won 31–28 on Brian Schmitz's 37–yard field goal with eight seconds to play. Photo courtesy of the Illinois High School Association.

Ernie Wulff (32) of St. Laurence breaks away from a tackler and sprints seven yards into the end zone for the game-tying touchdown against Glenbard West in overtime in the Class 5A championship game in 1976. Matt Oskielunas converted the extra point for a 22–21 victory. Photo courtesy of Ernie Wulff.

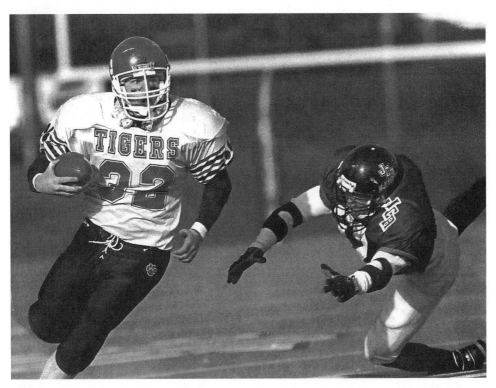

In one of the most exciting and bizarre championship games in the history of the state playoff, Wheaton Warrenville South's Phil Adler (left) rushed 24 times for 186 yards and three touchdowns to beat Joliet Catholic 40–34 in double overtime for the 1992 Class 5A title. Adler ran 10 yards for the game-winning touchdown. Photo courtesy of the Illinois High School Association.

5
Small Schools

Aledo: Rekindling a Tradition

Michael O'Brien shared the disappointment of his teammates. In fact, O'Brien and the other underclassmen were devastated. Aledo had finished 11–1 in 1998, losing to Stillman Valley in the state quarterfinals. Townspeople said it was the best team in school history, a dominant squad that averaged 40 points per game. Worst of all, there was speculation that Coach Bill McCarty was going to leave. Then he did.

"McCarty revamped the program and rekindled the tradition," O'Brien recalled. "He brought us back to the playoffs. He coached from 1990 to 1997 and turned Aledo into more of a football town. He brought hope to a lot of kids who trained hard but never were able to put it all together. When he left [for Port Byron Riverdale], there was a lot of disappointment. But the kids banded together and hoped for the best."

O'Brien feared that McCarty's successor would be a second-rate coach. But athletic director Fred Nessler called O'Brien, the team leader, into his office during the summer and assured him that he wanted to continue what McCarty had started. He said he was focusing on a young coach who had taken his Colfax Ridgeview team from 2–7 to 9–3 and the state quarterfinals in four years.

Cullen Welter was the answer. He was a good fit, too. A former four-sport athlete while growing up in Mahomet-Seymour and a sprinter on Illinois' track team, Welter was looking to move closer to his wife's family in the Quad Cities. He did an extensive background check on Aledo and its football program. He liked what he saw.

Aledo, the seat of Mercer County, is a rural farming community of 3,500 located on Highway 17 about 25 minutes from Interstate 74. Many of its residents work in the Quad Cities. There are two stoplights, a McDonald's, a Hardee's, a Wal-Mart, a YMCA, two golf courses, Scooter's bar, and four pizza restaurants. Happy Joe's, by most accounts, is the most popular. The town's most famous product is country music singer Suzy Bogguss, a 1975 graduate. In 2007, Aledo celebrated its 125th anniversary.

Welter was more interested in determining if he could build a winning football team. It had been done in the past. George Pratt, for whom the football field is named, won 76 percent (89–27–5) from 1946 to 1962. He is credited with making football a Friday night event in Aledo. Jim Smith, who had a cup of coffee in the NFL, was a great player in the 1960s.

For the first 15 years of the state playoff, however, Aledo qualified only once (1975). In 1988, Coach Brian Applegate's team was 13–1 and lost to Carlyle for the Class 2A championship. But Applegate left and Aledo went 0–9 the following year.

Then McCarty arrived. He won 71 percent (62–25) of his games in eight years. He qualified for the state playoff in four of his last six years, winning 53 games. His 1997 powerhouse, led by quarterback Colin Conway, halfback Travis Boswell, and flanker Todd Baldwin, was 11–1. Then he left. Enter Welter.

"McCarty's shoes were very big and hard to fill. He was the hope of the town as a coach," O'Brien said. "When he left, we thought nothing would work out."

At a team meeting to introduce Welter, only one third of the squad showed up. The others remained despondent and not too interested. Five of them were so discouraged that they opted not to play football in 1998. But O'Brien was impressed. Welter was very inspiring and professional.

"He was very much in tune with the current tradition we had at Aledo," O'Brien said. "He wanted to further our tradition. And he brought something new to the game. He is a chess player, a mind-oriented coach, very articulate. He knows what he wants. He doesn't tolerate people who are lackadaisical or have bad attitudes. He gets very angry when players don't meet expectations he knows they can fulfill."

Welter's record speaks for itself. In 11 years at Aledo, his teams have posted a spectacular winning percentage of .837 (113–22). They won state titles in 1998, 2001, and 2002 and finished second in 2005 and 2006.

"Why have we been successful?" he said. "It comes down to building rapport with your kids. Anyone can learn the Xs and Os if they study the game. But if you develop relationships and the kids know you care about them, they will do what it takes to win. Your ability to relate to kids is the most important attribute in coaching. Our kids believe they work harder than other schools. When they step on the field, they believe they will win."

Welter got off to a good start. He was 29 years old when he inherited an 11–1 squad that had graduated all but three starters and returned only seven seniors. One of the best, Brandon Hofmann, didn't show up for the first day of practice. He was supposed to be the quarterback but he was a star basketball player and wasn't sure he wanted to play football. He ended up being a receiver.

Andy Frye, a junior, stepped in at quarterback. Wyatt Thomas rushed for more than 1,000 yards. O'Brien keyed the defense at middle linebacker. His twin brother, Andrew, was a two-way lineman. Other standouts were free safety Michael Bipond, two-way lineman Zach Harlan, safety Kent Brown, and wide receiver Richard Bigham.

The Green Dragons were 7–2 in the regular season, losing 49–0 to Olympic Conference rival Rockridge before beating Sherrard in Week 9 to clinch a playoff spot. In the playoff, they upset Tolono Unity by two on Frye's game-winning, third-down, 40-yard scoring pass to Bigham. In the state final, they avenged their earlier loss to Rockridge, winning 25–16 as Frye set a record for completions, Bigham scored three touchdowns, Brown made 13 tackles, and Michael O'Brien scored once, rushed for 60 yards, and stood out on defense.

Quarterback Brett Lee was the leader of the 2001 and 2002 state championship teams. As a junior, he wasn't sure he would play at all. He was coming off a 6–4 season in which he threw nine interceptions and fewer touchdowns. But he was the only quarterback on the roster. Privately, Welter had a "sneaky suspicion" that his team would "really be good" but he kept it to himself.

"Our big thing was to prove everyone wrong. That was our motivation," Lee said. "My goal was to be efficient, not kill drives, not turn the ball over, do whatever I had to do to get the ball in the end zone."

Lee completed 70 percent of his passes for 2,800 yards and 24 touchdowns as Aledo went 13–1, outlasting perennial state power Carthage 48–36 in the first round and beating Moweaqua Central A&M 27–24 for the state title after trailing 24–14 at halftime. Troy Blaser was Lee's go-to receiver, catching 70 passes for more than 1,000 yards. He caught a 35-yarder from Lee with four minutes to play in the state final to account for the game-winning touchdown. Middle linebacker Cody Hessman was the defensive leader.

In 2002, with five starters returning on offense and defense, Aledo was rated No. 1 in the state in the preseason. Welter went from a passing game to an option attack. Lee passed for 1,800 yards and rushed for 900, Chris Dixon rushed for 1,200 yards and 33 touchdowns, J. J. Dunn rushed for 1,000 yards, and middle linebacker Matt Randall was the team's emotional leader and the conference's leading tackler. They averaged 45 points per game.

In the state final, in a duel of unbeatens, Aledo trailed Carthage by 18 points with eight minutes to play but rallied to win 41–40 in overtime in what Welter described as "the most incredible game I've ever been part of." Lee triggered the magnificent comeback with a 49-yard scoring pass to Sam Salmon. Brad Franks' interception at Carthage's 41 with 3:38 to play set up the tying touchdown, Lee's one-yard sneak with 34 seconds left.

In overtime, Carthage All-Stater Ashton Gronewold ran 10 yards to score on first down but was stopped on a two-point conversion attempt. Aledo scored on Dunn's one-yard run on third down. Josh Bigham kicked the winning point.

"It was a freak accident. We had no business winning. But we kept plugging away and the ball kept bouncing our way," Lee said. "For us, it was gratification. We set a goal to win another state title and to go undefeated. It was all about going unbeaten. If we had lost, it was a failure. We didn't know if we were better than the 1997 team but our goal was to do everything we could to go undefeated. We wanted to carry on Aledo's football tradition. And the best way was to go undefeated."

Arcola: The Monahan Brothers Ride Again

The Monahan family has left an indelible mark on Arcola, a small farming community south of Champaign-Urbana that dates to the 1860s, when Tim Monahan's great-grandfather arrived in the area and began to dabble in broomcorn.

In 1922, Monahan's grandfather founded the Thomas Monahan Company, which became the world's largest producer of broom handles (200,000 a day) and earned Arcola a tagline as "the broomcorn capital of the world."

But football is almost as important as corn in Arcola. The high school fielded its first team in 1894. Turkey Ray was a legendary star from 1928 to 1931. In the 1930s, Coach Kile McWherter was 32–1–1 in four years. Popeye Pullen scored 224 points on teams that won 33 games in a row. Lou Baker produced three unbeaten teams in the 1950s, and then went to Illinois to become Dick Butkus' linebacker coach. In 1999, Kolin Peterson emerged as the leading rusher in school history with more than 5,000 yards.

Tim Monahan's father played for Knute Rockne at Notre Dame. Tim played on Lou Baker's unbeaten teams in 1954 and 1955, and then played for Terry Brennan and Joe Kuharich at Notre Dame. His brother Jim played on a 30–2 basketball team in 1962 and went on to captain the basketball team at Notre Dame.

He fathered nine children, six boys. And all six—Tom, Jon, Patrick, Matthew, Chris, and Mark—were instrumental in the success that Arcola experienced during Steve Thomas' brilliant 30-year coaching career that produced 210 victories, three state championships, and two seconds from 1964 to 1993.

The Monahans rushed for 14,245 yards among them. Tom was a freshman linebacker on Arcola's first state championship team in 1978. Jon rushed for 1,700 yards and 42 touchdowns on the 1985 state champion, surpassing Red Grange's single-season scoring record. Patrick was his backfield mate. Matthew and Chris played on the 1988 state championship team. Mark was the tailback on the 1991 state runner-up and cousin Jim Monahan was the center.

"I was fortunate," said Tom, the oldest of nine children. "I didn't have to fill shoes. I didn't feel the pressure that the others did. At that time, I didn't have to live up to something. I was out to prove that we were winners after all those bad seasons [eight losing seasons from 1965 to 1975]."

"No one could be harder on me than my older brothers, particularly Chris and Matt," said Mark, the youngest. "Mom sent Matt to kindergarten a year early to get him out of the house because we fought so much. It was survival of the fittest. We had to be careful because we dated some of the same girls. It was more important to make the All-Conference team than to date the homecoming queen."

There were bragging rights at the dinner table. Which brother was the best athlete in football, basketball, or track? In a family survey, disputed by one and all, Mark was voted the best male athlete in the family. The coaches agreed that Mark was the best all-around football player among the Monahans.

"That's a pretty significant accomplishment," he said. "The difference maker was I played all three sports. I was on a 1,600-meter relay team that won state. I ran high and low hurdles and went to state in four events in 1992. I anchored the relay and placed in the 300 hurdles."

He walked on at Notre Dame, as Tom and Jon had done before him, and earned a scholarship as a nickel back on special teams. His crowning achievement was intercepting a pass against Purdue in 1992.

But even Tim Monahan contends that Terry Miller was the best player in Arcola history. A 1964 graduate, Miller played quarterback, fullback, guard, safety, and linebacker as a senior for Coach Lloyd Atterberry. He also starred on Bob Avery's basketball teams that were 26–2 and 25–6. He played basketball at a hoop outside the Monahans' house.

After seeing Miller play basketball in a sectional final, Illinois football coach Pete Elliott told Miller that he didn't have any football scholarships to offer but he would arrange for a basketball scholarship, then Miller could decide later which sport to concentrate on. Miller played freshman basketball with Rich Jones, Rich Dunlap, and Bennie Louis, and then switched to football. He was a freshman when Butkus was a senior. Later, he played in the NFL.

"Arcola was a town where there was a lot of trust," Miller said. "No one locked their doors. I never recall my parents taking the keys out of their car. That's the way it was. Kids didn't dare get into trouble because they knew everyone would know about it. No one had any worries."

Arcola was a football town. "It you wanted to be part of the system, you had to go out for football," Miller said. But he dreamed of being a basketball player. He felt he was a better basketball player in high school than football. However, after going one-on-one with Rich Jones in Illinois freshman drills, he conceded he didn't have much of a future in basketball.

"In Arcola, football was handed down for many years," Miller said. "My grandfather talked about getting guys together and playing the old Staley Bears in Decatur. It started way before me. It became a great tradition."

Miller's brother Dan quarterbacked the 1978 state champion. The team was led by running back Jeff Fishel, whose father, Jack, quarterbacked the unbeaten 1954 and 1955 teams and brother John quarterbacked the 1977 state runner up. Other standouts were defensive back Marty Thomas, the coach's son, tackle David Cook, receiver Jeff Moore, and 135-pound lineman Randy Wright. They smashed Hampshire 42–14 for the title.

But everybody agrees that the 1985 state champion, Thomas' only unbeaten team, was the best of all. The 1988 state champion might have had a better defense—it allowed only eight points in five playoff games—but the 1985 team averaged 38 points per game and the defense allowed only one touchdown in the first half during the course of a 14–0 season. Their only regret was beating Durand by only 14–6 in the state final after sweeping past four earlier playoff opponents by a 141–25 margin.

Standouts were Patrick and Jon Monahan, who rushed for 118 yards and scored both touchdowns against Durand, running back Mitch Thomas, quarterback Duane Boyd, linebacker Mike Davis, and linemen Joe Schrock and Tommy Reece, Ramie Silva, Bert and Roi Ray, Jeff Butler, and Duane Beachy. The offensive line was called the "Crunch Bunch." Jon Monahan rushed for 1,900 yards, Mitch Thomas 1,200.

The architects for the success in the 1970s and 1980s were Steve Thomas, Byron Bradford, and Randy Rothrock. Bradford assisted Thomas for 29 years. They retired together in 1993. Rothrock assisted Thomas for 17 years.

Thomas, who died in 2004, was an All-State running back for Warren Smith at

Urbana, then played at Illinois and had a tryout with the Dallas Cowboys. He was very structured, very organized. Practices lasted for 1 hour and 45 minutes. No one stood around. The system was simple: run the ball and play defense, like Woody Hayes. He never forced kids to lift weights in the summer. He loved to hunt and fish.

"His philosophy was: 'If I make a kid lift weights, how can I count on him?' He expected kids to know how to block and tackle and run a play without a mistake or we'd run it until we did," Rothrock said. "He never cared about scores or statistics. He was more interested in getting a lot of kids to play."

"You can't talk about Thomas without putting Bradford in the same sentence," Chris Monahan said. "Both were stoic men of great character. You wanted to play well for both of them. Bradford was more outgoing, more of a players' coach. Thomas was the strong, silent type. They stressed fundamentals. They taught them so well that the players bought into the system."

It was the emphasis on fundamentals and the culture of winning that were key to Arcola's success, not the talent or presence of college recruits, according to Patrick Monahan, who graduated No. 1 in his class at Arcola and earned a degree in aerospace engineering at Notre Dame.

"Coach Thomas was part of the wallpaper when we grew up," he said. "The attitude was we expected to win. We expected to have a good season. Mentally, we knew we could win. Others hoped they could win. We sensed we were at the beginning of something big."

Bloomington Central Catholic: Building a Foundation

Bloomington Central Catholic (Bloomington CC), once called Trinity, opened in the early 1900s. But as late as 1974, the school was still conducting classes in an old downtown building with old blackboards and white chalk.

The football program was a low-budget operation and the players had to find ways to get to practice at old McLean County fairgrounds, three miles away. They lifted weights in the basement of Holy Trinity Church across the street from the school.

But the school administration was committed to building and supporting a winning program. John Snyder was basketball coach and athletic director for 41 years. All programs were financed by gate receipts and fund-raising efforts by boosters. But facilities didn't become first-class until the new school was constructed in 2003.

"I was young [31 years old] and wanted to be a head coach," John McIntyre said. "We were feeling our way through getting the program together. What really helped was the football playoff. Once we got into it, we got better as we went along. The playoff system helped to build incentive for football."

Ed Murphy produced two 7–0–2 teams in 1952 and 1953 but the school didn't enjoy much success until McIntyre returned for a second time in 1979. He was hired in 1974 but posted a 9–18 record in three years, then took two years off to serve as interim principal at Octavia. In his second stint, he won two state championships and settled for a second in nine years. From 1982 to 1985, his teams were 43–7.

Ironically, McIntyre said his two best teams didn't even qualify for the state play-off. His 1979 team was 7–2 but lost to Bloomington by three points. His 1983 team, featuring several veterans from the 1982 state championship squad, finished 11–2 and lost to Marian Central in the state final.

"We had a three-year series with Kankakee Bishop McNamara in the early 1980s and split with them 3–3. One year, both schools won state titles. It told us we were on our way," McIntyre said. "We played on Sunday afternoon in Bloomington and it was a big event in town. After 1982, when we won the first state title for the area, it got everything going."

One of the primary builders of the program was Bob Brady, now president of Brady Homes, a building development business based in Bloomington. Brady followed his two older brothers to the school and got caught up in Bloomington CC tradition. He was a sophomore on the 1982 state champion but broke an ankle three days before the playoff.

"When they won, everyone signed the game ball and gave it to me," Brady said. "We were always looked upon as the underdog but we came out fighting. We all had great pride. Our school was much smaller than anyone we played. We had 57 in my senior class. We were building a foundation for what was to come in the 1980s. The beauty of a small school is you need the participation of all students to succeed, regardless of athletic ability."

McIntyre took the cards he was dealt and produced a winning hand. He surrounded himself with good position coaches and delegated authority. His scouting reports were 20 to 30 pages long. His wife cooked breakfast on Sunday morning while the coaches and players looked at film. Future coaches Don Boynton and Bobby Moews, who played for McIntyre, paid their dues and worked their way through the ranks. It was all about preparation.

"He was one of a kind," Brady said of McIntyre. "He wouldn't tell you to run through a brick wall. He'd run through it first and ask you to follow. He always found ways to win, not cave, in fourth-quarter situations. We became a team, not a selfish group. He was all about teaching us about life situations, whether it was fourth-and-goal or how to deal with academics."

The 1982 team featured running back Dave Schilkoski, quarterback Doug Moews, linebacker Kendall Eyre, offensive linemen Tom and Tim Kraft, Matt Johnson, Dan Krause, Dan Welch, and Jim Killoran. It was a gritty group that won two playoff games in overtime—23–22 over Ottawa Marquette in the first round and 17–10 over Richmond-Burton in the semifinals—before trouncing Casey 38–0 in the final as Schilkoski rushed for 135 yards and two touchdowns.

"It was a group of seniors that had mental toughness that I hadn't seen on a football field before. It wasn't a group of gifted athletes but they were tough and aggressive," Brady said. "The game that stands out was Ottawa Marquette. I was standing on the goal line with crutches. They went for a two-point conversion on the last possession and we stopped them on the six-inch line. To this day, they still think he scored."

Brady, Schilkoski, Moews, and Krause returned in 1983 but Bloomington CC was overpowered by Marian Central and Chuck and Andy Hartlieb and Dan Fortin 34–14. But the 1984 semifinal loss to Jacksonville Routt was harder to swallow. Starting quarterback Dan Flynn was injured and couldn't play. Brady, a free safety, came running up on a sweep and when the ball carrier cut back, Brady's cleats flew out from under him. The runner went on to complete a 60-yard scoring run, and Routt won 10–7 and went on to win the state title.

"All I could do was watch," Brady said. "I was there, I pursued properly, but the grass gave out and that was that. When we came off the field, we felt we were the better team. A loss like that is hard to accept."

The 1987 state champion, McIntyre's last team, was described as "survivors." As freshmen, the senior class numbered only 13 players. They didn't win a game until the final game of their sophomore season. They were small but quick. They lost to Monticello by one point early in the season and McIntyre decided to install sophomore Brian Flynn at quarterback and move quarterback Jim Horton to wide receiver, where he caught seven touchdown passes during the rest of the season. Other standouts were fullback/safety Kurt Thoma and slotback/defensive back Scott Connors.

The first-team defense allowed only two touchdowns in its first nine games. In the playoff, they dispatched Elmwood 28–7, Bradford 35–0, Roseville 31–8, Freeport Aquin 17–14, and Hardin-Calhoun 20–12 to finish with a 12–2 record. The victory over Hardin-Calhoun marked the 100th of McIntyre's career.

Boynton grew up in St. Charles and attended Illinois State. His ambition was to be a head coach by his 30th birthday. He met McIntyre at a fund-raiser after the 1982 championship and was impressed. But there were no jobs available. He scouted for a season, was hired in 1984, and became head coach in 1988. In five years, his teams were 44–10, a .815 winning percentage.

"I was an outsider coming in. I was the only one on the football staff who wasn't a graduate of the school," Boynton said. "But there was a great atmosphere of success. I was made a financial offer that I should have refused. My role was not to take this great program that McIntyre had built and go downhill with it. I wanted to try to continue the same level of success that he had established."

The 1990 squad had great leadership with center Jeff Flynn, the class valedictorian, and quarterback Rob Zononi, the salutatorian. Others were fullback Tony Kiley and tackle Kenny Rhodes. Zononi passed for 2,400 yards and 25 touchdowns. But they lost to Sterling Newman 6–3 in overtime for the state title.

Bobby Moews (pronounced Mays) played and coached for McIntyre, then succeeded Boynton as head coach in 1992. After a 7–3 debut, his second team went 2–7 and committed 35 turnovers in 36 quarters. But the 1994 squad had only 15 turnovers in a 13–1 season. The leaders were quarterback Tom Bardwell, who had concentrated on golf and didn't play football until his junior year; 5–8, 165-pound junior linebacker Chris Kiley, who was credited with 140 tackles; 5–9, 155-pound noseman Bob Crawford; two-way lineman Andy Hoenigis; and tailback Kori Parker, who rushed for 1,500 yards.

It was a second-half team. In Week 4, they beat defending state champion Pontiac 24–20 on the final drive, snapping Pontiac's 16-game winning streak. In the playoff, they beat Canton 17–3, Pontiac 7–6, Spring Valley Hall 28–20, Aurora Central Catholic 27–21 in overtime, and Du Quoin 22–12 after trailing 12–0.

Moews, who is 125–51 for the past 16 years, produced a state runner-up in 2007 despite the presence of only nine seniors. They finished 13–1, losing to seven-time state champion Driscoll. Tailback Ryan Waldron rushed for 1,900 yards, quarterback Adam Rebholz passed for 1,800, and 235-pound Zach Eyre and 245-pound Joe Ring anchored the line. But Moews conceded that Driscoll was one or two steps faster.

Moews' 2008 squad never missed a beat, however. The Saints, led by Rebholz, Ring, running backs Brad Connor and David Murray, and linebacker Sean Stokes, swept through a 14-game schedule by averaging 40 points. Rebholz passed for 319 yards, ran for two touchdowns, and passed for two others in a 37–28 victory over Aurora Christian in the Class 4A final.

"We preach to our kids to play hard all the time, like every play means something," Moews said in explaining his philosophy. "Coach McIntyre was one of the best game-day coaches I ever was around. I liked his style, what he expected of kids. Demand is a hard word. But we ask a lot of our kids, a lot of time during the season. But the kids who have followed saw what was being asked and realized success at the end of the rainbow."

Carthage: The Unruh Era

A lot of things have changed in Carthage. The school has been renamed Illini West. The nickname has been changed from Blueboys to Chargers, though old-timers admit they never will get accustomed to the new name. And the school colors have changed from royal blue and white to navy blue, orange, and white.

But some things will never change. You can't erase history. Carthage, the seat of Hancock County, dates to 1837. Lincoln and Douglas conducted one of their famous political debates in the town square. But the biggest tourist attraction is the town jail, where Mormon founder Joseph Smith was killed by an angry mob.

Most kids grew up on cattle or grain farms. They socialize in the parking lot at the local Dairy Queen or Hardee's and drive back and forth on Highway 136. There are no stoplights in town, just a four-way stop. Students and parents and alumni celebrate victories at the Pizza Hut in nearby Keokuk, Iowa, across the Mississippi River.

The boys play football and the girls play basketball. And football coach Jim Unruh always wears the same old stocking cap on the sideline in cold weather. Well, not really the same. When the school became Illini West, he began wearing a navy blue cap.

Since he became head coach in 1986 as a 21-year-old college graduate, Unruh has never changed his pregame speech. After discussing the game plan, he finishes with the same directive: "Gentlemen, always remember that the game of football is about being physical. You have to be more physical than your opponent."

The message never has failed to resonate. Unruh, whose father, Paul, coached West Chicago to a state championship in 1974, won 200 games in his first 20 years. In 23 seasons, his teams are 230–44, a .839 winning percentage, one of the highest in state history. He has won five state titles, including three in a row from 1998 to 2000, and finished second four times. From 1998 to 2008, his teams were 118–13.

"I still remember that I sent out resumes to everybody," Unruh said. "At the time, I wasn't looking for a coaching job, just an elementary school teaching job. Then I got a call from the superintendent at Carthage. Was I interested in the head coaching job? There was a sign outside of town. It said: 1984 state runner-up. I thought I would be in way over my head.

"But my mom and dad said to go for it. I thought they were desperate and didn't have any football success. But they had success in the past. I got a quick education. I learned they had a lot of tradition in football and girls' basketball. I was stepping into a place that took them very seriously."

Art Keller started the tradition in the 1940s and 1950s. When he left for Carthage College, Ed Test came along and produced unbeaten teams in 1969 and 1972. His 1974 team qualified for the first state playoff. Bob Steinman took teams to the state playoff in 1979 and 1980. Ken Miller's 1984 team finished second. Then Unruh was hired.

"I still look up to Rusty Willey, a center/linebacker on the 1984 team, with awe," said Zak Huston, the athletic director at Illini West who started on three of Unruh's teams before graduating in 1995. "I recall the 1984 team losing to Jacksonville Routt in the championship game and [future Jacksonville and Illinois basketball star] Andy Kaufmann intercepting a pass in the game.

"I remember the 1988 team [13–1 state runner-up] with Richie Hopkins, Mike Adams, Lance Brown, and Warren Clayburn. I like to say I was part of a group that showed the 1995 state championship team how to play football. We were 10–1 as juniors and seniors and lost to Hardin-Calhoun, which won back-to-back state titles."

Unruh knocked on the door a couple of times before breaking it down. After 1988, his 1994 team was ranked No. 1 in the state and won 10 in a row before losing to Hardin-Calhoun in the second round.

"I still remember asking myself, 'What does it take to get to the championship game?' We had such high expectations. That was the best team I coached that didn't get to the state final," Unruh said.

But Carthage won in 1995, smashing Arcola 45–13 for the school's first state football title. Kenton Patrick rushed 20 times for 239 yards and four touchdowns, including an 81-yarder, and Joel Morehouse carried 13 times for 145 yards and one touchdown. The Blueboys amassed 506 yards rushing on 51 attempts. They threw only one pass. The defense was keyed by noseman Sid Huls. The offense rushed for 5,164 yards, third most in state history.

Wyatt Green led Carthage to state titles in 1998, 1999, and 2000. He rushed for 4,800 yards and more than 60 touchdowns in his career, averaged 9 yards per carry, and set a state record by rushing for over 100 yards in 39 games. The Blueboys won 32 games in a row at one point. They were so good that they attempted to arrange for an exhibition game with a Joliet Catholic team led by J. R. Zwierzynski that Coach Dan Sharp said was the best he had produced. But the Illinois High School Association wouldn't permit it.

Green grew up in Burnside (population: 80), located eight miles from Carthage. When he was five, he painted a football field in his yard. He would simulate running against someone and throwing passes to himself. He had his own helmet and pads. He played six-on-six pickup games once a week in his backyard. In sixth grade, he participated in a YMCA-sponsored league in Keokuk.

Carthage was 14–0 in 1998 with Green, noseman T. J. Menn, fullback Luke Wessel, quarterback George Toubekis, center Jeremy Kerr, flanker Bart Ellefritz, running back Andy Dietz, and wide receiver Eric Huston. The 1999 squad also finished 14–0 as Jared Murphy threw a 54-yard pass to Willie Thompson to the 23 and Curtis Bisby scored with 1:10 to play as Carthage edged Galena 14–12.

In 2000, after having its 32-game winning streak snapped by LaHarpe in Week 4 when the two teams were ranked 1–2 in the state, Carthage bounced back to beat LaHarpe 14–0 in the state final. Green carried 27 times for 152 yards and two touchdowns and Aaron Fink rushed 28 times for 106 yards. They didn't throw a single pass. Mark Jacob and Jason Jefferson keyed the offensive and defensive lines.

"I got so mad with running the same plays for four years," Green said. "Finally, as a junior, we were doing a two-minute offense and I said I'd throw a pass off a halfback sweep. We did it on our own. [Unruh] didn't say anything and I ran it for a 50-yard touchdown pass in a game. We added four plays to our offensive playbook in my last two years."

Unruh didn't want to tamper with success. He ran a Delaware wing-T that his father ran at West Chicago and Bob Reade ran at Augustana College. He didn't try to trick anyone, just do a better job of blocking and tackling than his opponents. For the last 15 years, he ran a double tight end, wing right set for 99 percent of his snaps. His only rules? Something he learned from his father, Reade, and Lou Holtz: Obey the law, act like a gentleman, do what's right.

Aston Gronewold was a promising freshman in 2000 when Green was a senior. He was promoted to the varsity after the loss to LaHarpe. Unruh said Green and Gronewold were the best players he ever coached. Gronewold said the 2000 team was the best he saw and Green was the player that he looked up to the most. The team set state records by scoring 81 touchdowns and 694 points in 14 games. It rushed for 5,093 yards, fourth most in state history.

"I was a little kid with a bunch of grownups," Gronewold said. "I learned the way to win. I worked hard and never took a play off. The 2000 state championship game was the seniors' Super Bowl. They poured their hearts and souls into it. That was our best team. I idolized older people when I was growing up."

Gronewold didn't experience the success that Green did. As a junior, he rushed for 1,800 yards and his team was 13–1 and averaged 48 points per game but lost to Aledo 41–40 in one of the most exciting state finals in playoff history. As a senior, he rushed for 2,222 yards and scored 42 touchdowns but his 13–1 team lost to Iroquois West 32–14 in the state final. In four years, those were the only games he lost.

"Those were some of the most fun years of my life because we worked hard and put in an effort," he said. "It set the tone for what I wanted to do. If you don't let anyone outwork you, things will fall into place. For me, we lost. But I didn't have any regrets because I knew I had done everything I could to win."

After finishing second in 2002, 2003, and 2004, Carthage, now Illini West, once again claimed the big trophy in 2008 as Sean Flynn rushed 30 times for 213 yards and two touchdowns and Mike Lafferty threw an 18-yard touchdown pass to Jacob Schmudlach with 25 seconds to play to beat Du Quoin 21–14 for the Class 3A crown.

Decatur St. Teresa: Decade of the 1970s

Dick Munn insists the football tradition at St. Teresa High School in Decatur began long before he enrolled as a student in 1957. But the truth is the program, which had experienced some success under Joe Venturi in the 1950s, had suffered 10 losing seasons in a row before Munn became head coach in 1968.

"Munn was the guy who started it all. All the credit for starting the program goes to him," said Scott Davis, a Decatur native who has served as St. Teresa's football coach and athletic director since 1987.

"He set the mold for what was to follow," said Terry Howley, a 1965 graduate who was an assistant under Munn and coaches Ed Boehm and Ralph McQuiggan and later was mayor of Decatur. "He changed the attitude, got the weight program going, and persuaded kids to come to St. Teresa."

After struggling at 2–6–1 in 1969, St. Teresa went 7–1–1 in 1970, and then went 8–1, 9–0, and 9–0 in the next three years. When Munn left for West Aurora, Boehm took over and won 32 of 35 games in three years, including state championships in 1974 and 1975. Then McQuiggan won 19 of 22 games in two years and won a state title in 1979.

Dale Patton produced a state runner-up in 1986 and Davis has logged a record of 165–57 in the past 21 years. From 1992 to 1996, his teams were 49–7. In the past six years, they went 61–9.

"The 1970 team set the tone for what followed," said Phil Jones, who was the team's leading rusher, pass receiver, and punt/kick returner. He and his older brother Jessie were the only black students in the school. He also had a white girlfriend, something that was difficult to deal with in the racial turmoil of the 1960s and 1970s.

"My mother didn't want me to go to public schools, where there was a lot of racism," Jones said. "St. Teresa was a religious school. There was some racism but my mother taught me not to expect everyone to be a racist. She expected me to handle myself as a man. Some kids hadn't seen a black until they saw me. It turned out to be a great thing for me."

Jones credited Munn and the school administration for supporting him. His brother Jessie was a senior when he was a freshman. His cousin Jerry arrived the year after Phil graduated. Jerry was one of the stars of the 1974 and 1975 state championship teams that keyed a 45-game winning streak.

"It was a great learning experience for me," Phil said. "I look back and see what I went through and I wouldn't take it today. But my mother had an influence over me. I held my temper and composure. I couldn't go to parties because parents were racist and didn't want blacks in their house. I got rid of my frustrations by being a good athlete, by being better than others. They made me push harder."

By all accounts, St. Teresa was a family. When Munn became head coach at 25, St. Teresa had an enrollment of 320 students. He drew athletes from four parishes and competed against four public high schools that dwarfed St. Teresa. He was accused of recruiting but he insists he never recruited a single athlete.

"Once we started winning, we were able to draw from the entire area," he said. "People were told that if they were moving to Decatur, St. Teresa was the only place to go if you wanted to play football. We were ahead of our time. We ran a multiple pro offense and no one else did."

Jackie Jackson came from Blue Mound, which didn't have football, and became an outstanding linebacker. Marty Leech wasn't Catholic but his mother wanted him to play football at St. Teresa. Mark Feldman, another non-Catholic who quarterbacked the 10–0 team in 1973 and the 1974 state championship team, transferred from La Grange. Jerry Jones' father came to Munn's house and said his son wanted to play for him.

"To this day, I tell [Munn] that I went into coaching because of the influence he had on me," said Craig Bundy, a 1974 graduate who played on two unbeaten teams and has been head coach at Bradley-Bourbonnais for the past 11 years.

"What separated him was we were in better shape than anyone we played, more mentally tough. We had a simple offense but we were so well coached and prepared. I didn't have a father around so I needed discipline in my life. I had a bad temper but I couldn't get away with that with Munn. You couldn't act like a fool or you would pay for it. If you didn't say 'Yes sir, no sir,' you would be in trouble."

Munn's 1972 and 1973 teams are regarded as the best in school history but Boehm's 1974 and 1975 squads received more name recognition because they won championships in the first two years of the state playoff. But Boehm admitted that Munn's 1971, 1972, and 1973 teams were "better, bigger, and stronger" than his 1974 and 1975 teams.

Marty Bushell was the star of the 1974 team. Munn had left. So had 20 seniors from 1973. Boehm, the logical choice to succeed Munn, was a familiar face. But the team lacked experience and had a lot to prove. Could they continue the winning streak? Would they be competitive in the first year of the state playoff?

"We had a buzz. We knew we would win. We didn't know if we could win it all but we were ready to prove ourselves," Bushell said. "Boehm challenged us to rise to the level that people expected. He said it was our turn to continue the tradition and domination. 'Let's keep this thing rolling,' he told us."

They did. Bushell rushed for 1,300 yards, including 131 in a 15–6 victory over Alexis in the state final. He scored on a 58-yarder with 8:24 left to seal the victory.

"That was the most memorable game to me," Bushell said. "It was our first state title, it capped an unbeaten season, and we proved ourselves to the rest of the state. We were leading 7–6. They were looking for us to pass. The play was called—fake pitch to the left and give to me over right guard. One block by Bob Burtschi and I saw daylight and took off."

The 1975 team was more dominant. Bushell and Jerry Jones were leaders. Bushell rushed for 1,300 yards, Jones for 1,100. Jones set a state record by rushing 32 times for 250 yards and scoring five touchdowns in a 35–0 rout of Stockton in the state final. Bushell averaged nearly 10 yards per carry. The team averaged more than 40 points per game, crushing Warrensburg-Latham 47–7, Arcola 41–0, St Joseph-Ogden 72–0, and Sullivan 46–0 in the regular season and stomping on Gillespie 46–0, Dupo 33–0, Danville Schlarman 45–0, and Stockton in the playoff. They shut out their last eight opponents.

They were so quick, Boehm said, that they once took the ball off a punter's foot. Other standouts were linebacker Chuck Vercellino, noseman Chris Schroth, guard/defensive end Marty Leech, end/defensive back Jeff Hannapel, tackle Greg Hahn, two-way lineman Scott Feldman, and quarterback/linebacker Russ Hollingsworth.

St. Teresa's domination of the decade of the 1970s continued when McQuiggan arrived in 1979. The 1978 team was 7–2 and failed to qualify for the state playoff but there was plenty of talent returning, including Ben Pothast, Mike Regan, Keith McRedmond, Bob Moody, Mickey McNamara, Steve Neisman, Scott Tabscott, Mike Sheehan, and Gary Burgess. In the state final, they smashed Amboy 36–12. Howley describes McNamara, a 6–0, 210-pound defensive tackle, as the best defensive player he coached in 14 years. He was the leader of the 1979 defense.

"Looking back, I learned that you get a different perspective when you get older, how winning and a sports program bring a school and a town together," Bushell said. "Decatur had been a basketball town before. But I recall coming back on the bus after winning in 1974 and people coming out to cheer us and welcome us home.

"Our football program finally had a chance to show the state how good we were. It uplifted the spirit of the town. Joe Cook, Rex Spires, and Bob Fallstrom wrote about us for the *Decatur Herald & Review*. Everybody got involved and turned it into a big city celebration. It was a great time to be part of St. Teresa sports."

Galena: Not Just a Tourist Attraction

Ed Cichy had a reputation and a record of going into a small school with a limited amount of players and talent and turning them into a winner. But when he interviewed for the head coaching position at Galena in 1978, he wondered if he had bitten off more than he could chew.

"When I came to Galena, there were only 17 varsity players, 11 sophomores, and 12 freshman," he recalled. "When I interviewed for the job, Stockton was the power in the area. I was the junior coach in the league and [Stockton coach] John O'Boyle was the senior coach. The guy who interviewed me said I had to beat Stockton."

When Cichy retired from coaching 10 years later, O'Boyle only had a one-game edge in their rivalry. Cichy, by his own admission, had "created my own monster." His teams were 78–22 and qualified for the state playoff five times, a more difficult feat in an era of fewer classes in a format that allowed for only conference champions.

Cichy wasn't so much interested in qualifying for the state playoff as he was in generating interest in his program. Four years after he was hired, he put 99 players on the field—and the school's total enrollment was only 350. He built a solid foundation but tired of the expectations and turned the program over to Chuck Korte and Ed Freed, who took it to the next level.

"Kids saw that, if they go out for football, they will play," Cichy said. "Some parents were dissatisfied because of the policy of playing so many kids. But it built the program.

"One of the things I noticed when I got here is kids were tough. They had a native wildness. Galena kids like to bash kids around. That was the style we played. I was a big Woody Hayes person as a kid. I liked to run the ball, plow away. Some people chanted, 'Boring, boring, boring.' But we won games. Once kids saw they could win, it changed their attitude. Fifth graders began to say they couldn't wait to play football at Galena."

Cichy's 1980 team, led by Ron Smith, Kendall Hartwig, Mark Mueller, and Kevin Nicholson, was ranked No. 4 in the state and qualified for the playoff for the first time. Even though it lost its first game, Cichy said it was the team that "started to put Galena on the map in football."

But old-timers claim the 1985 team, led by Buzz Harris and Jeff Zeal, was the best in school history. They finished 11–1, losing to Marian Central 8–3 in the mud in a state quarterfinal in Woodstock.

"People got the fever," said Mike Hyland, who has served as defensive coordinator since 1980 and athletic director since 1999.

Even Pete Kieffer, who never dreamed that he'd see a Galena football team play in a state final, caught the fever. Kieffer hasn't missed a game in 40 years and volunteers to take care of the football field.

Chuck Korte caught the fever, too. Born and raised in Galena, he didn't play sports in high school. He had to work on the family farm after his father died of cancer when he was a sophomore. After college, he returned to Galena to teach and coach in middle school and the lower levels. When Cichy retired, he was ready for another challenge.

"He was a pied piper, very dynamic, a wonderful motivator," Hyland said. "He said, 'Why can't we win a state title? Why aren't we working for that? With O'Boyle's teams doing so well at Stockton, why can't we do that?' The community embraced him. The kids bought into what he was teaching. He wasn't a typical football coach. He was a riverboat gambler as far as taking chances, unconventional, creative, double passes, trick plays."

In 16 years, Korte's teams won 148 of 188 games, including state championships in 1997 and 2003 and second in 1999. In a six-year period from 1995 to 2000, Galena was 71–7. His successor, Ed Freed, who served as co-coach in 2003, has won 77 percent (43–13) of his games in the past five years. His 2007 squad won the state championship.

"Galena didn't used to be as much of a tourist town as it is today," Korte said. "We had a lot of kids who grew up on farms, blue-collar kids who weren't afraid to put out an effort. What I remember most in the summer is the kids kept looking forward to the start of the season. Football was fun for them."

After losing to Chenoa in the state semifinals and finishing 12–1 in 1996, Galena wouldn't be denied in 1997. They completed a 14–0 season by beating Stark County 14–0 for the school's first state title. The team was led by running backs Michael Cox and Michael Gratton, linebackers Tim Vincent and Matt Ohms, quarterback Brian Murphy, and defensive linemen Nate McCoy and Casey Kaiser.

The 28–15 loss to Chenoa was the only setback that Vincent's class suffered in four years. But Vincent, a 6-6, 240-pounder who later played at Northern Illinois, never has forgotten one play that could have turned the game around. Trailing 8–6 and faced with a fourth-and-goal at Chenoa's three, Chris Miller swept around the end and dove for the end zone pylon. But he missed.

"I had a feeling in the pit of my stomach that you don't want again," Vincent said. "Assistant coach Dan Tranel brought the juniors together. He said, 'Remember this feeling right now because you don't want to have this feeling next year. What are you going to do to change it?' We dedicated ourselves."

The 1997 team was dominant. It averaged 35 points per game, recorded nine shutouts and didn't permit an opponent to get closer than the 14–0 margin in the state final. Cox, who walked on at Northwestern, rushed for 2,000 yards. But the team had so much depth that when Cox tore up his knee in the first playoff game, backup Michael Gratton stepped up and rushed for a state-record 292 yards in a semifinal victory over Arcola.

"After the state final, on the way to the bus, somebody noticed that a letter was missing from the state championship trophy, the I from champion," Korte said. "The kids said, 'No, don't replace it. There is no I in team.' So the trophy still is sitting in our trophy case without the I. That was the thing about that team. Everybody cheered for everybody else. Our goal was to go 14–0 and we did it as a team."

Freed, who has Iowa roots, was coaching at the University of Dubuque when he heard about Galena. "I heard more about football than the tourist attraction," he said. He switched to a pro-set I formation offense (instead of Korte's wishbone) and purchased new, tighter fitting uniforms, but stuck to most of the old traditions—Hyland's 5-2 defense, spaghetti night on Thursday planned by the senior mothers, and yearly team mottos (last year's was "Respect All, Fear None").

It all came together again in 2003. Korte and Freed ran the offense, Korte called the plays and Hyland ran the defense. Galena was coming off a 9–2 season in which they had lost to eventual state champion South Beloit 35–24 in the second round. There was a lot of talent returning—quarterback Justin Carter, running backs Alex Dupessis and Matt Randecker, defensive back Nick Heitkamp, and two-way lineman Chad Wienen were the leaders—and there were high expectations.

The Pirates struggled at first and were only 6–3 going into the state playoff. They avenged a 40–3 loss to Stockton by eliminating their conference rival 13–10 in overtime in the second round. They had to drive 95 yards to beat Orangeville and edged Leroy 21–20 in overtime for the state title.

"With two and a half minutes left in the fourth quarter, Leroy had the ball on our one-yard-line and was going in to score," Freed recalled. "A quarterback sneak didn't get in. They ran another sneak and the quarterback got stood up. Defensive end Jared Fleege stripped the ball but nobody saw the ball come out. He burst out of the pile and the officials didn't know what was going on. They caught him past midfield and sent the game into overtime. In Galena history, that play never will be forgotten."

Neither will Gavin Kaiser's performance in the 2007 state championship game. Galena, coming off a 10–1 season in which it had lost to Lexington in the second round, capped another 14–0 campaign by trouncing Tuscola and All-State quarterback John Wienke 35–7 for the 1A crown.

Kaiser scored on a 91-yard kickoff return and runs of 1 and 55 yards and completed a 28-yard touchdown pass to Matt Hillard. He rushed nine times for 96 yards, completed 10 of 15 passes for 145 yards, averaged 33.5 yards on two punts, and accounted for 217 all-purpose yards. He also made six tackles and broke up three passes.

"This senior class had been talked about for years, the one that could go to state," said Kaiser, who teamed with Logan Flack, Spencer Dupessis, Vince Newton, Michael Decker, Cody Johnson, Matt Hillard, Ryan Stodden, and Irving Pulido.

Kaiser passed for 1,500 yards and 18 touchdowns. Decker rushed for 950 yards. Pulido was credited with 125 tackles as a strong safety. The offense averaged 38 points per game while the defense, keyed by Decker, Stodden, and Pulido, shut out three playoff opponents.

"You must make the game as much fun as you can, especially in your senior year," Kaiser said. "Good things will happen if you work hard and relax."

Pittsfield: "The Streak"

In Pittsfield, old-timers still refer to it as "The Streak." Sixty-four victories in a row, including 44 shutouts. Seven consecutive unbeaten seasons. One team was unscored upon in nine games. Two others allowed only one touchdown, one when the second-stringers were on the field. They once had a string of 15 shutouts in a row.

It was the most successful stretch of invincibility in state football history. And it makes everyone wonder what kind of a punctuation mark the Saukees would have left in the record book if they had played in the post-playoff era.

After starting 1–4–3 in 1965, Coach Donald "Deek" Pollard built a dynasty at the small (500 students) Pike County school. He produced seven 9–0 teams in a row, then resigned to become an assistant coach at Western Illinois and left what he considered his best team to assistant Fred Erickson, who went 9–0 in 1972.

"The most difficult thing was to find a way to motivate players for the next game, maybe an opponent without success or with a lot of success," Pollard said. "We had success on defense. I was big on shutouts. I sold them on the principle that if you can make the starting defensive team at Pittsfield, you will play and we won't take you out. If you are tough, we told them, you will play. Motivation was easier when the shutouts began to come game after game."

"If Pollard had stayed, the streak would have gone on for many more years," said John Ruzich, a lineman who starred on the 1968 and 1969 teams and earned a scholarship to Michigan State. "Everyone believes if there had been a playoff system, we would have won every year."

Fred Ruzich, John's younger brother, recalled that nobody wanted to be on a team that got scored upon, much less one that lost a game. In 1971, athletic director Glenn Smith, looking far and wide for opponents that would agree to play Pittsfield, scheduled a game at Westville, which was a strong program in eastern Illinois near Danville. Westville scored 26 points but Pittsfield scored 50. But Pollard didn't celebrate.

"He never let us eat on the way home," Fred Ruzich said. "You'd have thought we lost. It was so quiet on the long bus ride home, no snickering, not a word. We didn't think about losing. We didn't feel any pressure. We just felt there wasn't anyone we couldn't beat. But we didn't want to be scored on."

Kevin Lowe, who starred on the 1969 and 1970 powerhouses and later played at Illinois, said there was talk of scheduling a game with Geneseo, which had a string of five unbeaten seasons in a row from 1966 to 1970.

"Both schools were in big hog-producing counties at the time and there was talk of scheduling a game with Geneseo at Western Illinois University and calling it the Hog Bowl. But the Illinois High School Association wouldn't go along with it. I'd like to think we could have won several state titles during that era."

But the 1969 and 1970 teams, which included Lowe and running backs Charlie Hubbard and Bruce Callender, set the bar so high. In 1969, as the players ran from the locker room to the field, they chanted, "Thirty-six and O." In 1970, the chant was "Forty-five and O."

"We fully believed that was a realistic goal," Lowe said. "We would have loved to have had a chance to play in the state playoff. We wouldn't have won 64 in a row with a state playoff. I'm not naïve enough to think we could have gone 14–0 against the best teams in the state. But we would have loved to try."

Tom McCartney, who quarterbacked the 1968 and 1969 teams and is described by Pollard as the best player he coached, agrees the streak wouldn't have extended as long as it did if a state playoff was in place. "But it would have been fun to participate in what they have today. We would have found out how good we really were," he said.

But McCartney, who later played at Illinois, said "what sticks out the most in my mind" about the Pollard era at Pittsfield was how many kids had a chance to go beyond high school and play in college and get a college education.

"That was important," he said. "I could go to college on scholarship to play baseball or football. But a lot of guys got to college who otherwise wouldn't have."

Charlie Hubbard, who started on three unbeaten teams, said the players prided themselves on believing that they would shut out every opponent—and they almost did. He was a running back as a sophomore but played defensive end as a junior and strong safety as a senior. "We looked forward to playing defense," Hubbard said.

Perhaps the closest the streak came to being snapped before September 21, 1973, was in 1969 when Pittsfield hosted Quincy Christian Brothers Catholic. The game was played in a monsoon with two inches of water on the field. As black clouds rolled over the field, Pittsfield elected to receive the kickoff and proceeded to drive 80 yards for the game's only touchdown. Quincy reached Pittsfield's eight-yard-line with eight seconds to play but Lowe sacked the quarterback as time ran out.

"We started taping at 5:30 and it got dark," Pollard recalled. "The principal said there was a big storm coming. Should we cancel the game? No, I said, the rain would be to our advantage. Over 100 games were canceled that night. We were the only one played in western and central Illinois. You couldn't see the lines on the field when it started. The water was up to our ankles and you couldn't set the ball on a tee. But the rain stopped at halftime. I think the only people who stayed to watch were my father, mother, wife, and two daughters."

Which was the best team?

Pollard insists the 1972 team was best of all, the team he left behind. It has the best talent, he said. Most of the seniors had started as juniors on the 1971 squad, his last team. It was led by linebackers Ron Ghrist and Kevin Lowe, who played at Missouri and Illinois, respectively, tackle Fred Ruzich, guard Mike Barton, quarterback Rich Bergman, center Brett Irving, and running back John Carlton.

McCartney picked the 1967 squad. He was a sophomore and played tight end at the time. "It was the best team I played on," he said. The stars were John Ruzich, running back Dave Shaw, fullback Mark Beattie, center George Roodhouse, guard Tom Henderson, tackle Parker Zumwalt, quarterback John McMackin, and tackle Bart Crawford.

Pollard said Crawford was one of the toughest kids he coached. The 6–2½ country kid weighed 350 pounds as a freshman, 285 as a sophomore, then 260. Because he had a D-minus grade point average in high school, he didn't qualify for a Division

I scholarship. So he played for four years at Truman State in Missouri. At the end of the first semester of his sophomore year, he was on the dean's list. He graduated with a degree in zoology. Today, he is director of a habitat in Florida.

Lowe, Hubbard, and longtime Pittsfield sports historian Wayne Ator cited the un-scored-upon 1970 squad that didn't allow one opponent to get a first down and didn't permit two others to cross the 50-yard-line. Callender rushed for over 1,000 yards for the second year in a row. Jay Carlton succeeded McCartney at quarterback. Lowe and Ghrist, a budding sophomore, were devastating blockers and linebackers.

"On Friday night, you could have walked away with everything downtown because no one was there, they were all at the football game," Fred Ruzich said. "Sportswrit-ers from St. Louis came to the games. Players from the St. Louis Cardinals NFL team would show up. We felt privileged to be part of the program and a lot of responsibility went along with that."

After he graduated and left for Michigan State, John Ruzich subscribed to the weekly county newspaper and called home every week to learn if the team had won or lost and what the score was.

"After Pollard left, we knew the streak would end," he said. "We started to get into close games. Someone asked the new coach, Fred Erickson, what he should do in a certain situation. He said he would do what Pollard told him to do the year before. We knew the streak would end before too much longer. It's amazing we didn't have one bad game or drop the ball for so many years."

Sterling Newman:
Building a Tradition

Jeff Riney grew up as a self-described "basketball fanatic." It figured. His father Charley was the longtime basketball coach at Sterling Newman. He guided his 1980 squad to the Class A supersectional round and was inducted into the Illinois Basketball Coaches Association's Hall of Fame. Jeff played football only to keep in shape for basketball.

As a freshman, however, the youngster began to realize that basketball wasn't in his future. There was no place for a 6–5 center beyond the high school level. He discovered a passion for football. As it turned out, he became a starter as a sopho-more, a rarity, and triggered the success of one of the winningest programs in the state in the past 20 years.

"It was a basketball school at one point and it was becoming a wrestling school," Riney said. "But the class ahead of me [1990] and my class [1991] had a strong mix of athletic guys who were very competitive and wanted to do well and started a weight-training program. When I was a freshman, our sophomore team went unbeaten.

You could tell there was something special about that group. People would show up for the sophomore game and not care about the varsity."

In the 1990s, Sterling Newman was one of the most dominant programs in the state. Coach Mike Papoccia produced state champions in 1990 and 1994 and state runners-up in 1993 and 1998. His 2004 team also won a state title. The Blue Machine was 101–18 in the 1990s, despite 4–5 and 6–3 records early in the decade. In 29 years, Papoccia has a record of 229–83, a .734 winning percentage.

Papoccia is homegrown, a 1970 graduate of Sterling Newman. He knew the school had enjoyed some football success before he became coach in 1980—they had a string of seven conference championships in a row at one point—but nobody outside Sterling was aware of it. Growing up, he had idolized Tom Dettorice, who played on the school's first undefeated team in 1967 and whom he described as "the meanest 175-pound fullback/linebacker I ever saw," and two-way tackle Dan Hermes, who played in 1963 and turned down a scholarship to Notre Dame to become a priest.

He didn't try to reinvent the wheel. He tried to carry on old traditions while instituting new traditions. He put his indelible stamp on the program. But he wasn't stubborn. He accepted change. For example, he once ran a run-oriented, double tight end, wishbone, full-backfield offense. Without the size and numbers he once had, he switched to a pass-oriented, four-wide-and-let-it-fly shotgun attack.

"We try to get kids to be successful. We don't talk about winning," Papoccia said. "In 1985, I read a book by [UCLA basketball coach] John Wooden, *They Call Me Coach*. It's my coaching bible. All he talks about is trying to get kids to believe they were a success, that they played up to their potential. Ever since I quit talking about winning, we have been winning. That's the truth."

He organized a father/son campout on the first Saturday of practice. He also instituted a mother/son banquet on the Friday before the first playoff game. He removed NC (Newman Catholic) from the helmet for a cross. He used to have a lot of team rules and had his players sign a contract. Now the contract simply says, "Do what's right." No earrings, no tattoos, no hair over the ears. Anyone caught swearing must do 25 pushups.

Four years ago, Papoccia added a Walk of Fame that the players take on the first day of practice in August. It reminds them of what is important about the school and the program. They walk to different spots in the school that pertain to aspects of life—classroom, chapel, trophy case, weight room, locker room, the field, Cory Dawson's tree (donated by parents of a youngster who died of pancreatic cancer in eighth grade), and ends with a prayer and the school song.

"You learn what you are becoming a part of, being accepted into the Newman family, learn who has given back to the school and the program," said Clayton Norberg, who was a running back and safety on the 2004 state championship team.

In 1992, Papoccia started another tradition, after a 6–3 season. "Carry the flag like those before you," he told his players. They still use the saying today. It reminds them that they aren't playing for themselves but for the people who played before them—and for those who will come after them.

"Our goal was to put Sterling Newman on the map. We wanted to be there with East St. Louis and Geneseo and Mount Carmel," said Matt Hoffmiller, who played on the 1993 state runner-up and the 1994 state champion. "That's what drove us every day. The idea was to make Newman a powerhouse.

"We had won state in 1990. We had heroes. We saw them every day. We looked up to them—Jeff Riney, Jason Graham, Rob Sprungman, Brian Burris, John and Jay Krick. After going 4–5 and 6–3, we felt we had to work harder. After the postseason banquet in 1993, after we lost to Hardin Calhoun for the state championship, the junior class vowed we would win as seniors. We didn't want to lose again. We didn't want that feeling."

Papoccia said the 1989 team set the tone for the 1990 state championship team and what was to follow. It finished 11–1 and lost to Orangeville in the quarterfinals on a long pass in the fourth quarter.

"It was the most talented team I ever had," the coach said. "They were the ones who started bonding together and getting in the weight room together, the ones who set the tone and showed the way."

The 1990 team took a while to get the message but once they heard it loud and clear, they dominated their opponents. After starting 1–2, they won their last 11 games in a row, smashing Franklin Center 47–7, Stockton 49–8, Durand 35–8, and Annawan 28–6 before edging Bloomington Central Catholic 6–3 in overtime for the state title. Jay Krick ran behind Jeff Riney for the winning touchdown on fourth-and-one.

"Once we got rolling and winning, we wanted to annihilate everybody," said Riney, a 6–5, 245-pounder who went to Notre Dame. "We were trying to hold teams to negative yards. We won one game 63–3 and the mood in the locker room was like we lost because we had given up a field goal. We wanted to be perfect."

Newman led Erie 40–0 at halftime and Papoccia said he would leave the first string in the game until it scored one more touchdown, then put in the reserves.

"I said to myself, 'So we're only going to be in for one more play?' We ran 'right half dive' over me and David Molina ran 80 yards for a touchdown on the first play from scrimmage. The coach told us to sit down. Eighteen years later, it still sticks in my mind. That's who we were."

Papoccia wrote a Vince Lombardi quote on the chalkboard. It said, "Perfection is unattainable but if we chase perfection we might achieve excellence."

"That's what we wanted to do, score on every play, get a sack on defense," Riney said. "It was neat to be part of what has turned out to be the beginning of a tradition. We had no idea we were starting something. We thought it was a two-year window, that after going 4–5 the following year we'd go back to the way it used to be."

It didn't happen because Papoccia and assistants Tim Nelson, Chuck Rosenberry, and John "Cheeks" Ybarra wouldn't let it happen. They instilled a new sense of pride in Newman football, in off-season training, in wanting to be a part of something special.

Sterling Newman got on a roll beginning in 1993, losing only eight games in the next seven years. The 1994 championship team, led by Hoffmiller, Dave Miller, Ryan

Velasquez, and Chris Hemminger, didn't produce a single Division I player but it played as a team and capped a 14–0 season with a 27–0 victory over Lexington for the state title.

Another leader was safety Chad Law, who had lost the starting quarterback position. He intercepted a pass at midfield with two minutes to play to seal a 14–7 victory over Stockton in the state semifinals. A month later, he was killed in an automobile accident. At his funeral, all of his teammates wore their football jerseys.

"We would have given the state championship trophy back if we could have Chad back," Papoccia said.

The 1998 team lost to Carthage 30–26 for the state title. It featured running back Andrew Papoccia, the coach's son, who later played at Illinois State. Many old-timers feel he was the best player in school history.

According to Mike Papoccia, the 2004 state championship team was the best he produced but not the most talented. "It played so well together," he said. The Comets finished 13–1, beating Carthage 21–7 for the state title. The defense was led by Norberg and Charlie McGinn, the offense by Chris Salvatori and Chris Welty. They were inspired by senior Jake Harrison, who was injured in a car/bike accident in the summer but still came back to serve as a punter and kicker.

"As a team, we were so close. We called ourselves 'Band of Brothers.' That's what is written inside our state championship rings," Norberg said. "A lot of us had wrestled together since sixth grade and a lot of our dads had gone to Newman.

"The coach set an example. He gave every player a chain link. At a team meal on Thursday night, someone got emotional and talked about life. Each person said he pledged a 100 percent commitment to the team. In the fourth quarter of every game, Jake would grab the chain and we'd all grab onto it. We knew it didn't take one single person to win a game but all of us."

Stockton: The John O'Boyle Era

Mike Toepfer spent 20 years in the U.S. Marine Corps, the last 12 as a judge advocate. Throughout his military career, Toepfer said the guide he would use for leadership was his old high school football coach, Stockton's John O'Boyle.

"He was molding folks on how to succeed in life," Toepfer said. "I didn't realize it then. But it began to dawn on me in college when I saw things I had to do and how to get along with people. There were no real stars on our team but we all worked together for a goal. Everyone wanted to do their best for John O'Boyle."

O'Boyle advised all of his players, "If you work hard and keep your ears open and your mouth shut and try hard, you'll get to play." He insisted that his teams should "play hard, play clean, and play smart." He hated quitters more than Democrats and wouldn't tolerate a player who offered excuses rather than results.

"His rules served me in the Marines and in law school," said Toepfer, who is an attorney and partner in his own law firm with offices in Warren and Galena. "I found out if you lived your life like you played for John O'Boyle, you'd succeed. He brought that out in everybody."

Toepfer was the leader of O'Boyle's 9–0 powerhouse in 1969, the school's first great team, the one that put Stockton football on the map. He and Charlie Krahmer were co-captains, started at offensive guard, and played key roles in the offense. In Week 7, they rallied from a 7–6 halftime deficit to beat Dakota 13–7 in the most important game of the season.

"We were big on sweeps, traps, and crossbucks. I stayed very busy as a guard," said Toepfer, who also started at linebacker. "Dakota had a big defensive tackle. I pulled and could feel the air going out of him when we hit him.

"O'Boyle had trick plays, like a guard around. I had to step up, turn my back to the goal line, then come around and the quarterback would hand me the ball. We practiced it a few times but I never got to do it in a game."

John Vanderheyden, a sophomore backup guard on the 1969 team, said it was a shame that there wasn't a state playoff at the time. It was the beginning of a long string of Stockton successes. Vanderheyden played on teams that were 25–2. As a senior, he was the biggest lineman at 5–11 and 195 pounds.

It was the pre-playoff era, before Gatorade, before summer programs, before weight rooms, before personal trainers and speed coaches, a time before coaches and team trainers and even physicians knew how to deal with heat. O'Boyle never allowed his players to take a drink of water during two-a-day practices in the hot days of August.

"I'd work as an apprentice electrician for Jeff Eastlick's father in the day, then run the streets of Stockton in the evening. That was our summer program," Toepfer said. "We learned ways to get around the heat. We filled our helmets with ice cubes to keep our heads cool. I'd have killed for a drink of water. But I can't recall any heat casualties."

After finishing second in the state playoff in 1975 and 1977, Stockton was ready to claim the top prize in 1978. Eastlick, who spent most of his time blocking for leading rusher Tim Finn the year before, emerged as the leader of a team that featured 160-pound guards and only one starter heavier than 200.

Eastlick and his teammates didn't forget about 1977. The team was ranked No. 1 in the state throughout the regular season. They recorded five shutouts in nine games. Finn rushed for 1,650 yards. After playing on two state runners-up in Illinois, he coached two state championship teams in Texas City, Texas, in the 1990s.

Finn expected to win a state title in 1977. It didn't happen. After beating Polo 17–0 in the first round of the playoff, Stockton fell behind (14–0) for the first time all year against Monmouth, then rallied to win 46–38. In the semifinals, they were locked in a scoreless tie with Alexis in the fourth quarter when Eastlick fumbled on Alexis' five, his brother Pat recovered, and Jeff scored on the next play. Stockton went on to win 14–0.

But Finn chipped a bone in his ankle in the first quarter of the championship game against Mahomet-Seymour and had to sit out the rest of the game. Before the injury, he rushed twice for 26 yards. But Stockton lost 19–0.

"I felt we were in for a big day," Finn said.

The 1978 team lost to Polo 10–8 in the opener but won 12 in a row, closing with a 9–0 victory over Carlinville for the Class 2A championship. Dan Rhyner kicked a 30-yard field goal, Eastlick rushed 22 times for 83 yards and one touchdown, and Mike Woolcock averaged 46.2 yards on five punts. Eastlick, Greg Frank, Tim Zueger, Bill Kupersmith, and Gene King anchored the defense, which yielded only 89 yards and never permitted Carlinville to cross midfield. They allowed only one touchdown in four playoff games.

Stockton drove 48 yards at the outset of the fourth quarter to score the game's only touchdown. Eastlick carried eight times in a row, capping the march with a three-yard plunge over Woolcock, the right guard.

After the game, a reporter asked O'Boyle, "Did you realize you gave Eastlick the ball eight times in a row?"

"No, I didn't," he replied.

"Why did you do it?" the reporter persisted.

"Because I knew he would have the ball in his hands eight times in a row," O'Boyle responded.

O'Boyle produced his second and last unbeaten team in 1991, a 13–1 powerhouse that shut out three opponents in the playoff and capped it off with a 32–6 trouncing of perennial power Arcola for the Class 1A title.

Troy Wright, the last of five brothers to play for O'Boyle, was the team's leading rusher. Linebacker Tony Arand and end Steve Smith keyed the defense. In the final, Neill Cahill caught a 15-yard touchdown pass from Jamie Minshall and was credited with 15 tackles while Troy Alderman had 11, Smith 10. Smith also picked up a blocked punt and ran 37 yards to score.

"O'Boyle was the second biggest influence in my life, after my father," Eastlick said. "He taught you to always give your best effort. If that isn't good enough, that's the way it is. But if you do give your best effort, good things will happen. He didn't say it as much as he lived it. We believed in him and he believed in us.

"There was a sense of big things happening in our lives and O'Boyle was the center of it. He taught us to respect ourselves, to do things a certain way. He said, 'Measure a man by the opposition it takes to discourage him.' It was a Lombardi-ism.

"O'Boyle never said a bad thing about you. He always said good things about you. You always wanted to play for him. I'd go to war for him. He'd lead us in and out safely. He was a leader of men and you wanted to be a man for him. He led men, not boys."

Woodstock Marian Central: Decade of the 1980s

The Hartlieb brothers—Chuck, Andy, Jim, and John—were the drum beaters but Don Penza was the bandleader who wrote the music for the Marian Central teams that dominated the pop charts in the 1980s.

Penza, an All-America end and captain of Frank Leahy's unbeaten Notre Dame football team in 1953, was an outstanding coach in Wisconsin. He won two state championships at a small Catholic school in Wisconsin Rapids, and then became mayor of the town. In 1981, after he failed to get reelected, he looked at a bulletin board one day and found an opening for a football coach at Marian Central in Woodstock.

In 19 years, he had a record of 147–34–2. In eight years at Marian Central, he was 79–17, a .823 winning percentage. From 1983 to 1988, he was 69–10. He won state championships in 1983, 1986, and 1987 and was second in 1985. He died of a heart attack in 1989. He was 57. His successor, Dale Patton, guided Marian Central to another state championship in 1989.

"He was a one-of-a-kind coach. There aren't too many like him. He was unique for his time," said Chuck Hartlieb, who quarterbacked the unbeaten 1983 state champion. "He concentrated on the individual, not the athlete. He tried to help us in our maturation process. His job was to prepare us for life after football."

Penza was 6–2 and weighed 260 pounds. He was intimidating, gruff, and rough around the edges. He let his quarterbacks and linebackers call their own plays on offense and defense. They worked on their own skills in practice. He wanted them to succeed or fail on their own decisions, not his. Hartlieb recalls sitting in study hall and sketching plays that he wanted to work on that day.

Andy Hartlieb, president of the American Community Bank and Trust in Woodstock, credits Penza's approach for his business success. "His message was, 'I'm not here to teach you football but to teach you how to make decisions and become a man, to make decisions under pressure, carry the responsibility, it's your game to win or lose," Andy said. "It makes you grow up pretty fast. You take ownership of your situation.

"That meant a lot to me in my life. He taught me how to conduct business, how to handle problems and issues. Today, everybody rescues their kids from trouble. Don didn't do that. He taught us determination and competitiveness, to make it happen, not to make excuses. The environment was 'This is your team, this is your problem, you push it, you make it go.' He was teaching you to be a leader. He had a knack for that."

Penza was old school. He earned his pedigree and philosophy from Leahy and Notre Dame. He wore a suit on game day. "He built the program on the premise that football coaches were no different than academic teachers. We taught kids during the week and the test was on Friday," said Patton, who assisted Penza from 1985 to 1988.

"Coach 'em up and let 'em go," was Penza's advice to his coaches.

"During a game, he stood opposite of where the action was," Patton said. "It looked like he was detached from the game but he was a very keen observer. He saw things. When he would intervene on offense or defense, it was masterful, usually a key correction or insight.

"At halftime, he was an incredible genius. We never went to the locker room, always to the end zone, no chalkboard. He'd have kids tell him what they saw. Then he'd walk them through adjustments. He wasn't emotional or motivational, always businesslike. He expected his kids to find it within themselves to prepare."

Marian Central opened in 1960, the only Catholic school in McHenry County. Family oriented, it had a reputation for sending over 90 percent of its 400 students to college. Tom Parsley had produced a conference champion in 1965. But the football program knew little success and had established no tradition until Penza arrived.

After starting 2–7 and 3–6, Penza was ready to put his program on the map in 1983. Chuck Hartlieb fit right into his coach's philosophy. There was a lot of fresh blood, plenty of enthusiasm, and a sense of renewal. The Hurricanes enjoyed a lot of success in the preseason passing leagues and Chuck's creative offense, utilizing two tight ends and two wide receivers, with Andy at fullback and Dan Fortin at tailback, set the tone for what was to be seven years of invincibility.

"There was not a lot of momentum in the program after the 1982 season," Chuck said. "We were struggling to find a way to win and come together as a team. His [Penza's] style took some time to get used to, calling my own plays at 16. I had to mature quickly. We never had a goal of winning the state title."

But momentum started to build. Despite a lack of size in the line, the Hurricanes averaged 30 points per game as Chuck passed for 200 to 225 yards per game. Most players went both ways. Chuck rarely came off the field. Jim Mass and Rich Hoover were reliable receivers and Darren Fortin, Dan's brother, keyed the defense from his linebacking position.

They got better and better. They smashed Johnsburg 42–6 and Grant 42–0. Confidence grew and grew. They couldn't wait for their first-ever appearance in the state playoff. In their opener, they fell behind Hampshire 14–0 after two minutes, and then erupted for a 63–35 victory. They went on to trounce Ottawa Marquette 33–0, Polo 26–0, and Bloomington Central Catholic 34–14 to complete a 13–0 sweep.

After going 11–1 in 1984, the 1985 team started 1–2 but finished 10–4 behind sophomore quarterback Jim Hartlieb and tailback Jeff Hill. But they lost to Casey 34–6 in the state final. All of which set the stage for the state championship teams of 1986, 1987, and 1989.

The 1986 team, which finished 12–2 after losing to Crystal Lake South in the opener and to Grant in Week 5, is often judged to be the best of all Marian Central teams. Jim Hartlieb was the junior quarterback. Rich Powers and Joe Remke were a pair of 6–1, 185-pound linemen who wreaked havoc on both sides. Powers went on to become a national champion wrestler at Northern Iowa. Two-way end Sean Noonan also was a standout. In the state playoff, they defeated Richmond-Burton 35–0, Genoa-Kingston 28–14, Momence 40–21, Amboy 42–8, and Decatur St. Teresa 24–20.

In 1987, Jim passed for nearly 2,000 yards as the Hurricanes, who lost their opener to Crystal Lake South for the third year in a row, went on to win 13 in a row, beating Hampshire 35–21, Richmond-Burton 35–14, Morrison 35–7, Stockton 27–11, and Deer Creek-Mackinaw 35–6 in the playoff.

There were so many injuries that Penza was forced to bring up his fifth-string full-back, sophomore John Hartlieb, for the playoff. He replaced Tom Parsley, who broke his leg. He led the team in rushing for all five playoff games. Other standouts were wide receiver Pete Huinker, lineman Pete Havlis, and fullback Tony Lawrence.

"I recall getting in the huddle for the first time and looking at Jim, like we were in the backyard," John said. "We would copy things from college games that we watched our older brothers playing in, all the way to getting into stances and barking out phony signals. There was a lot of winking back and forth."

There wasn't much winking in 1988. The team finished 9–2, losing to Forreston in the second round. It hadn't played up to its potential. It was Penza's last team. He suffered a massive heart attack while raking leaves in the spring of 1989. He should have had heart bypass surgery years earlier but he was fearful of doctors and didn't want to have it done. In truth, he worked himself to death.

But there was another factor. Ricky Church, who played on the 1987 championship team, got on drugs and killed his girlfriend's mother and father and tried to kill his girlfriend and her brother. He disappeared, and then was found years later.

"It hurt Don a lot. It killed him to the soul, to have one of his players that he was so proud of do something like that," said Terry Stenger, a longtime assistant coach at the school. "He didn't ever truly get over it."

The 1989 team was motivated to honor Penza's memory. Quarterback Jim Parsley, tight end Tom Kruse, running backs Brian Huinker and Brian Kaminski, and linemen Brad Harding and Mike Lawler stood out as Marian Central went 14–0, beating Burlington 38–0, Byron 23–21, Galena 42–7, Momence 12–0, and St. Joseph-Ogden 27–13 in the playoff.

"After Coach Penza died, I was hesitant to follow him," Patton said. "But it was a family, all very supportive. It was the right thing to do. I didn't change anything. I just wanted to help guide the kids and stay out of their way. Everybody knew it was about and for Coach Penza."

The Hartlieb brothers led Marian Central of Woodstock to four state championships and a second-place finish in the 1980s. Left to right, Jim, John, Andy, and Chuck. All went on to play college football. Photo courtesy of Jim Hartlieb.

Arcola's Jeff Fishel was stopped cold (22 carries, 14 yards) in an 18–0 loss to Genoa Kingston for the 1977 Class 1A championship. But he carried 20 times for 137 yards and Marty Thomas added 148 yards and two touchdowns as Arcola trounced Hampshire 42–14 for the Class 1A crown in 1978. Photo courtesy of the Illinois High School Association.

Decatur St. Teresa's Marty Bushell (41) breaks loose on a 58–yard run for the clinching touch-down in a 15–6 victory over Alexis for the Class 2A championship in 1974. Bushell rushed for 131 yards in the game. Photo courtesy of the Illinois High School Association.

Aston Gronewold led Carthage to second-place finishes in the state playoff in 2002 and 2003 and emerged as one of the most prolific ground-gainers and scorers in state history. He rushed for 1,800 yards in 2002 and amassed 2,222 yards and 42 touchdowns in 2003. Photo courtesy of Aston Gronewold.

Coaches Mike Papoccia (left) of Sterling Newman and Jim Unruh of Carthage shake hands before their epic showdown in the 1998 Class 1A championship game. Carthage won 30–26 to seal the first of its three successive 14–0 seasons. They met again for the Class 2A title in 2004 and Sterling Newman prevailed 21–7. Unruh won four state titles in six years at one point, a fifth in 2008. Papoccia guided Sterling Newman to state titles in 1990 and 1994. Photo courtesy of the Illinois High School Association.

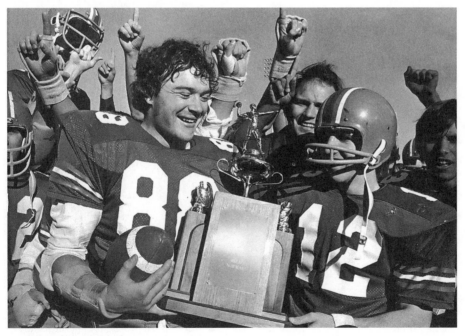

Greg Creamer (left) and Mark Feldman celebrate with Coach Ed Boehm and their teammates after Decatur St. Teresa defeated Stockton 35–0 for the Class 2A championship in 1975. Photo courtesy of the Illinois High School Association.

Barry Pullen (12) of Arcola cuts back to avoid Carthage's Brian Brun (27) during the 1995 Class 1A championship game. Carthage won 45–13, marking the first of four state titles the school would win in the next six years. Photo courtesy of the Illinois High School Association.

The Monahan brothers played major roles in the success of Arcola's football program in the Steve Thomas/Brian Bradford/Randy Rothrock era. Thomas guided Arcola to a 210–90–2 record and three state titles from 1964 to 1993. Back row, left to right, Chris, Matthew, and Mark. Front row, left to right, Tom, Patrick, and Jon. Photo courtesy of the Monahan family.

Stockton's Steve Vanderheyden (44) breaks away for a sizeable gain in the 1977 Class 2A championship game against Mahomet-Seymour. But Stockton lost 19–0. Photo courtesy of the Illinois High School Association.

The defensive front of Pittsfield's 1971 and 1972 teams that capped off a state-record 64–game winning streak. The 1970 team was unscored upon in nine games. Of the 64 games in the streak, 44 were shutouts. Left to right, Mike Barton, Ron Holst, Mark Deeder, Terry Lyman, Walter Stolte, Fred Ruzich, and Charles Coultas. Ruzich went on to play at Michigan State. Photo courtesy of Deek Pollard.

Jerry Jones (22) of Decatur St. Teresa set a state playoff record by rushing 32 times for 250 yards and four touchdowns in a 35–0 victory over Stockton for the Class 2A championship in 1975. He also scored on a 24–yard pass from Russ Hollingsworth. Photo courtesy of the Illinois High School Association.

6

Midsized Schools

Addison Driscoll: Eight Titles, Seven in a Row

Football has always been Mike Burzawa's passion. But it was Rod Molek's successful baseball program and the promise of a good education that lured Burzawa to Driscoll Catholic in Addison. The football team had experienced only three winning seasons from 1974 to 1988. Then Gene Nudo arrived and the game changed forever.

Nudo was a salesman—he once was named Rookie of the Year while working for Kellogg's food division—and a journeyman coach who assisted at Ridgewood High School in Norridge, his alma mater, guided the River Grove Cowboys to the national semi-pro championship in 1984 and seconds in 1985 and 1986, worked in the Arena League, and served as a volunteer on Coach Rich Marks' staff at Driscoll.

After he was hired to succeed Marks as head coach in 1989, he took the program on a meteoric rise that put Driscoll's name on the map. The Highlanders qualified for the state playoff in Nudo's first year, advanced to the state semifinals in his second season, and went 14–0 in 1991 en route to the school's first state championship.

Burzawa was one of the leaders of the team. He and Mike Kamienski each rushed for more than 1,000 yards. They ran behind an offensive line that called themselves "the Overlords"—center Tom Ciccone, guards Joe Angelino and Joe Coglianese, tackles Dan Hennessey and Dave Sciortino, and tight end Rich Marks. Coglianese, also an outstanding linebacker, was singled out as the Player of the Year in the conference. Quarterback John Mika passed for 800 yards.

"Nudo set the tone for the football program. He established the winning tradition," said Burzawa, who coached Driscoll to a 41–1 record and three state championships before leaving for Evanston after the 2007 season. "We'd talk a lot about what happened in 1991, how much fun it was. It was a lot of work but he made it fun."

The 1991 team had a motto. Nudo wrote it on the chalkboard before the first playoff game. It said, "Refuse to lose." It was written inside a big heart. The motto was written on the 1991 state championship rings.

"I coached against them when I was at Ridgewood and I noticed there was a lot of talent there and they wanted to win but they didn't know how to win. They were struggling to find an identity," Nudo said.

He hit the ground running. His staff included friends he had known for a long time—Frank Battaglia, Mike Loconsole, Steve Ache, and Larry Orrico, a former quarterback at Ridgewood. The freshman squad, led by Burzawa, lost only one game. Nudo could see that it was a special group. "Everything was lined up," he said.

He also gave the program a fresh look. The Chicago Bruisers semi-pro team had gone out of business. Nudo packed up the equipment and took it to Driscoll—helmets, pads, videotaping system and all. The Highlanders used to be called "the egg yolks" because they wore yellow jerseys with black pants. No longer. Nudo switched to a Pittsburgh Steeler appearance, black-on-black. Nobody laughed after 1991.

Nudo wasn't finished. He installed a structured off-season conditioning program, a pro-style offense, and a 4-4 defense. And he recruited within the building. Of the 185 boys enrolled in the school at the time, he persuaded 120 of them to come out for football in his first season. To promote the program, he published a media guide for the local press.

"I knew we were on the cusp of something good and I wanted people to take notice of it," Nudo said. "I liked working with kids. I wondered, 'How good could we be if we could work with the kids every day?' I felt we weren't giving them enough, that we could always give them more. The greatest crime against youth is to under-challenge them."

The 1991 team trailed Elmwood Park 13–0 in its opener, then rallied to win 28–13. They beat Immaculate Conception (IC) and Tony Mondragon twice in legendary coach Jack Lewis' last season, 14–7 after trailing 7–0 at halftime and 10–0 in the second round of the playoff before a crowd of 6,000. "IC was the second best team in the state," Nudo said. The Highlanders allowed only one touchdown in their first three playoff games, then trounced Robinson 42–20 for their first state title.

"When we were down 13–0 to Elmwood Park at halftime, Nudo told us we were about an inch from being 0–9," Burzawa said. "The next Monday, we ran Pittsburghs, timed laps around the football field. They amounted to a 300-yard sprint. I don't know why Nudo called them Pittsburghs. We did that every week for the entire season. They made us physically and mentally stronger. You had to make a certain time or it didn't count. We had to do four within a certain time. Sometimes we did seven, eight, or nine. Since 1998, everybody who plays Driscoll football knows what a Pittsburgh is."

"The things that we established are things they still talk about today, even though I've been gone since 1995," said Nudo, who left to become director of football operations for the Arena Football League and later coach of the Arizona Rattlers. "My three-year span at Driscoll was the best time of my professional life, to see how successful those kids have become. That's the reason you get into coaching."

Tim Racki, a 1986 Driscoll graduate, became head coach in 1998. He took the program on an unprecedented run of success, a seven-year record of 76–14 and four state championships in a row from 2001 to 2004 before leaving to become head coach at Nazareth Academy in LaGrange Park. Then Burzawa picked up where he left off.

Greg Turner starred on the 2002 and 2003 championship teams. Racki said Turner was the best all-around player he ever coached. John Tranchitella played on four teams that went 53–2. Other leaders were Anthony Gebhart, Luke Mroz, Jason Schultz, Dan Oliverio, Mike Freeman, Matt Mahaney, Mike Segretti, Dan Cwik, Phil Pedi, Shane and Tim Franken, David Schwabe, and Kevin Palermo.

Pedi remembers it all. He is one of only three players in state history—Tranchitella and Schwabe are the others—who has four state championship rings, two with Racki and two with Burzawa, and started on three of them. He passed for 1,900 yards and 24 touchdowns for the unbeaten 2005 squad, which crushed Newton 42–7 for the state title and is generally considered to be the best in school history. The offense averaged 40 points per game and the first-team defense allowed only 20. Other standouts were Tranchitella, Justin Nudo, and Mike Redpath.

"The 2005 team was the best but my favorite year was 2006 because, for the first time since I was in high school, I was playing with my friends," said Pedi, who passed for 2,400 yards and 25 touchdowns. "We lost 27 seniors. Only three starters were back. We didn't want to be known as the team that screwed up and ended the streak. There was an enormous amount of pressure. If we don't win the state title, what have we done? Knowing what I had been through helped me. The streak will end sooner or later but I'm glad it's not going to be me."

It almost was. In the first round of the playoff, Driscoll had possession on its 35 but had no timeouts and trailed Downstate Morton 7–6 with 1:45 to play. Pedi threw the ball into an opponent's hands but he dropped it. On fourth-and-nine, he passed 10 yards to David Schwabe, who made a sensational diving catch for the first down. Pedi completed eight passes in a row as Driscoll drove to Morton's five, then passed to Danny Taylor for the winning touchdown with 12 seconds remaining.

"It was an unreal experience," Pedi said. "I never had to execute a two-minute drill to win a game but I always dreamed of it, like a John Elway two-minute drill to win the Super Bowl. I did it a lot of times in my backyard with my friends, throwing a game-winning touchdown pass. But it was never like this."

And it will never be the same again. Driscoll closed after the 2008–09 school year.

Belleville Althoff: Time to Retire

After closing out the 2007 season with the most prolific running back ever produced in the St. Louis metropolitan area, Belleville Althoff's Glenn Schott decided it was time to end his 47-year coaching career. He always enjoyed the kids and the practices and the teaching. But the games, the parents, and outside influences had taken their toll.

"It was an emotional situation at the time but then I felt a sense of relief," he said. "You come to a point in time where you say you enjoyed the kids and the practices and the teaching but you didn't enjoy the games anymore.

"In today's society, our educational system has deviated from an academic institution to a parental institution. Coaches and teachers are being asked to do things that parents don't want to do or can't do. I want to raise my two sons, not yours.

"And there's a pet peeve of mine: two words that go around in society today—exposure and specialization. Parents look at athletics to possibly pay for college expenses. They want their kids involved in outside teams, traveling teams, AAU. No teaching is being done. It's the I theory, no team concept."

So Schott has retired. Oh, he'll help out with the football team and do some public relations for the school, maybe even serve as assistant athletic director. But he won't teach. He plans to fish and spend more time with his six grandchildren.

He leaves a considerable record of achievement. In 37 years at Althoff, his teams won 66 percent (245–127–6) of their games. He won state championships in 1980, 1989, and 1990. He sent players to 33 different Division I colleges and he produced two of the leading ground-gainers in state history, Hickey Thompson and Jason Ford.

An admirable legacy for a man who started teaching in a one-room country schoolhouse outside his hometown of Perryville, Missouri. He taught seven students—two in second grade, two in third grade, one in fifth grade, and two in seventh grade. The facility included an outhouse, an oil stove, and a cistern for fresh water.

His high school coach, Max Hamilton, brought him to Belleville in 1962. He served as line coach until 1971, and then became head coach when Hamilton left. Schott copied some of his mentor's philosophy and added some wrinkles of his own.

"Hamilton's philosophy was when you stepped on the field, no matter who you played, you were as good as they were and had to go out and work at it," Schott said. "Coaching is 85 percent psychology and 15 percent Xs and Os. I had to make sure the kids understood what they had to do. We were getting middle-class kids who were hard-nosed, willing to work hard, had a good work ethic, and were aggressive and willing to hit."

On the field or on the court, Althoff was in a class by itself. In a survey of the past four years, the *St. Louis Post-Dispatch* ranked Althoff's boys' and girls' programs No. 1 or No. 2 for schools with enrollments under 1,000 students. Althoff is 560, half boys and half girls. According to Schott, Althoff sends more kids (98 percent) to college at all levels than any school in the St. Louis area.

To contend with opponents that usually were three or four times larger than Althoff, Schott chose to run the ball. "To give us a chance to win, we had to control the ball. If I have it, you can't score. And we had to play good defense, too. That's what we've done," he said.

In the past six years, he bowed to change by switching to a double slot motion, no-huddle offense. Surprisingly, it attracted more youngsters to come out for the team and it revived Schott's enthusiasm and interest in football.

"It was a lot of fun," he said. "We still ran the ball but with different looks. And we threw a lot more. The quarterback was like the tailback in the old single wing. We were fundamentally sound. Our kids played the game the way it should be played. I hope that's how people will remember the program."

There are lots of memories, beginning in 1980 when Althoff won its first state title. The Crusaders had reached the state semifinals in 1979. The playoff system was new to them. They had to play teams from Chicago Heights, Champaign, and Peoria, and Schott had to persuade his leading rusher, Mike Laney, to come out for the team as a senior.

But it all worked out. Althoff finished 12–1, rallying to beat a De Kalb team led by Mike and Doug Mallory, sons of Northern Illinois and Indiana coach Bill Mallory, by a 10–7 margin for the Class 4A crown. Laney ran for 94 yards and a touchdown in the final, Jeff Junker kicked the decisive field goal and averaged 38.8 yards on five punts, including a 61-yarder. Bob Totsch and Ken Blacharczyk also stood out.

"The whole experience had a great effect on the school and the community," Schott said. "The first title generated great enthusiasm that can't be duplicated. It was something new for everybody."

In 1989 and 1990, Althoff was dominant. The Crusaders lost their opener in 1989 to Hazelwood East, which went on to win the Missouri championship, then went on to win 25 games in a row and two state titles. They were so good that Hickey Thompson suffered a broken ankle in the third game of 1989 and was lost for the season but DaRond Stovall was shifted from quarterback and Armando Fisher stepped in and the offense never lost a beat.

In 1990, Thompson returned and set a state record by rushing for 3,010 yards and scoring 42 touchdowns—and he never played in the third or fourth quarter except in the state final. Stovall returned to quarterback and Nebraska coach Tom Osborne said he was one of the top four quarterbacks in the nation. But Stovall preferred baseball. The St. Louis Cardinals picked him in the fifth round of the major league draft.

Stovall, described by Schott as "the best overall athlete that Althoff ever produced," was set to go to Iowa to play football. Curiously, basketball was his first love but he admitted that he was most skillful in baseball. When he was drafted by the Cardinals, he opted for professional baseball. He played for the Cardinals, Expos, Marlins, Dodgers, and Angels organizations but spent only one season in the majors (with the Expos in 1998) before retiring in 2002. He had no regrets.

Subbing for Thompson, Stovall rushed for 950 yards in 1989. He gained 100 yards and scored once in a 38–7 rout of Princeton in the Class 3A final. Quarterback Bernie Ysursa passed for 106 yards and one touchdown. It was a prelude to greatness in 1990 and great motivation for Thompson, who watched from the sideline.

"I wondered if I would ever get a chance to play on a state winner," he said. "Watching my teammates win the state title motivated me. I was supposed to be part of it. They made me feel good but it isn't like being out there playing. I began to work out in the summer, pulling tires, lifting weights, running up hills."

It all paid off in 1990, as Thompson became the leading rusher in state history. The Crusaders went 13–0. Their closest game was in the state final, a 13–6 decision over Rock Island Alleman, coincidentally the only game that Thompson, a 5–11, 180-pounder with 4.4 speed, didn't break at least one long run during the season. Other standouts were Stovall, Luther Hardin, Jim Stiebel, and Rich Sauget.

"Bernie had graduated and Hickey was back. [Schott] asked me to start at quarterback. I said I'll play quarterback if it is best for the team, if we can repeat as state champion," Stovall said. "We ran the I formation. I ran a few pass plays. My main target was Vic Faust. I also had some running plays but Hickey ran 25–30 times a game. The 1990 team was quicker than 1989. We had fun. We expected to win. We were dominating."

Was Thompson better than Jason Ford, who set a career rushing record in the St. Louis area with 6,418 yards? After originally committing to Iowa, the 5–10, 225-pounder with 4.4 speed changed his mind and opted for Illinois.

"Ford is right up there with Hickey," Stovall said. "Ford is a more hard-nosed runner, stronger than Hickey. But Hickey was flashier and quicker. Ford has great lower-body strength, great leg drive. He runs over people. I'd pick Hickey to run behind me. He could make guys miss and break away."

"I didn't know about the Althoff tradition until I got there," Ford said. "I knew who Stovall was because he and my dad were friends. But I didn't know who Hickey Thompson was. When they compared me to Hickey, I got filled in who he was. When I was a freshman, I went to the library and there was a big banner on the table about the three state titles. It was disappointing that we didn't win one."

Du Quoin: Stanhouse and the Hambletonian

By most accounts, Don Stanhouse is the greatest athlete ever to come out of Du Quoin. It is hard to argue the point. He signed a letter to play football for Dan Devine at Missouri. And he was the ninth player selected in the major league baseball draft by Charlie Finley and the Oakland Athletics.

The youngest of six children, whose father died when he was 10, Stanhouse grew up in a small farming and coal-mining town of 4,500 people. He baled hay, fished, played football, basketball, and baseball, and went to church. When he was 18, after he was drafted, he found himself in a hotel with a swimming pool for the first time in his life.

But he loved football. He was a quarterback and safety. He kicked off, returned kicks, punted and returned punts, and also kicked field goals and extra points. He was 6–2 and weighed 187 pounds, big for that time, the late 1960s. He once scored 44 points in a 62–7 victory over Benton. In a game against Sparta, in a dense fog, he returned the opening kickoff for a touchdown and nobody knew it.

As a senior, his 1968 Du Quoin team went 10–0, the first unbeaten team in school history. After the last game against West Frankfort, he handed his No. 11 jersey to his backup, Al Martin. "It's yours now," Stanhouse told him. He was passing the torch. Today, he understands he was a steppingstone to building a foundation for all the success that was to follow.

Galen Davis, now 86, a 1942 Du Quoin graduate and a longtime coach, athletic director, and administrator at the school, recalls the 1939 unbeaten football team and playing basketball against Centralia's legendary Arthur Trout and Dike Eddleman. He claims Stanhouse and Nick Hill, who quarterbacked the 2002 state runner-up, were the best football players in Du Quoin history.

"Stanhouse was so natural in all sports. He made it look easy," Davis said. "Football was his best sport. He had a flowing motion. He could look ahead and see what he had to do."

"Stanhouse was the best football player I ever saw in Du Quoin," Martin said. "He could kick and punt the ball a mile. He could run and throw and play defense. He was a Brett Favre type of guy. He had savvy about him. People wanted to play for him. He was the best athlete we've seen."

Stanhouse's 1968 team set the tone. It was Coach Bob Karnes' first team at Du Quoin and, by his own admission, his best. In 20 years, he won 69 percent (136–59–4) of his games and finished second in the state playoff in 1986. His last four teams were 43–7.

Du Quoin (DQ) was a baseball town—baseball and the Hambletonian and the fairgrounds. Football was an afterthought. Don Anderson rekindled some interest with a 6–3 team in 1966 and an 8–1 team in 1967. Then he left for Taylorville and recommended his assistant, Karnes, to succeed him. The principal, who also was the baseball coach, approved the hire.

"We broke the ice," Karnes said. "It's a catchy thing. Once you turn the corner, kids in fifth and sixth grade are putting DQ on their helmets and deciding who will be quarterback and running back. You can fool kids with Xs and Os and knowledge of the game. But if they think you don't care about them, they will smell it out real quick."

Karnes cared a lot. He asked his players to conduct summer workouts on their own. Since he lived only five houses from the school, he could see who was there and who wasn't. He said he couldn't guarantee he could outsmart a rival coach but he could outwork him. His philosophy was to mix discipline with passion.

"My dad told me, 'When you are in charge of men, there are three ways to handle it. If they are doing the job they are supposed to be doing, leave them alone. If they aren't doing the job, kick them in the butt and encourage them. If they are going beyond what is expected of them, give them a pat on the back.' He said it was more important to know young people than to know the game of football," Karnes said.

His 1986 team lost to West Frankfort in the opener, then won 12 in a row before losing to Kankakee Bishop McNamara for the state title. The team was led by fullback Tris Greenwood and Karnes' oldest son, Jason, a junior who played quarterback and safety. But it was a traumatic season because two-way lineman Monte Chasten was diagnosed with leukemia after the sixth game and died on the day before the last regular-season game. He had moved to Du Quoin only two years earlier from Canton, Illinois.

Karnes retired after the 1987 season. It could have been Karnes' best team, maybe as good as 1968. They finished 11–1, losing to Alton Marquette in the second round of the playoff. His son Jay suffered an ACL injury in the fifth game and missed the rest of the season. Two-way tackle Brian Pryor keyed a defense that shut out eight opponents. But it wasn't to be.

When Karnes left, the cupboard was full. Martin, Stanhouse's former backup, a 1972 graduate and Karnes' former assistant, was picked to succeed his mentor. His 1988 team went 14–0 and won a state championship. He said his unbeaten 1992 team was even better. It was quarterbacked by Jason Karnes, Bob's son.

In 21 years, Martin's teams have posted a record of 215–43, a .833 winning percentage. He has won two state titles and finished second four times. In his first 10 years, his teams were 112–16. Under Karnes and Martin, Du Quoin has qualified for the state playoff for 25 years in a row.

Martin learned from Karnes and John Helmick, who coached at Carbondale and Metamora. His stamp? "We always have a large number of kids who get involved. We play a lot of kids each year. Very few kids go both ways. Kids know they will get a fair chance to play the game," Martin said.

It is a great challenge to coach football in Du Quoin. It is located in Perry County, which has the highest unemployment rate of any county in Illinois. The Hambletonian, the greatest harness race of all, left in 1980. Many businesses closed. School enrollment has dropped to 430. Kids hang out in the McDonald's parking lot or the Wal-Mart parking lot. Some coal mines are being reopened but a lot of kids leave and go to college and don't come back.

"There always is a group of kids that are very determined to carry on the tradition," Martin said. "It is a great challenge to coach in a rural area, a challenge to get kids to come out and motivate them. Some parents don't have jobs. Some kids are homeless. Coaching is more important than ever before. It is very rewarding but very challenging. The football program remains a source of pride for the entire community."

In 1988, Martin felt a lot of pressure. The team was coming off an 11–1 season. Martin was just hoping to have a "decent" year so he could gain tenure. He brought in a wishbone offense, an outside veer he had picked up in Carbondale. To his surprise, quarterback Scott Baxter demonstrated great ability to handle the ball. Other standouts were twins Sid and Shane Boyett, who was born with one arm, and fullback/linebacker Gonnie Morgan.

They seized momentum by beating Hillsboro 48–13 in a matchup of unbeatens in the first round. In the quarterfinals, they recovered a fumbled punt on the 12 in the fourth quarter and went on to edge Harrisburg 15–7. And they beat Herscher 25–13 in the final as Baxter broke off some big plays and Martin called the outside veer six times in a row during one series. "We found one play that would work," he said.

In 1992, Du Quoin was rated No. 1 in Class 3A from start to finish and played up to its billing. But it wasn't easy. Jason Karnes ran 47 yards for a touchdown and passed to Dennis Phillips for a two-point conversion in a 15–14 semifinal victory over Robinson as the defense stopped a two-point conversion with 10 seconds to play. Karnes passed for a career-high 160 yards and one touchdown, rushed for 100 yards, made eight tackles, and tied a state record with two interceptions as Du Quoin beat Marengo 14–10 in the state final.

"I'll never forget the way the town rallies around you in playoff time," said Hill, who passed for 4,000 yards in three years. "The streets are decorated with jerseys hanging on telephone poles. Everyone is at the game. You might not appreciate it as much as we do if you are from a big suburban school in Chicago. But it's a big deal in Du Quoin. It's all we've got."

Geneseo: Five Decades of Excellence

It began in the 1960s with a streak of 52 games without a loss, continued in the 1970s with three state championships, then carried on with another state title in the 1980s and three second-place finishes in the 1990s. In five decades, five coaches have produced teams that have won more than 80 percent of their games.

"It's not about me, it's about the kids," said current coach Larry Johnsen Jr., who played for or assisted former Geneseo coaches Bob Reade, Vic Boblett, and Denny Diericx but not his father, former Geneseo coach Larry Johnsen Sr.

"They are the highlight. We want to give them an opportunity to succeed. We have done the same thing for 50 years—the Delaware wing-T and the 5-2 defense. It's what the kids know. We do it in Little League, middle school, and high school. I'm a traditionalist. We've tinkered with the shotgun but we still run what we've always run. We still look like the Green Bay Packers since the 1970s."

Johnsen Jr. grew up in the 1970s. Wayne Strader, perhaps the most celebrated player in school history, was one of his heroes. He was a ball boy until eighth grade, when his father coached Geneseo to its last state championship in 1982.

"There is pressure to win here," he said. "Sometimes if you win, it isn't good enough. All the coaches worked for good administrators who understood the value of a good football program. Sometimes you wonder what people are thinking. But I would rather have high expectations than no expectations. That's part of the job here."

Johnsen Jr. was born to be a coach, to follow in his father's footsteps. He recalls watching film on old reels in his basement. He thought coaching was the greatest profession in the world since the first time Reade gave him a chance to be on the field during the 1978 state championship game.

He sought advice from his father, former coaches, and longtime assistants Elmer Reedy and Ron Clary. They said, "Don't let the monster get you. You have to maintain a family life and fulfill the religious part of your life. You have to be yourself and have to do what you know and keep things in perspective."

Three years ago, he was part of a group that raised $2 million for an indoor facility for physical education classes and indoor track.

Tradition is everywhere in Geneseo, a one-time agricultural community that has grown into a suburb of the Quad Cities. It is a very white, Anglo-Saxon, middle-class landscape that could have been painted by Norman Rockwell. There are more churches than bars. At the high school, there is a wall filled with pictures of All-State players.

"Any community finds something to hang its hat on, the high school, a business, football or basketball, something they identify with," said Ted McAvoy, a 1960 graduate who was Reade's statistician and later served as principal from 1990 to 1999 before retiring.

"Cobden was the Appleknockers. Hoopeston was the Cornjerkers. Like most small towns, the high school is the focal point of our community. Once they started winning, it really gave the community something to hang its hat on. One of the great things that happened is Reade stayed for 17 years. The continuity was tremendous. He was doing the same thing at the end as when he came. He had success and the community bought into it."

Reade's success trickled down to the youth football league. From fifth grade on, half of the boys in every class, 50 or more, would try out for football. Parents, alumni, and fans could identify with "46 counter" and other plays that were being called. Reade passed the baton to Boblett and Diericx and others who had grown up in the program. The Green Machine was the biggest attraction in town.

"I sensed that expectations got too high," Diericx said. "Sometimes the community never got into it until we got to the playoff. They expected too much. But that's better than the alternative. It was said Bud Wilkinson created a monster at Oklahoma. Bob Reade created a monster at Geneseo. Other coaches have to keep feeding it. It was our job to maintain it."

The monster was created in the 1960s when Steve Penney and Barry Pearson, tagged the "touchdown twins" by the local media, starred on teams that went 8–1, 9–0, and 9–0 and started the 52–game unbeaten streak. In 1967, Penney scored 21 touchdowns, Pearson 20. Guard Rich Quayle and tight end Ray Hansen also starred on the two unbeaten teams. Bob Orsi, a 5–10, 165-pound sophomore guard, showed signs of becoming a future star.

"The loss to Rochelle in 1965 shouldn't have happened," Pearson said. "We held them on our one with two minutes left. We had the ball back but couldn't move it and had to punt. They scored in the last 30 seconds to beat us. It was the only game I ever lost in high school. We sensed something special was about to happen."

Orsi and 5–11, 140-pound sophomore quarterback Rick Penney, Steve's brother, were the leaders of the 1968 team that was unbeaten but tied by Princeton. The team won several games by close margins, including 21–20 over Rock Falls.

"We probably could have lost four times but didn't," Orsi said. "We won on pride and determination and hard work. It told us that we didn't have to win by 50 points and still feel good. We had a winning attitude. We felt we could win any game, no matter what the competition."

The 1969 team with Orsi, Penney, Vic Boblett, Doug Arnold, and Mark Skelton went 9–0. Orsi, a 195-pound fullback/linebacker and regarded as the state's top player, had over 30 scholarship offers. He chose Missouri over Illinois, Michigan, Ohio State, Northwestern, Iowa, and Wisconsin.

"The program was more than any coach or player," Orsi said. "It was established and should perpetuate itself. The commitment to playing the game and the system was established. Even when Reade left, the program was established and kept winning. The program was bigger than one person."

Penney and Arnold were back in 1970 and the Green Machine went 9–0, overpowering Ottawa 42–6 before a crowd of 13,000 in the biggest game of the season. Jerry Hart, Tommy Nelson, Jim Gray, and Steve Klemmer were other standouts.

The streak finally ended in 1971 at Spring Valley. Hall Township went ahead with 49 seconds to play and stifled Geneseo's last desperate drive to win 14–12.

"It had to end sometime, some people said. I agreed at the time. But when we had a 60-game winning streak at Augustana College, I said why? Why does a streak have to end sometime? We didn't play well enough to win against Hall. But those kids didn't want to be the ones to lose," Reade said.

When the state playoff began in 1974, Reade set a goal to be a state champion as quickly as possible. In 1974, Geneseo lost to eventual state champion West Chicago in the quarterfinals, then lost to Geneva in the 1975 semifinals. But the Green Machine, led by Wayne Strader and Lance Hofer, went 13–0, 12–1, and 13–0 to win state titles in 1976, 1977, and 1978. It was soon enough.

The 1976 squad, with Strader rushing for more than 2,200 yards and 33 touchdowns, may have been the best in school history. The 1977 team avenged an earlier loss to Rochelle in the first round of the playoff. And the 1978 team, which Reade insisted wasn't big enough (the linebackers weighed 150 pounds) to win a state title, was noteworthy because of Hofer, who was sidelined with a broken thumb on his throwing hand in the third game.

Hofer played quarterback and safety, kicked off, punted, and kicked extra points. Jay Penney, the third brother to play for Reade, stepped in at quarterback. He was a 6–0, 160-pound junior with a big name and no experience. In the second round against Sycamore, Hofer came back and threw a touchdown pass with his other hand.

After losing to Wheaton North in the 1981 state final, Johnsen Sr. guided Ron Tracey, Randy Clary, Travis Mackey, Pat Mitchell, Chet Carey, and his 1982 squad to the state title. After Carey, the quarterback, recovered his own fumbled snap in the end zone for a touchdown to beat Rockton Hononegah in overtime in the playoff opener, Geneseo went on to outlast Springfield Griffin 44–36 in the final as Tracey rushed for 104 yards and three touchdowns and Clary ran for 116 yards and one touchdown.

Boblett produced a state runner-up in 1990 and Diericx had second-place finishers in 1992 and 1993. Johnsen Jr. got to the semifinals in 2004.

"What used to strike me on Friday night, as we waited for the sophomore game to end, a number of little kids would be standing around the back door of our locker room," Diericx recalled. "These were their idols and they were looking forward to when they would play for the Green Machine.

"The senior class knew they wouldn't be remembered for what year they graduated but for what team they played on. Each class was motivated to equal or surpass what had been done before. It was ingrained in the kids from the time they were little. The emotions of Geneseo would rise or fall with how the team did on Friday night."

Joliet Catholic: Four Coaches, 13 State Titles

When you walk through the main entrance of the Student Activities Center at Joliet Catholic Academy, you immediately are struck by the huge trophy case in the middle of Alumni Hall. It contains 13 state championship football trophies, aligned in two rows. Someone is always looking at it. But that isn't all there is to see.

Upstairs in the center, down the hall, there are dozens of plaques, Tom Thayer's spikes from Super Bowl XX and Mike Alstott's jersey. In football coach Dan Sharp's office, there are mini-helmets and signatures of every player he coached who went to a Division I school. And, of course, there is a picture of former coach Gordie Gillespie.

"At first, I didn't know who Gordie Gillespie was," admitted Nick Clancy, an All-State linebacker on the 2007 state championship team who is playing at Boston College. "He started the success, set the foundation for everything. The first day of summer camp when I was a sophomore, I saw this guy with gray hair walking his dog along the football field. He went over to talk to Coach Sharp. I asked someone, 'Who is that?' He said, 'Are you serious? That's Gordie. He's a legend.' All you hear about is the legend of Gordie Gillespie.

"The first time he talked to me as a sophomore, I was with the punters doing special teams on a Tuesday. I shanked one right. He was staring at me. I was so nervous. He said, 'Young man, here's what you do.' He put my right leg behind my left leg and explained how I should punt. I did it the right way and the ball sailed 50 yards. He has so much knowledge of the game."

Joliet Catholic's football program was barely a blip on the radar screen until Gillespie became head coach in 1959. And it took seven years for him to produce a championship squad. The school began playing football in 1920 and had only seven winning seasons until the 1950s. During one span, it had 10 losing seasons in a row.

Until Gillespie's arrival, the lone bright spot was 1953, when Phil Cantwell coached an 8–0 team that was led by Bob Wright and Al Prospero.

Gillespie produced four state champions in a row from 1975 through 1978 and added another in 1981. Jim Boyter won a state title in 1987. Bob Stone won in 1990. Dan Sharp has won six in the past nine years. Since 1959, Joliet Catholic is 450–103–6, a spectacular .812 winning percentage.

Mike Alstott (1991) and Chris Jeske (2004) were named *Chicago Sun-Times* Players of the Year. J. R. Zwierzynski (5,070 yards in 1998–2001) was the school's all-time leading rusher, surpassing Alstott (3,839 in 1989–1991) and James Randle (3,136 in 1995–1996). Zwierzynski also was the school's all-time leading scorer with 89 touchdowns and 598 points. Alstott accounted for 54 touchdowns and 332 points.

The school also produced a wealth of outstanding linebackers. Gillespie had Pat Lennon, Roger Hewlett, and John Piazza. Sharp had Mike Goolsby, Nick Clancy, and

Jeske. Zwierzynski was moved to linebacker in college. And it also produced out-standing linemen such as Pat Mudron, Tom Thayer, Bill Draznik, Tom Gullickson, John Meade, John Horn, Kevin McShane, Mike Maloney, and Mike Kolodziej.

"Anybody would like an opportunity to coach in a program that is so successful," said Stone, a 1974 St. Francis de Sales graduate who coached at Wilmington for four years before joining Gillespie's staff at Joliet Catholic in 1981. As head coach from 1989 to 1996, his teams were 80–19.

"I had heard Gillespie talk at clinics. I wanted to further my career by getting into a program like that. That's where I got my idea about coaches coaching. Gillespie wanted his coaches to coach. He didn't run everything. He had input and expected you to do what was right. It was a great way for any coach to develop.

"He also taught me that you don't have to get things out of a book. If you had an idea and proved to him that it worked, he would use it. As tough as he could be, he always had time for kids and family. A lot of him is in me. He advised me, 'Bob, the best play you called is the last play you called.'

"There was the pressure of high expectations all the time. Sometimes it was dif-ficult. But Gordie seemed impervious to that. It wasn't winning but winning state titles and point spreads and how you won. It was a pressure cooker. Anyone likes that atmosphere because you want the success that goes along with it."

John Fitzgerald Piazza, who was born two days after John F. Kennedy was inaugu-rated in 1961, traces his success to the fundamentals he learned while playing for three of Gillespie's state championship teams. He later played for four years at Yale and currently is the mayor of Lemont, Illinois, just a few miles up the road from Joliet.

"The best times I've had were playing football at Joliet Catholic, head and shoulders above my college experience," Piazza said. "Gillespie had a presence about him. He got the best out of what he had. He saw the pool of talent, or lack of it, and made something out of it. He made the best out of 5–7 and 5–8 kids who weighed 170 or 180 pounds and played defensive line.

"We knew if we listened to him and did what he taught us, we would be success-ful. He gave me the best advice I ever received. He encouraged me to go to Yale. It was the best decision I ever made. I wanted to hang around home and be with my friends. Yale was culture shock for a kid from Lockport. But it helped to make me what I am today."

Joliet Catholic is a family-oriented school and the Larsens epitomize that bond. Larry Larsen graduated in 1961. He sent four sons to the school—Mike (1982), Len (1984), John (1985), and Matt (1993). A fifth son, Adam, graduated from Joliet Central in 1997.

Ironically, only Mike played on a state championship team, Gillespie's 1981 team. But Matt participated in one of the most exciting state finals in playoff history, Joliet Catho-lic's dramatic 40–34 double overtime loss to Wheaton Warrenville South in 1992.

Matt also was a student when school administrators chose to merge with all-girls St. Francis Academy and seriously considered changing the school name and colors, much to the chagrin of tradition-conscious alumni.

"A lot of kids didn't want the schools to merge," Matt said. "Would we stay or leave? Some kids were walking out of school. The new nickname was going to be the Royals. The new school colors were going to be royal blue and silver."

The administration finally rethought the situation and opted to stick with tradition, the boys' teams retaining their colors and name, and the girls' teams retaining their colors and name. In the end, however, the program that Gillespie had built continued to prosper. Nobody dared to tamper with his double wing offense.

"In my day, I had a swagger and I wore my brother John's jersey and his t-shirt under my pads," Matt said. "They didn't let us wear the victory light on our helmet, which was a part of Joliet Catholic's history. Now they've gone back to the victory light.

"We were in a big transition period when we were there. We wore a powder blue stripe on our uniform, which irritated us. But living in that town and going to that school, it was like going to Notre Dame. You got haircuts for free and you ate at restaurants for free. Alumni took care of everybody. Kids wanted to be part of the excitement."

Kankakee Bishop McNamara: Rich Zinanni Era

To this day, Rich Zinanni rates Kelly O'Connor among the best football players he has produced in his 33-year career at Bishop McNamara in Kankakee, in a class with college stars Thomas Guynes (Michigan) and Kurt Belisle (Notre Dame), and NFL standout Tyjuan Hagler (Colts).

O'Connor, who never played in college, was a freshman when Zinanni was hired as head coach in 1975. As a senior, O'Connor quarterbacked McNamara to the state championship game for the first time. It set the tone for what was to follow in the 1980s—four state titles, two seconds, a 47–6 record from 1985 to 1988.

"In the early 1970s, we didn't have much to brag about," said O'Connor, who was 5–9 and weighed 160 pounds as a senior. "Jimmy Smith was at Kankakee Westview. He was a great player, the biggest name in town, a man among boys. We beat him in overtime when I was a junior but lost 21–17 as a senior.

"We were trying to make a name for ourselves, trying to do something that no other team in the Kankakee area had done, go to the state championship. We felt it was realistic. No one talked about the state title. Our goal was to make the playoff and see how well we could do. For the teams of the 1980s, it was the beginning."

McNamara lost to state power Geneseo 55–8 in the second round of the 1977 playoff. "It was a motivator. We wanted to play them again. We felt we were a better team as seniors. And we didn't think they were as good," O'Connor said.

O'Connor was named to the *Chicago Sun-Times* small-school All-State team. He rushed for 1,000 yards and 17 touchdowns and passed for 1,500 yards and 13 touchdowns. Other standouts on the team were tight end Rory O'Connor, Kelly's cousin, offensive tackle Keith Winowski, and linebacker Ron Young. In the state final, they lost to Geneseo 14–7.

They weren't as talented as the teams of the 1980s but they shared a common thread. "You believed in him [Zinanni], you wanted to play for him," O'Connor said. "He never sugarcoated anything but treated you as a young man. You knew you would get a fair shake from him," Belisle said. "He lets kids be kids but when it is time to get serious, you get to work," Hagler said.

Zinanni's best advice? "Do the right thing," he told Belisle. "If you don't know what is right, ask your parents. If you can't talk to them, look in the Bible."

Zinanni's philosophy is based on his relationship with his athletes. "I wanted to make our kids understand their responsibilities and make them confident about what they do. If you take a kid and make him confident because he knows what he is doing, he feels better about himself and he plays better. If you give me a group like that, I'll take my chances against any team, some with more talent," he said.

Zinanni, a 1965 graduate of Bishop McNamara, played one year of football at Northern Illinois but was forced to quit after suffering a hip injury. He served as a teacher and counselor at Sheridan prison for one year, and then was asked to fill an opening at McNamara in 1970. He tried it, liked it, and has enjoyed the ride ever since.

After finishing second in 1978 and 1981, McNamara was ready to take the next step in 1982. Team leaders were quarterback Mike Van Mill, tackles David Buck and Tim Highland, running back Steve Wertz, and wide receiver/safety Mike O'Connor. After slipping past Geneva 30–24 in overtime in the semifinals, they beat Alton Marquette 17–6 for the title.

By all accounts, the unbeaten 1985 squad was the best of all. No opponent got within 12 points. There was so much depth that only two players went both ways. Led by quarterback Brian Hassett, tackle Bobby BeDell, wide receivers Kevin and Kurt Cassidy, linebacker Darren Zinanni, the coach's nephew, and fullback/linebacker Mike Zuccollo, McNamara crushed Momence 42–14, Herscher 34–7, Rockridge 20–0, Lisle 23–8, and Stanford Olympia 34–7 in the playoff.

They repeated in 1986 with quarterback David Wertz, the Cassidy brothers, Zuccollo, and running back Eugene Edwards, and in 1987 with quarterback Joel Pallissard and linebackers Matt Brace and Tony Swain.

Domination of Catholic schools such as McNamara, Marian Catholic, and Belleville Althoff forced the Illinois High School Association to revise its playoff format. McNamara, an independent, had to travel to Milwaukee, East St. Louis, Springfield, and South Bend to fill out its schedule because no one in its neighborhood would play them.

So McNamara finally joined the Chicago Catholic League, arguably the most competitive conference in the country. In the 1980s, when they were dominant in the state playoff, they weren't playing Mount Carmel or St. Rita or Fenwick. Now the competitive bar was being raised. In the past six years, McNamara has had only two winning seasons. But Zinanni and most alumni love the challenge.

"We made the step to get in because we were playing common interest schools," said Zinanni, who has a career record of 274–98, a .737 winning percentage. "When we had a chance to join the Catholic League, we felt we could fit in the middle somewhere. It has been great for us."

"It was great that McNamara was winning state titles in the 1980s," Kelly O'Connor said. "But to me, when we went into the Catholic League and began competing with Mount Carmel, that's when McNamara football was at its best.

"It's a tall order to compete against those schools. To win in football, you have to have Tyuan Haglers. They haven't had many of them in the last few years. But Zinanni has had a long career and has continued to have teams that compete against schools that are bigger and stronger. Our kids are always better because of it.

"I'm glad that they went to the Catholic League. I couldn't be prouder that they did it and compete at that level. We always wondered what it would have been like to play them. Today, we beat teams because we fool them or finesse them or have better skilled players or better-coached players, not stronger or more physical players. We can't line up and run over people."

Belisle grew up in Limestone Township near Herscher and grew up hating McNamara. They were a bunch of privileged kids, the opposite of Herscher, Belisle thought. And they had stolen all of the talent from Herscher, including Kurt Quick, the town hero. But Belisle opted to enroll as a junior—his parents moved to Bourbonnais so he had a choice, Bradley or McNamara—"because McNamara was the school that would give me the best opportunity to showcase my talent to college scouts."

He played on two outstanding teams in 1992 and 1993 that included quarterback Ryan Spielman, running back Jason Schroeder, wingback Lee Lafayette, tight end John Burns, safety Casey Kinkaid, and lineman Pat Sandusky. But they lost to eventual state champion Oswego in 1993 and to Morris on a last-second field goal in 1994.

"We didn't achieve our goal of winning a state title," Belisle said. "I had set the goal when I was 9 years old. But we fell short."

Hagler always felt that his cousin, Lee Lafayette, who was four years older, was the best player in McNamara history. "He was my idol. I wanted to be better than he was," said Hagler, a 2000 graduate who played on the 1998 state runner-up team.

"Lee Lafayette showed me how you can go through a school like McNamara and go to any college you want. His dream had come through. Now my dream was next. It was my turn. I'm making progress. I played on a Super Bowl champion, then became a starter last year. My next goal is the Pro Bowl, then another Super Bowl ring as a starter. I still have a lot to accomplish—and it all started at Bishop McNamara."

Metamora: Coming of Age

Marty Stromberger is universally described as "the architect of Metamora football." He built a program from scratch and groomed coaches who produced teams that have won two state championships, claimed six second-place finishes, and become one of the most prolific winners in Illinois.

But Stromberger never saw it coming.

"The program had been .500 before I got there," he said. "It didn't have a winning attitude. I made two mistakes. I didn't know the ability of the conference I was getting into and we were 0–9 in my first season. And I started nine sophomores at the end of the year and they weren't ready for the competition. The town wasn't excited about football."

To change the mind-set, Stromberger knew he had to win some games and develop a winning attitude among the athletes. He became the first coach in Illinois to run a belly series, an offense he stole from Georgia Tech coach Bobby Dodd. And he befriended Illinois coach Ray Eliot, who taught him the wide tackle six defense, forerunner of the 4-4.

Winning soon followed. After his 0–9 start in 1962, Stromberger produced two unbeaten teams and a 45–6–1 record in the next six years and won seven conference championships in the next nine years. After 10 years and a .738 (62–21–3) winning percentage, he retired to become principal at Metamora.

Bill Roper followed with an 11–0 team in 1973. John Helmick had a .833 (82–16–1) winning percentage in nine years, winning a state title in 1975 and logging a 71–10 record from 1975 to 1981. He handed the torch to Pat Ryan, whose .819 (186–41) winning percentage in the past 19 years includes a state title in 2007, five seconds, and an 84–10 record from 1995 to 2001.

"The greatest thing I did was change the attitude of the kids," Stromberger said. "We didn't consider losing. If we lost, it was a mistake. Kids developed that attitude from their freshman through senior years. They still have that feeling."

Metamora is an old German town, a bedroom community across the Illinois River from Peoria. The courthouse is a historic landmark. Lincoln, the circuit lawyer, stopped there. The school draws students from four feeder schools, the only thing that unites the school district—Metamora, Germantown, Cazenovia, and a few small housing developments. Class pictures date to 1918. Seventy percent of the residents are professional people. Most of them work in Peoria or at Caterpillar in Morton and all of them expect their children to do well.

"The basketball coach has a tough time here," said Chuck Leonard, who has scouted Metamora football opponents for 43 years. "We're usually in the football playoffs so the kids start basketball late in the season. They are willing to work. One of the keys is we never have a situation where we say, 'I wish that kid had come out for football.' The parents and kids want to be part of a winning program."

Dick Schertz was one of the first great players to be developed at Metamora. A 1965 graduate, he was a sophomore on Stromberger's first team. Only 500 people would show up for games, quite a turnabout from the 5,000 who today make Friday night a weekly ritual. In the 1960s, the lights were so dim that spectators and even players had trouble determining who was who.

"Football was a big thing but not like it is now. It's grown into a monster," said Schertz, who had two sons play for Ryan. "I didn't sense it would become a big deal when I was a freshman. But we went 7–1–1 as juniors, then 8–1 as seniors. I was in on the beginning but I didn't realize we were starting something.

"Today, kids work on weights all year long, the whole team. Kids have to be on the team. If not, they aren't the main characters in the school. Everything revolves around football. In my day, good athletes played all sports. But now they concentrate on football. There is a culture of a winning atmosphere. It isn't just people who have kids in school now but also people who have been out of school for 40 years or aren't related to anyone who is playing. They all go back to see the games."

Stromberger said his 1968 team was his best. Some argue it was the best in school history. "If the 1968 team lost a game, they should have fired me," he said. His 1966 team was unbeaten, too, but it was small, a bunch of overachievers who lacked the talent and athleticism of the 1968 powerhouse. The team was led by quarterback Rick Hodel, linemen Gordon Hahn and Mike Rudolph, and halfbacks Dick Schertz and Dick Krumholz. They averaged 35.4 points per game and outscored opponents by an average of 26 per game.

The 1975 team might have been even better. It was Helmick's second team. He said it was his best. After serving as an assistant coach at Peoria Woodruff, which had lost 48 games in a row, Helmick wasn't the first choice to succeed Roper at Metamora. Some people told him not to take the job. But when he was offered, he didn't turn it down. He had no head coaching experience.

"Metamora was good but not great," he said. "What attracted me was they had been successful. Some people said it was hard to discipline the kids because they had been so successful. I felt if we could establish discipline, we could have a successful program."

Helmick didn't allow his players to unbuckle their chinstraps or remove their mouth guards in practice. They had to put on their cleats outside the locker room. He established rules and expected his players to abide by them. He was absolutely dedicated to teaching fundamentals. John Vogelsang, who assisted Stromberger, Roper, and Helmick, said Helmick was "one of the most dedicated Xs and Os coaches I've been around, a real student of the game."

In 1975, Helmick installed an option offense with the fullback as the primary ball carrier, an offense straight out of a Woody Hayes playbook with 230-pound junior fullback Larry Sommer pounding inside and senior tailback Paul Wernsman running outside. Quarterback Jim Garber was the team leader and tight end Phil Schertz, wingback Tom Miller, tackles Rocky Elbert and Greg Hill, defensive back Tom Miller, linebacker Scott Ruder and his cousin, guard Pat Ruder, formed a talented supporting cast. Sommer was the best defensive player at tackle.

They allowed only 35 points in the regular season, and then beat Alton Marquette 41–28, Kankakee Bishop McNamara 31–8, East St. Louis Lincoln 14–12, and Geneva 25–7 in the playoff.

The Lincoln game, played at Parsons Field in East St. Louis, marked what many old-timers regard as the greatest game in school history. Both teams were unbeaten and Lincoln had beaten traditional cross-town power East St. Louis earlier in the season. Lincoln's defense, led by linebacker Orlando Pope, was known as "the Mean Dudes" and they had vowed to limit Sommer to fewer than 50 yards. Their offense featured future NFL wide receiver Johnny Poe.

Metamora led 14–6. Lincoln scored and attempted a two-point conversion to tie but Garber came up to stuff the run and preserve the victory. Sommer, undaunted by Lincoln's defense, rushed for 150 yards. Helmick used only 13 players. His offensive line included two 170-pound tackles and a 160-pound guard.

"They called me the bowling ball," Sommer said. "I didn't have blazing speed but I kept on going. Helmick always started with 36 belly, me running inside to see how opponents would react. If they would try to stop me, he'd throw in a play-action pass by Garber or pitch the ball to Wernsman. If Helmick said, 'This will work,' you trusted that it would."

On fourth-and-two at midfield with two minutes to play, Helmick called time-out. "Coach, give me the ball. I'll get it," Sommer told him. Helmick said to go for the first down. Sommer got it. "They knew he was going to get the ball. It was the greatest three-yard run you'll ever see," Hill recalled.

Morris: Darlington to Dergo

Ed Brady was there when it all began. He remembers how it was. Dan Darlington was the sophomore football coach at Morris when Brady was a freshman. He brought Brady up to the sophomore squad, and then promoted him to the varsity when he became head coach the following year. It was the beginning of a beautiful friendship.

"I was intimidated by him. Most kids were," said Brady, who went on to play in the NFL for 12 years. "He pushed you hard to get the best out of you. You respected him for that. He stressed being physical. We did a lot of hitting in practice, similar to college and the pros, like an NFL training camp. He knew what he was doing to prepare you for the game."

Darlington was no stranger to Morris. A 1968 graduate, he was an outstanding three-sport athlete, an All-Stater in football and basketball and a state qualifier in the 440-yard dash. He once scored 50 points in a basketball game. He earned a scholarship to play football at the University of Illinois.

In 28 years at Morris, Darlington emerged as one of the winningest coaches in state history. His teams were 264–55, a .828 winning percentage. He won 23 conference championships, two state titles, and five seconds. From 1988 to 1995, he was 84–11. He had only one losing season. He sent 83 players to college on full scholarships and over 100 on partial aid.

"I was an old-school coach. I didn't tolerate a lot of stuff that is tolerated today," Darlington said. "Teams have to be disciplined. That's what I hung my hat on. I wouldn't permit long hair in a time when long hair was popular. If your hair was outside the helmet, you didn't get a helmet. The best players got to play, no matter who they were."

Preparation was Darlington's trademark. "You have 12 months to get ready for the opener so you should be ready for it," he said. He lost only one opening game in his career.

And he was flexible. In his first 10 years, he coached a Woody Hayes–style of offense. He would try to run over opponents. He rarely threw more than six passes in a game. The strategy worked. At a school that played its first football game in 1902, Darlington won more games than all coaches before him combined.

But he had to adjust. As the rival schools got larger with enrollments over 1,000 students and the opponents got heavier, Darlington realized he couldn't run over people consistently. He changed his philosophy to take advantage of his quarterbacks. Ten of them went on to play in college on scholarship.

Darlington was born and raised on the East Side of Morris, along the I&M Canal, by the Illinois River, what was described as the tough side of town. "I never had a silver spoon in my life," he said. Darlington was all about work ethic. He put in endless hours to build the football program and he expected his assistants—Denny Steele, Keith Laughery, Jay Roth, Gary Dergo, and his son George, now the head coach at Morris—to do the same.

"We had to change the mind-set of the kids," Darlington said. "In my first year, I had 28 kids out for varsity football. After that, we never had fewer than 45, as many as 65. We stressed hard work. We started to lift weights. I wouldn't let them leave the building until they lifted weights. Later, they all wanted to be there, wanted to be a part of it."

John Dergo remembers the feeling. Brady is the only Morris graduate to play in the NFL; but John, George's son, is the most celebrated player in school history. He led his team to the state championship in 2005 by rushing for 3,010 yards and 52 touchdowns. He set state records for points in a career (756), points in a season (376 in 2005), touchdowns in a career (110), and touchdowns in a season (52).

"When I was little, I couldn't wait to play for Coach Darlington, to be a Morris Redskin," he said. "My friends and I would play backyard football and pretend we were playing other teams. We couldn't wait to be on the varsity.

"Coach Darlington made football in Morris a way of life. It was a like a brotherhood. You became so close with your teammates in the spring, summer, and fall, every day for hours at a time. He was very motivational. You felt like you were going into battle with a fearless leader and felt you were unstoppable."

It took three years for Darlington to turn around the program. He was 6–3 in his first season but conceded he was closer to 4–5. But he felt his team earned its 6–3 record in his second year. Then Brady's 12–1 team went to the state final in 1979, beating perennial state power Geneseo 14–8 in the semifinals and snapping the Maple Leafs' 33-game winning streak, before losing to Mascoutah and Kris Jenner 7–6 for the state title.

"It was a crushing loss. Our goal was to win the state title in our first appearance at state," Brady said. "It was similar to losing the Super Bowl [in 1989]. I'll think about that loss for the rest of my life. You're playing with your buddies in high school. It isn't like college or the NFL. Those guys are still my best friends. We could have pulled it off but we didn't."

Darlington still remembers that loss, too. Morris was on Mascoutah's 16. It was third-and-one with 30 seconds to play. Brady was the center, Jeremiah McNulty the guard.

The play called for fullback Randy Butler to run over Brady and McNulty for the first down. Then quarterback Bill Button would throw into the end zone (incomplete to stop the clock) and Morris would kick a field goal to win the game.

"Butler broke to the six, they stand him up, and one of my halfbacks knocks over the pile," Darlington recalled. "An official calls a penalty for aiding the runner. I had never seen a call like that in high school. We would have had first-and-goal at the six. I said it was a bush league call but I said we'd be back the next year."

Button, the *Chicago Sun-Times* Player of the Year, and running back Mark Sharp returned in 1980 and led Morris to the state championship. The Redskins smashed Harrisburg 40–0 in the state final as Button completed 11 of 21 passes for 123 yards and three touchdowns and Sharp rushed 10 times for 101 yards and one touchdown. He also caught two TD passes from Button.

"The 1980 team was as good as any of my teams," Darlington said.

The 1984 state championship team was 0–9 and scored only two touchdowns as freshmen. "They were so terrible, parents used to ask what we could do with them," Darlington said. But they got in the weight room, got stronger, and developed. As seniors, quarterback Jim Feeney, running back Doug Sharp, linebacker Dan Almer, tackle Brian Barkley, and their teammates went 13–0 and rallied from a 7–0 deficit to beat Benet 31–14 for the state title.

"I told that story to all freshman teams after that," Darlington said. "Winning is important but not that important as freshmen. How many come back as sophomores? That's how I evaluate my coaching staff, how well they prepare the freshmen."

After that, Darlington experienced a lot of winning but also a lot of frustration. He finished second on five occasions. In 1989, he lost to Richards 12–6 in overtime. "It was a great game, as good as any game I've been in," he said.

But his toughest loss was in 1993. Led by quarterback Todd Schultz, who later played at Michigan State, the team was unbeaten, had averaged 52 points per game, and had beaten eventual state champion Oswego 41–14. But the Redskins lost to Marian Catholic 26–20 in the quarterfinals after leading 20–0 in the first quarter.

Darlington retired after the 2004 season, after guiding Morris to another second-place finish and following a dispute with the school administration. Who would succeed him? Steele, his longtime assistant, was retiring, too. George Dergo, who had coached with Darlington for 25 years, planned to retire as wrestling coach after his son John graduated in 2006. In May, Dergo was offered the job. He accepted.

"I was the last one standing," he said. "My son is a senior and I'm not going anyplace. The program didn't skip a beat in the summer. My son was a senior and all the kids he grew up with were playing and I had coached them as freshmen. We knew we should have another run at a state title. I wasn't thinking about how good they were but how to finish it off with a group of kids I'd know since they were in diapers."

After losing to Joliet Catholic in the state final in 2001 and 2004, the 2005 squad eliminated Joliet Catholic 28–21 in the quarterfinals and went on to beat Normal Community 14–9 for the title. John Dergo rushed for 300 yards to beat Joliet Catholic and ran behind an offensive line that included ends Jamie Cumbie and Dane Zumbahlen, tackles Alex Perry and Mark Kopczick, guards Alberto Diaz and Sam Farber, and center Darin Haas.

"We're lining up in an I formation with a returning All-State running back and seven very big linemen and we're coming right at you. That was our mind-set," John Dergo said. "I didn't really expect what happened. I had better numbers than I thought I would. But being best friends with every one of them, playing sports from soccer to baseball to football while growing up since we were six years old, then going out with a state championship. How good is that?"

New Lenox Providence: The Matt Senffner Era

Eric Steinbach, a first-round selection in the NFL draft and a three-time All-Pro offensive lineman, reflects on his days at Providence Catholic in New Lenox and how he was motivated to succeed by Coach Matt Senffner.

"I was there for the best part of the dynasty," Steinbach said. "I came in 1994 and watched the older guys go 14–0. I could tell the work ethic and determination, how the program was run. They did a great job of molding kids on and off the field. They taught so many life lessons."

As a freshman, Steinbach's team was 2–7. But they were in the weight room, training in the summer and playing seven-on-seven. He observed the older players, how they handled themselves. "They taught us what it takes to be a winner," he said.

Providence already was emerging as one of the state's elite programs when Steinbach enrolled. The Celtics won their first state championship in 1987 behind sophomore linebacker Pete Bercich, running back John Martin, and defensive standouts Kevin Kickles, Mark Masters, and Doug Ternik. Martin rushed for 213 yards and scored the winning touchdown in a 14–7 victory over Roxana.

Bercich went to Providence to play baseball for Coach Jaime Garcia. A catcher, he dreamed of being the next Carlton Fisk. Providence had a reputation for baseball, wrestling, and basketball, having won state titles in each sport in the late 1970s and early 1980s, but football was struggling. If you were growing up in New Lenox and you were a good football player, you likely would enroll at Joliet Catholic, not Providence.

But after winning a state title and leading his team in sacks as a sophomore, Bercich realized football might be his calling. "Mentally, I was more suited to play football than baseball," he said. It was a wise decision. Later, he played for four years at Notre Dame and had an 11-year career with the Minnesota Vikings in the NFL, seven as a player and four as a coach.

"Looking back, the coaching I got at Providence was fantastic," Bercich said. "Senffner was a Joe Paterno kind of guy—ugly uniforms, ugly games, three yards, and a cloud of dust. If you weren't mentally tough, you couldn't make it through the program. He worked us hard and taught us what it was like to grind through a football season."

They won again in 1991 with running backs Frank Pflugradt and Jeff Schley, quarterback Chris Orr, linebackers Tom Manzella and Craig McPartlin, and defensive backs Alan Lakomskis and Greg Keigher. Lakomskis had a record 14 interceptions. Chris Orr's 17-yard scoring pass to Justin Orr with 10:29 to play lifted Providence to a 14–7 victory over Bloomington for the state title.

That was only the beginning. In Steinbach's four years, Providence went 14–0, 14–0, 14–0, and 13–1, winning 50 games in a row and sweeping four state titles. He didn't play on the varsity as a freshman, only participated in kickoffs and a few defensive plays as a sophomore, missed his first few games as a junior following knee surgery, and established a state record with 26 sacks as a senior but saw the winning streak snapped by Bishop McNamara.

"We kept evolving every year," he said. "By the time we were seniors, we took over and knew how to carry on the tradition. We had no blue chippers. Pete Bercich was the last graduate to go to a major college program. If you bought into the program, it would make you better than the guy next to you. You'd come in as freshmen and take notes in the back of the room, then keep moving up to the front. It taught me how to be a professional, how to get ready for college."

Robert Cruz quarterbacked the unbeaten 1995 and 1996 state champions. In 1995, after upsetting Richards 17–0 in the semifinals, Providence trailed Springfield Sacred Heart-Griffin by 10 with three minutes to play. But the Celtics rallied behind Cruz to win 22–17.

"They were taking it to us for three quarters, kicking our butts. It never had happened to us before. The coach looked at me and said I would have to win the game for us and throw passes that we hadn't used in games," Cruz said. "On a third-and-15 play, I threw a 25-yard pass to Dan Joyce and we scored from the three with 14 seconds left. It was a pass we had practiced but never had completed in a game. I still remember the call—97 X option 3 delay robin."

In 1996, Cruz and running back Louis Medina triggered the offense. Cruz passed for 2,600 yards and 35 touchdowns and Providence capped another 14–0 season with a 28–21 victory over Metamora. In 1997, Eric Steinbach had a coming-out party on defense and Justin Ruggio, Mark O'Reel, and David Popp sparked the offense as the Celtics beat Metamora 26–12 for another state title.

Senffner was the guiding force. From 1994 through 2004, he lost only 12 games, won seven state titles, and finished second twice. He was fond of his first two state champions but didn't hesitate to single out the 2001 squad as his best. The offense, led by running back Mike Mentz and quarterback Mike Budde, averaged 32 points per game and crushed Richards 41–0 in the state final. Senffner said the defense, anchored by linebackers Rory Steinbach and Matt Eggert and defensive backs Matt Gannon and Mark Reiter, was even better.

"You heard about [Senffner] when you came in. You respected him. You were a little bit afraid of him but you always wanted to bust your hump for him," Eric Steinbach said. "He always did a great job of motivating kids. He got the best out of his players and coaches. He prepared for games like colleges did."

The 2002 team was exceptional, too. In Week 4, they beat Joliet Catholic 10–2 in an ESPN showcase game at Joliet Memorial Stadium. In the last 10 games, they averaged 48.5 points. In a rematch with Joliet Catholic in the state quarterfinals, Providence romped 41–0. The defense shut out seven opponents, including Pontiac 43–0 in the state final, and allowed only 52 points in a 14–0 season. The offense was led by quarterback Nick Stanton and running back Clay Cleveland. The defense featured Mark Reiter, Marty Marino, Mike Stephens, and Brian Kulczak.

"The defense was called the circus. John Pergi, the linebacker coach, said because of the way we ran to the ball, we looked like a circus. A lot of crazy stuff would happen in our games," said Dan Olszta, who played outside linebacker and later earned a scholarship at Iowa as a long snapper.

"Each class had a superstition and we had tons of our own. We had the same routine before every game. We'd walk through the same doors. On Friday before a game, we'd go to my house, only two minutes from school, and my mother would cook a lunch. Clay Cleveland would have the same thing, macaroni and cheese, in the same bowl. Marty Marino and I had to play the same college football game on PlayStation. No matter what, I had to lose. And Andy Hopkins, the kicker, didn't make it to my house the first week so he couldn't come the other 13 weeks. It didn't make much sense but it worked for us."

The 2004 team, behind the passing of Clay Colbert and the running of Parker Cleveland and Jordan Farrell and a defense anchored by Matt Mazurowski, Pete Corriveau, and Pat Lenahan, averaged 37 points per game and allowed only 89 points in a 13–1 season. After edging Mount Carmel in a dramatic double overtime semifinal 16–15, they dismantled Bloomington 40–0 for the school's ninth state title.

"We had beaten Mount Carmel 42–16 in Week 9 but they were ready for us in the state semifinals," recalled Ryan Doyle. "The defining play was when they went for a two-point conversion and the win and our defense stopped them. It was the last play of the game and the season for somebody.

"I'm an offensive lineman and never usually watch the defense. My football career wasn't in my control at that point. I was watching a Mount Carmel receiver who was on the goal line looking for the ball, then dropping to his knees and pounding his fist into the ground. I knew he would tell me if they had won or lost.

"He would be jumping up and down or he would be emotionally crushed as we were in 2003, when we lost 14–13 to Minooka, when Clay Colbert threw an incomplete pass into the end zone on fourth down as time expired."

Patrick Doyle, Ryan's identical twin and also an offensive lineman, was standing a few feet away and observed the play from a different point of view. "It was a hand-off, our defense came through and stopped him less than an inch from the goal line. Derek Sexton made the first hit and Matt Mazurowski hit him before the goal line. It was over," he said.

Oak Lawn Richards: Moving On Up

In the late 1960s and into the 1970s, Richards wasn't the football program of choice for kids who grew up in Oak Lawn, Chicago Ridge, and Robbins. The Chicago Catholic League was in its prime and there were other options. Why go to Richards when you could go to St. Laurence or St. Rita or even Blue Island Eisenhower?

"When I was in seventh grade, my dad took me to a game and I saw Thornridge's Quinn Buckner run back two punts against Richards," Ron Pratl recalled. "They were a doormat. When I was a freshman, we finished 2–6–1, lost to Thornridge 62–0, and had only 15 players on the team at the end of the season. But we won Coach Gary Korhonen's first conference championship in 1975."

By the time Joe Montgomery came along in the 1990s—his mother didn't permit him to play football until he was 16 because she was afraid he would get hurt— Richards was established as one of the powers in the state. It was a program of choice for anyone who wanted to play the game and go on to the next level.

"My father wanted me to go to Eisenhower because it was closer to our home," said the future NFL player. "But I wanted to go to the school where my father went. I thought Richards had cool gold helmets. There was a mystique, a swagger, a hard-nosed feeling about Richards, something I wanted to be a part of."

After starting 28–26 in his first six years, Korhonen had only one losing season in his last 30, retiring after the 2007 season as the winningest coach (306–91) in state history. From 1985 to 1992, he was 87–12 with two state championships. From 1994 to 1998, he was 52–8. And he sent more than 275 players to college, five to the NFL.

For John Rutkowski, it was a no-brainer to enroll at Richards. He had watched Korhonen put the program on the map in the late 1970s. His father knew Korhonen and had joined his staff as offensive line coach in 1982. His older sister Debbie had attended Richards. He idolized Rob Pratl, a left-handed quarterback on the 1985 team. He even was a ball boy.

By the time Rutkowski enrolled in 1986, Korhonen's reputation had preceded him. "He can be intimidating because he is a man who knows what he wants. He is passionate about winning and his program and about kids. He intrigued me from the beginning. You always knew where you stood with him. He didn't hide anything. If he didn't think you were doing your job, he'd tell you," Rutkowski said.

Korhonen kept building for the day that his program would reach the top, when it would be ranked with the best in the state. After going 10–2 in 1985 and 1986, then finishing 10–3 in 1987 after losing to Providence 25–12 in the state semifinals, everyone felt it was time to take the program to the next level.

"We played year to year, trying to build on the previous year. Our goal in 1988 was to win the state title. That was the tone that was set by all of the coaches going into the 1988 season," said Rutkowski, who was backup quarterback to Efrem Haymore. "We sensed in the first day of double sessions that we could win state."

The senior leaders were Haymore, center Darrin Grove, linebacker Scott O'Connor, tackles Hal Mady and Jerry Cook, running back Tony Jansto, and two-way back Rich

Albon. Korhonen said it was his best defensive team. He was influenced by Buffalo Grove coach Grant Blaney, an old high school classmate who had guided his team to the 1986 state championship.

In the second game, playing in near 100-degree heat, Richards and Simeon were scoreless at halftime. In the second half, a Simeon receiver dropped a sure touchdown pass and Richards went on to win 12–0. After that, no one got closer than Rockford West, which lost 28–8 in the state semifinals. Richards crushed Hirsch 61–8, Bremen 51–20, and Providence 20–6 in earlier playoff games, then stomped Peoria Central 40–6 in the final to complete a 14–0 season.

"I often thought if that Simeon kid had caught that ball in the second game, what kind of a season would we have had," Korhonen said. "We won two state titles but there is nothing like the first one."

"Everyone was under the realization that if we didn't win state in 1988 and 1989 that we didn't achieve what we should have with all that talent," Rutkowski said. "We wouldn't have been satisfied with anything less. It doesn't happen very often when you have a wealth of talent that we had in 1988 and 1989."

Despite returning only three starters from 1988—receiver/defensive back Johnny Newton, tackle Hal Mady, and receiver Tommy Lyons—Korhonen and his players thought the 1989 team could contend for another state title. The Bulldogs were dominant with Rutkowski at quarterback, running back/linebacker Arthur Russell, running back/defensive back Kevin Jackson, guard Ed Elsouso, and sophomore linebacker Chris Koeppen.

Korhonen knew Koeppen was the best linebacker in the program but he was stubborn about bringing sophomores up to the varsity. After Richards swept through the regular season at 9–0, he decided to promote nine sophomores. Koeppen started every one of the five playoff games.

Rutkowski said 1989 was the better of the two state champions. Why? The offense averaged 38 points per game and the first-stringers rarely played more than a half. The defense allowed only eight points per game and had 30 interceptions. The roster featured 10 Division I players.

The ninth game pitted Richards against Providence in a duel of unbeatens in Oak Lawn. Linebacker Pete Bercich was Providence's standout. Richards won 39–6 in what Rutkowski said was the team's best game of the season. Rutkowski passed for three touchdowns and Russell rushed for 180 yards behind an offensive line led by Mady, Elsouso, center Bill Oldham, guard Brian Gerk, and tackle Mark McGrinni.

"We were coming off a 14–0 season and everybody was looking for us. Opponents geared up for us each week," said Rutkowski, who passed for 2,200 yards. "The pressure was on me because I was following Haymore and it was my team. A lot of people were wondering if I could fill his shoes. I was curious how I would respond to the pressure."

Richards, in the midst of a 34-game winning streak, went on to smash Sullivan 45–12, Oak Forest 32–20, Joliet Catholic 34–12, and Woodstock 45–13 before nudging Morris 12–6 in overtime in the state final. It was the closest game the Bulldogs played all year. Korhonen described it as the most satisfying victory of his career.

Tied at 6 with 30 seconds to play in the fourth quarter, Richards was on Morris' 30. Rutkowski attempted a pass to Russell but Morris' Mike Wright intercepted and appeared to be running for a game-winning touchdown. But Rutkowski caught him at Richards' 14.

In overtime, Rutkowski scored on a bootleg on third down from the two. But Rutkowski's two-point conversion pass to Newton was incomplete. On its possession, Morris attempted four passes that fell incomplete. Rutkowski passed for 110 yards and Russell rushed for 104.

"It was one of the best championship games I have seen," Korhonen said.

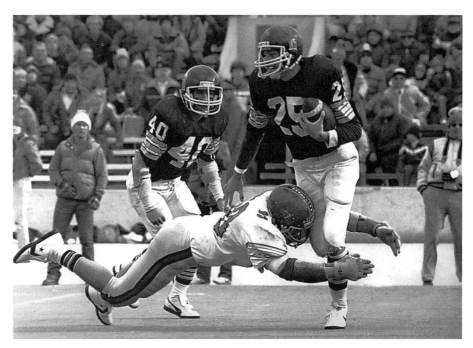

Joliet Catholic's Tom Seneker (25) runs into some formidable opposition in the form of a Deerfield tackler in the 1981 Class 5A championship game. Seneker's two-point conversion run after Andy Bebar's seven-yard touchdown run with 6:27 to play lifted Joliet Catholic to an 8–7 victory. Photo courtesy of the Illinois High School Association.

John Dergo (left) led Morris to the 2005 state championship by rushing for 3,010 yards and 52 touchdowns and scoring 376 points. He scored 110 touchdowns and 756 points in his career. Also an outstanding wrestler, he opted to accept a wrestling scholarship to the University of Illinois rather than continue to play football. Photo courtesy of MorrisRedskinsFootball.com.

George Dergo (left) and Dan Darlington coached Morris to three state championships and six second-place finishes. Darlington had a sensational .828 winning percentage (264–55) in 28 years and won state titles in 1980 and 1984. Dergo won a state title in 2005. Photo courtesy of MorrisRedskinsFootball.com.

The Penney brothers were instrumental in Geneseo's success in the 1960s and 1970s. Left to right, Steve, Jay, and Rick. Steve, a 1968 graduate, played on three teams that were 26–1. Jay, a 1980 graduate, was a junior quarterback on the 1978 state championship team. Rick, a 1971 graduate, played on three teams that were 26–0–1. Photo courtesy of Steve Penney.

After catching a pass from quarterback Phil Pedi on a fourth-and-seven play, Driscoll's David Schwabe (9) breaks loose for a big gain on the winning drive that propelled the Highlanders to a 12–7 victory over Morton in the opening round of the 2006 state playoff. Driscoll went on to win its sixth state title in a row. Photo courtesy of Driscoll Catholic High School.

Metamora's Larry Sommer holds the state championship trophy and celebrates with his teammates after beating Geneva 25–7 to win the Class 3A title in 1975. Sommer rushed for 159 yards and two touchdowns to spark the victory. Photo courtesy of the Illinois High School Association.

Members of Providence's 1996 team celebrate after beating Metamora 28–21 in a duel of unbeatens for the Class 4A championship. Photo courtesy of the Illinois High School Association.

Larry Sommer led Metamora to the 1975 state championship, a 25–7 victory over Geneva. The 5–10, 230–pound self-proclaimed bowling ball rushed for 1,973 yards during the season and emerged as the school's first All-State selection. Photo courtesy of Chuck Leonard.

Barry Pearson, who later played at Northwestern and in the NFL, was one of the standout players who helped to build Geneseo's Green Machine dynasty in the 1960s. Photo courtesy of Barry Pearson.

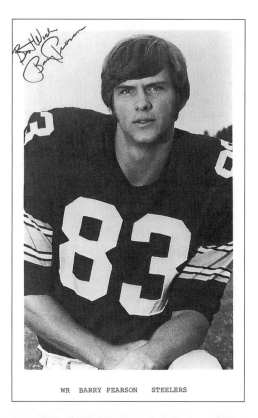

WR BARRY PEARSON STEELERS

Joliet Catholic's Dave Matichak (42) slips around his left end and attempts to elude a host of La Salle-Peru tacklers in the Class 4A championship game in 1977. Matichak scored two touchdowns as Joliet Catholic won 30–6. It was the Hilltoppers' third state title in a row under Coach Gordie Gillespie. Photo courtesy of the Illinois High School Association.

Geneseo's Randy Clary breaks away from Wheaton North's Jim Juriga (76) for a short gain in the 1981 Class 4A championship game. Wheaton North, with Darryl Richardson rushing for 122 yards and two touchdowns, prevailed 14–0. Photo courtesy of the Illinois High School Association.

The number 49 jersey worn by Geneseo's Wayne Strader during the 1975 season. Strader rushed for 2,200 yards and scored 33 touchdowns as Geneseo swept through a 13–0 season and emerged as one of the most celebrated teams in state history. In the state final, a 20–12 victory over Metamora, Strader carried 33 times for 188 yards and three touchdowns. Photo courtesy of Wayne Strader.

Nobody knew it then but this was the start of something special. Driscoll's Mike Burzawa (23) breaks away on a 64-yard touchdown run in the first quarter of the 1991 Class 3A championship game against Robinson. Burzawa, who coached Driscoll to three state titles in the 2000s, rushed for 152 yards and three touchdowns in a 42–20 victory. Photo courtesy of the Illinois High School Association.

Coaches Tim Racki (left) and Mike Burzawa formed an invincible combination at Driscoll Catholic High School in Addison in the 2000s. Racki produced four state champions in a row and his successor, Burzawa, who starred on the school's first state championship team in 1991, coached three in a row. Photo courtesy of Driscoll Catholic High School.

Coach Gene Nudo celebrates on the shoulders of his players after Driscoll completed a 14–0 season by beating Robinson 42–20 to win the Class 3A championship in 1991. The Addison didn't win another state title until 2001, then proceeded to win an unprecedented seven in a row. Photo courtesy of Gene Nudo.

Geneseo coach Bob Reade (left) gives instructions to running back Wayne Strader (49). In 17 years, Reade guided Geneseo to a record of 147–19–4 and three state championships. He produced eight unbeaten teams, including five in a row in the pre-state playoff period. Photo courtesy of Wayne Strader.

Jason Karnes was the only All-State quarterback on Du Quoin's 14–0 state championship team in 1992. Photo courtesy of Illinois High School Association.

Vic Boblett was an All-State running back at Geneseo in 1970. In four years, he never played in a losing game. Later, he coached at Geneseo and was 36–9 in four years and produced a state runner-up in 1990. He currently is head coach at Rock Island. Photo courtesy of Illinois High School Association.

7

Large Schools

Chicago Mount Carmel:
Frank Kiszka's Legacy

Frank Kiszka enrolled at Chicago's Mount Carmel a year after football coach Terry Brennan left to join Frank Leahy's staff at Notre Dame. He obviously liked what he saw. The 1957 graduate spent the last 36 years of his life, prior to his untimely death in 2005, working in the school's football program.

Kiszka was most visible walking the sideline at Mount Carmel games, serving as the team's one and only statistician since 1968. He didn't take statistics for the opponent, only Mount Carmel. And you didn't dare argue with his figures. The media guide and record book, which he published for 14 years, was testimony to his attention to detail.

The former grammar school football coach was Mount Carmel's Man of the Year in 1978 and Man of the Decade for the 1990s. He was inducted into the school's Hall of Fame in 1986. All the while, he also kept statistics for hockey, basketball, and baseball. For the last 20 years, he was the school's hockey moderator and worked in the Development Office, specializing in alumni affairs.

A single man, Mount Carmel football was the love of his life. He watched the program enter a golden era, beginning with Frank Maloney's 1967 Prep Bowl champion and continuing with Bill Barz' first state champion in 1980, then achieving dynastic proportions with Frank Lenti's run of nine state championships from 1988 to 2002 and the Caravan's mythic record of 122–12 in the decade of the 1990s.

"Mount Carmel was a unique and fascinating place," said Maloney, a 1958 graduate who was 30–12–2 in five years as his alma mater's football coach. "It reminded me of the Marine Corps. The spirit of the kids was remarkable. Everyone was involved—the kids, the faculty, the alumni. Sports were huge. Pep rallies on Friday were sensational. The school built its reputation on strong athletic teams.

"When I grew up, I saw all the games in 1950, 1951, and 1952. They were my heroes. I'd go to Eckersall Stadium on Sunday to watch them. There was something special about that. I was coaching in high school when I was 22 years old. I was very cocky. I thought I could invent the game."

His 1964 team lost to Weber and Chico Kurzawski for the Catholic League championship. But his 1967 squad, led by quarterback Dennis Connell, running back Dave Zuccarelli, end Bill Trapp, and tight end Jerry Schumacher, was 9–2, upset two-time city champion Loyola for the Catholic League title, and then smashed Public League kingpin Dunbar 37–0 in the Prep Bowl.

Although Dunbar's defensive strategy indicated that Mount Carmel should run the ball—and Zuccarelli took advantage of the opportunity, rushing 19 times for 127 yards and four touchdowns—the Caravan was noted for its passing game in 1967. After analyzing his returning players from 1966, Maloney determined he had an exceptional passer in Connell and a promising receiver in Trapp.

He attended a clinic in Atlantic City and, after hearing USC coach John McKay outline his passing game, came away convinced that it was the wave of future and he had the tools to pull it off with Connell and Trapp. They practiced daily at Jackson Park. Even after Trapp dropped 10 balls in an opening loss to Loyola, Maloney stuck with it. By the end of the season, Maloney was feeling very good about his passing game and opponents still weren't used to defending it.

"I'm an old Catholic League guy. Tom Carey was my coach. I admired Tony Lawless, Jim Arneberg, and Max Burnell from afar," said Maloney, who currently is the director of ticket operations for the Chicago Cubs. "It was smash-mouth football in those days, run them over. My 1967 team was the first team in my memory that played a wide-open game. We threw the ball first. That was our fundamental philosophy."

Barz, an All-State running back at Rich Central who played on two bowl teams at Notre Dame, arrived at Mount Carmel in 1977. In his last four years, before leaving for Illinois Benedictine College in 1984, he produced teams that went 13–1, 10–2, 10–2, and 8–3, won one state championship and two Prep Bowls.

"I didn't know what I was walking into," Barz said. "Fr. Dave Dillon interviewed me one day and hired me the next day. I was coaching at North Park College and he came to the school in person to offer me the job. I knew about the Mount Carmel tradition but I didn't know how to acquire players in the Catholic League at the time. Recruiting was legal at the time."

Kiszka set up appointments for Barz to visit young prospects in their homes. He saw three eighth graders every night and five on Sunday. Until the Catholic League joined the Illinois High School Association in 1974, it was legal to offer scholarships to athletes.

Fr. Dillon and Fr. Bob Carroll, now principal at Carmel High School in Mundelein, were great leaders. They brought the alumni back and virtually saved the school. In the 1970s, enrollment was slipping and there were rumors that the school was in danger of closing. Only 176 took the entrance exam in 1976. But 225 took it in 1977.

"The biggest day of the year, bar none, was the day of the entrance exam, even bigger than a football victory," Barz said. "Football was a magnet for enrollment. The football players we recruited would bring four or five friends with them.

"It was like college recruiting. It became apparent to me very quickly that kids wanted to be there. Ron Szczesniak, the freshman coach, had 130 kids out for football and won the league title nine out of 10 years. I wanted to bring Tony Furjanic to the varsity as a freshman. I wanted them to grow together as a class and learn winning ways. Football was really important to our kids. Our goal was to win the state title in 1980."

Mount Carmel was coming off a 4–6 season but Barz had high expectations for 1980. He wanted to get off to a good start. When Coach Gerry Faust of perennial power Moeller of Cincinnati, Ohio, called to guarantee a $10,000 fee for a Mount

Carmel/Moeller opener in Soldier Field, Barz turned him down. Ironically, the following year, Barz made the same call and the same offer but Faust turned him down.

Instead, Barz signed a contract with Joliet Catholic, which had won four state titles in a row under legendary coach Gordie Gillespie from 1975 to 1978. Barz admitted that he had better talent in 1981, 1982, and 1983 but he believed that 1980 was "our year" and his players, despite a 7–6 loss to Loyola in Week 3, went on to prove it.

The offense was led by All-State running back Andre Carter, quarterback Ray Gronowski, center Ardel McKenna, guards Tony Furjanic and Brian McDonough, and tackles John Loncar and Ed Kurasz. The defense was anchored by Furjanic, who was the *Chicago Sun-Times* Player of the Year as a senior in 1981, linebacker Rich Mosior, noseman Marty Walsh, tackle Mike Beneturski, and defensive backs Ed Barkowski and Darren Martin.

"I loved coaching them," Barz said. "They were a special group of guys who stuck together for four years to make a dream come true. They played hard for 48 minutes in every game."

In the state playoff, the Caravan beat Thornton Fractional North and quarterback Mike Tomczak, the *Chicago Sun-Times* Player of the Year, 22–13 in the semifinals, then got past Hinsdale South 15–10 for the state title.

In the state final, Carter carried 29 times for 151 yards and scored two touchdowns and Jim Sherlock kicked a 29-yard field goal as Mount Carmel built a 15–0 lead at the end of the third quarter. Hinsdale South closed to 15–10 and had possession with four minutes to play but Barkowski recovered a fumbled snap at his 43 and the Caravan ran out the clock.

"The 1980 state title was the highlight of my career," said Furjanic, who played at Notre Dame and the NFL. "I was MVP on defense at the Liberty Bowl, when we played Boston College and Doug Flutie in 1983. But that memory still pales compared to the state title. It was the only real winning team I ever was on."

Chicago St. Rita: 100 Years of Football Memories

St. Rita celebrated 100 years of football in 2008, rekindling memories of the school's first Chicago Catholic League champion in 1923 to Ed Buckley's 1963 national champion to Pat Cronin's 1970 and 1971 Prep Bowl winners to Cronin's 1978 state champion to Todd Kuska's 2006 state champion.

And the great players—Harold "Chick" Walsh in 1922, Jack McHugh in 1946, Bob Spoo in 1954, Ray Schaack and John Herman in 1956, Ewalk Herster in 1958, Dave McCormick in 1961, Jim Klutcharch and John Byrne in 1963, Billy Marek and Dennis Lick in 1971, Mark Zavagnin in 1978, John Foley in 1985, and Matt Conrath and Darius Fleming in 2006.

"The teams will be remembered, not the coaches," said Kuska, who has sustained a winning tradition that was built by Buckley, restored by Cronin and carried on by Todd Wernet. "Each team needs to set the tempo for what they want to be and leave their own legacy. Some of these kids might not remember Lick or Marek or Cronin. But we sell them on the community and teach them the history and tradition."

It isn't old St. Rita any more. Kuska graduated in 1990, the last class to study in the old building and play football in the old stadium at South 63rd Street and Claremont. The Augustinian Order moved the school to a 33-acre campus at 77th and South Western Avenue once occupied by Quigley South Seminary. The football field, named in Cronin's memory, was upgraded to include lights and an artificial surface.

"I recall the way it was," Dennis Lick said. "The Bears games were blacked out. There was nothing else to do but go to Catholic League games. The atmosphere at the old stadium was electrifying. There were so many great rivalries. Playing on Sunday afternoon was a great feeling. It isn't that way anymore.

"Today, there's a different feeling when I go back. Things have to change. The move to 77th Street was the right thing to do. They have wonderful facilities. But it isn't quite the same as the old field at St. Rita."

Ed Buckley, an ex-Marine from Minnesota's iron ore country who graduated from Harvard in 1942 and fought in the South Pacific, was recruited in 1959 by Fr. Cornelius Lehane, then St. Rita's athletic director. Fr. Lehane's hometown was Lawrence, Massachusetts, and he had read of Buckley's success at the local high school. Buckley had coached Lawrence to state championships in 1957 and 1958.

Buckley, who died in 1993, left St. Rita after the 1963 season and later scouted in the NFL for the Broncos, Chiefs, and Redskins. He earned a Super Bowl ring with the Chiefs. A disciplinarian with great organizational skills who had a reputation for being abrasive and difficult to deal with, he always was proud of what he accomplished at St. Rita in such a short time. His staff included George Perles, who later coached at Michigan State, and Larry Bielat, who was Perles' quarterback coach at Michigan State.

"They brought Buckley in to change things. There wasn't much tradition at all. He was going to change the attitude of the players and the school. He was going to treat us like Marines," said Jim Klutcharch, who quarterbacked the 1963 powerhouse that closed its magical season with a 42–7 victory over Vocational before 81,270 people in Soldier Field.

Buckley conducted a massive recruiting drive to lure the best players to St. Rita. Over 40 freshmen were on scholarship from all over the city. He wooed Klutcharch, who grew up in Roseland and figured to enroll at Leo. He also got John Byrne, who played on a championship team at St. Margaret of Scotland grammar school at 99th and Throop. Byrne's older brothers had attended Leo.

"He was as bad as the stories, sometimes worse. He demanded excellence," Klutcharch said. "He got more out of people than people were able to give. Kids would play better than they were. But he put St. Rita on the map. He brought St. Rita into the football fold with Mount Carmel, Leo, Weber, Fenwick, and St. George. Even today, I run into people who say how impressed they were with the 1963 team."

In the Prep Bowl, Klutcharch passed for two touchdowns while Byrne, a 175-pound running back, carried 30 times for 231 yards and scored five touchdowns. He was convoyed by center Larry Smith, guards Tom Labus and Mike Poehner, and tackles Joe Kosiak and John Gorman. Afterward, the leading scorer in the city and suburbs was named the *Chicago Sun-Times* Player of the Year.

But the toughest test for the 1963 team, which defeated nine opponents by scoring 348 points while allowing 60, came in the Catholic League championship game. St. Rita edged Loyola 16–15 as Klutcharch scored two touchdowns, ran for one two-point conversion, and passed for another.

Loyola led 15–8 late in the third quarter when Klutcharch triggered a 60-yard drive with a 37-yard pass to Casey Mitchel, then scored on a six-yard rollout. On the extra point, Buckley never considered a kick to tie, only a two-pointer to go ahead. He called for Klutcharch to roll out, then run or pass to Roger Niemiec. Niemiec ran a post-flag pattern and was covered initially but stopped, broke back to the middle, and was all alone when Klutcharch flipped the ball to him.

"People make more of us winning the national title now than they did then. It was just a footnote then, the first time that a Chicago team had accomplished that," Byrne said. "But the big thing was going to Soldier Field and winning the Prep Bowl in front of 81,000 people. That still is startling to people today, that we played in front of so many people for a high school game."

Lean years followed Buckley's departure until Cronin arrived from De La Salle and turned a 0–9 team into back-to-back Prep Bowl champions in 1970 and 1971. With Marek, Lick, Neil Sullivan, Sherwin Hunt, Ray Jagielski, John Rock, John Killeen, John Hannigan, Bruce Strimel, and Joe Norwick, the Mustangs beat Lane Tech 12–8 in 1970 and Morgan Park 18–12 in 1971.

"That started the Cronin legend; that's when the mystique started," Jagielski said. "He proved he could win in the Catholic League. He won in his second year. He took a team that was 0–9 as sophomores and won the Prep Bowl. He knew what he had in talent with Lick and Marek and produced the great 1971 team. His next quest was to win with a team of kids that he brought in. He wanted to prove he could win with his own kids and he did that in 1978, Zavagnin's team."

There were high expectations in 1978. Eleven starters were returning from a team that had won the Prep Bowl. The Mustangs were ranked No. 1 in the Chicago area in the preseason. In their biggest test, they beat second-rated St. Laurence 14–6 before 23,000 in Soldier Field as John O'Neill caught the winning touchdown pass. John's brother, Mike, was the St. Laurence coach.

In the playoff, St. Rita rolled past Willowbrook 24–0, East St. Louis 48–12, and Richards 28–0, then edged Buffalo Grove 15–9 for the Class 5A championship. Mark Strimel passed for one touchdown and ran for another, Scott Craig kicked a 33-yard field goal and Zavagnin intercepted a pass at his 37 with less than two minutes to play to preserve the victory.

After Zavagnin, O'Neill, Strimel, Craig, Mike Kingsbury, Mike Madea, Jim Lang, Jim Byrne, and their teammates celebrated on the field, Cronin gathered his squad in the locker room. It was the first time they could recall that the coach was brought to tears after a game.

"He told us, 'I had a dream that this could happen for you guys and it was the first time in my life that a dream came true.' He was very emotional," Zavagnin said. "It was very neat to see a guy who had worked so hard for so many years achieve something like that. For one night, he took off the mask of being a dictator and finally let his guard down to enjoy what he had accomplished."

Wernet, who played for Cronin, succeeded his old coach. Though he was successful, winning 73 percent (110–40) of his games in 13 years, none of his teams advanced beyond the state semifinals. When he left for Homewood-Flossmoor, Kuska stepped in. In the last five years, his Mustangs are 51–14 with one state championship. And Kuska admits he saw it coming.

"When those seniors [on the 2006 team] came in as freshmen, I knew there was something special about them," he said. "They were 5–4 as freshmen but they were always together. You saw 30 or 40 together, not 10. They were very united. As sophomores, they were 7–2, then 9–3 on a state quarterfinal team in 2005. There were high expectations, a lot of experience."

The leaders were quarterback Pete Balsam, defensive lineman Matt Conrath, linebacker Matt Murphy, defensive backs John Sullivan and Dan Jilek, and guard Pat O'Malley. After losing to Fenwick 19–17 in Week 3, they went on a roll. They rallied from a 14–0 deficit to beat Providence 17–14 on Steve Flaherty's 31-yard field goal with no time left. They trailed Mount Carmel 6–0 in the fourth quarter, and then drove 85 yards to win 7–6 and claim the conference title.

In the Class 7A championship, they stormed to a 21–7 lead in the first quarter and went on to beat Lake Zurich 35–21 as Balsam, Cliff Moore, and Darieon Hood rushed for 280 yards between them. Balsam and Hood each scored twice, including a 93-yard kickoff return by Hood. Darius Fleming, Kevin Galehar, Kenny Stoklosa, Sean Estand, and Steve McGowan developed into solid contributors.

"Every coach has pressure on him to win, especially in a program like ours," Kuska said. "Any time we had a really good team in the past, we ran into another good team to knock us out of the playoff. We never had all the right things clicking at the right time. In 2006, however, when we needed a bounce, we got it. It gave us renewed confidence that we can do it. It's been 28 years [since the 1978 title] but now we have tasted it."

East St. Louis: "Common Thread Is Tradition"

Darren Sunkett was born and raised in Camden, New Jersey. He played football for four years at Cheyney State, a Division II college in Pennsylvania. He had a tryout with the San Francisco 49ers. But he never knew anything about East St. Louis until he met his wife, Tamara, who had grown up there.

After serving as defensive coordinator for two years at Ladue High School, located in an affluent St. Louis suburb, he was hired as head coach at Riverview Gardens, another St. Louis suburb. In four years, he won one state championship. Then East St. Louis called. He was hired in 2000. It was a challenge he couldn't refuse.

"I called home and told my uncle that I was moving to East St. Louis," Sunkett said. "He told me, 'Son, you might as well come home.' I asked him what he was talking about. He said, 'You're about to move to North Camden.'

"It didn't scare me. I knew I'd feel at home. It didn't take long to learn that East St. Louis had a great history in football. I'm grateful that they gave me an opportunity to be part of a storied program. This is a sports town. The common thread is tradition. People in the city do a great job of passing the tradition down. Once you put on the orange and blue, you are expected to win."

Sunkett did his homework. He met former coach Bob Shannon, who had won six state championships and 202 games in 20 years. He did research on the legendary coaches of the 1940s, 1950s, and 1960s, Wirt Downing and Fred Cameron, whose pictures were on the wall with the great teams and players of the past.

"Camden is a spitting image of East St. Louis. So there was no shock treatment when I came here. Riverview Gardens also is an inner-city school," Sunkett said. "I'm quite sure my players would say I'm a disciplinarian. I'm tough on them because the world will be tough on them.

"I try to make them walk a straight and narrow line. I won't tolerate cutting class or skipping school. I firmly believe that without education you won't go anywhere in life. I don't like seeing kids hanging out and standing around in the hall.

"But one thing I really dislike and hear all the time about inner-city programs is that we just have great athletes. Sure, we do. But they have to be coached. Some say we win on speed alone. But you can't. Some say we win without coaching here. Not true."

Sunkett points out that Riverview Gardens, a Missouri power in the 1960s, didn't produce a winner for 15 years before his arrival. And East St. Louis struggled after Shannon left. Sunkett got off to a shaky start, too; Flyer fans aren't used to 7–3, 6–4, and 8–3 seasons. But he has gone 11–1, 11–2, and 13–1 in the past three years and the future looks every bit as bright with several talented underclassmen being groomed for the varsity.

Sunkett's 2008 squad won the Class 7A championship by beating Geneva 33–14 as junior quarterback Detchauz Wray passed for 198 yards and four touchdowns. The Flyers, who averaged 46 points per game, were led by two seniors who committed to Illinois—wide receiver Terry Hawthorne and defensive back Tommie Hopkins—and one wide receiver, Kraig Appleton, who went to Wisconsin.

"If you look for problems, you won't have trouble finding them in any city," Sunkett said. "But our kids want discipline. East St. Louis, like Camden, has positives, not just problems. We make our kids understand what is expected of them. Once you are part of this program, this is something you should know. We won't run from the history of this program."

To Sunkett, teaching the history of the East St. Louis football program is as important as biology and math. He likes to walk his players through the commons area to let them see the state championship trophies and pictures of the state championship teams and pictures of players and teams from the 1930s and 1940s. He also invites former Flyer stars such as Julian Brown, James Harris, Kellen Winslow, Bryan Cox, Dana Howard, and Ronnie Cameron to talk to his players.

"Our kids are expected to uphold the reputation of East St. Louis football," Sunkett said. "They feel it from the time they walk through the doors as freshmen."

Downing, who later served as the school's principal, laid the foundation. In 16 years, he was 145–17–7, a .895 winning percentage that is highest in state history. He closed with three unbeaten teams in 1952, 1953, and 1954 that were led by ends Hugh Campbell, Frank Rigney, and Jim Jones, center Jim Sims, quarterback Don Mason, and halfbacks Charles Rogers and Jack Purdy.

Cornelius Perry usually isn't mentioned in the same sentence with Downing, Cameron, and Shannon. He was head coach from 1971 to 1975. His record was 37–13–3. "He was a great coach, so underrated," Kellen Winslow said. Perry is best remembered for coaching the Flyers' great 1974 team that lost to Glenbrook North in the first Class 5A championship. After going 1–7–1 in 1975, he was gone. Shannon was hired.

Marvin Lampkin recalled those times. He was a sophomore on Shannon's great 1985 team and later played at Iowa. He grew up in one of East St. Louis' projects, Roosevelt Homes, which he described as "the inner city with promise."

"A lot of people hear only bad things about East St. Louis but they don't hear about the good things," Lampkin said. "Yes, there was a lot of crime and drugs. But I was fortunate that my mother was a very strict disciplinarian. She kept me away from crime and drugs."

Lampkin never knew his father. When he was 10 years old, the Vice Lords and Black Gangster Disciples invaded his neighborhood. They tried to recruit Lampkin. But many of them had grown up with Lampkin and knew he was gifted athletically and wasn't going to get involved with street gangs.

"I was a leader, not a follower," he said. "I knew I wanted to play football. I went to East St. Louis Lincoln with my junior high school coach and left after one practice. I grew up with East St. Louis. I knew I wanted to be a Flyer.

"I knew about the tradition—Fred Cameron, Cornelius Perry, Alvin Jones, Victor Scott, Kellen Winslow, Terry Hill. People talk about 1974 as the team that started the dynasty, the team that set the stage for what was to come.

"East St. Louis was like a pro team. We'd go to old Parsons Field to see a game and I was in awe of the players when they warmed up. They were always well disciplined in the midst of a city that had a lot of crime. I never heard anything about East St. Louis players getting into trouble. There was always a sense of how we would win, not if we would win."

The 1985 team, led by quarterback Kerwin Price, running back Michael Cox, end

Arthur Sargent, and linebacker Bryan Cox, was Shannon's best creation. It was *USA Today*'s choice as the No. 1 team in the nation.

But the 1979 squad, Shannon's first state champion, ranked No. 2 behind perennial power Cincinnati Moeller among the nation's elite. Quarterback Alvin Jones, running back Kerry Glenn, wide receivers Victor Scott and Gary Joshway, fullback Darryl Dixon, and tackle Jarvis Hall were the ringleaders. They beat St. Laurence 20–14 for the state title.

"Jones had a great year," Glenn said. "Against Alton, he missed two out routes and Shannon benched him. He stuck to his guns. He did what he said he was going to do. The media asked, 'Why did you pull an All-America quarterback?' Shannon replied: 'Because he needs to complete 60 percent of his passes, not 50 percent.' That team set the tone for everything that was to follow."

The 1989 team might have been just as good. They were coming off two 13–1 seasons in which they had lost to Mount Carmel and Hersey in the state finals. Led by running backs Chris Moore and LaGrant Suggs, quarterback Rollie Nevilles, end Ken Dunn, and linebacker Dana Howard, the Flyers went 13–0 and crushed Thornton 55–8 for the state title.

"What did I learn from playing football for Bob Shannon at East St. Louis?" Howard said. "You can't put the word *can't* in anything, in sports or business. For me, sports played a major part in developing into a person. Coming from a winning program all my life, I knew I could succeed in anything as long as I had an opportunity. If you can make it in East St. Louis, you can make it anywhere."

Harvey Thornton:
Football Gets Its Props

Perhaps no high school in Illinois this side of Centralia is as steeped in tradition as Thornton Township in Harvey. But while the school is most noted for its basketball achievements, dating to Lou Boudreau in the 1930s, it also has established a national reputation in football.

No one is more aware of Thornton's tradition than Bob Caress. His father played with Boudreau on the 1933 state championship team. He was a star on Thornton's 1961 state runner-up team and earned a basketball scholarship to Bradley University. As a freshman, he played basketball and baseball.

But football coach Billy Stone, who played for the Chicago Bears, recruited him to try out as a punter and quarterback. He started for four years. In fact, his picture is next to Terry Bradshaw in the NCAA record book. He passed for 7,000 yards in his career, 2,800 in one season. He once threw 78 passes in a game. As a senior at Thornton, he only threw 46 passes in nine games.

Caress lived two blocks from the football stadium. He walked with his friends to football and basketball games. He recalled when the gym was under construction in the 1950s, when the facility that Boudreau played in was torn down in 1960. He idolized Russ McKibben in basketball and Paul Golaszewski, Brooks Young, and Paul Jackson in football. Golaszewski later became Boudreau's son-in-law.

Like most traditionalists, he is drawn to the Boudreau Room, the shrine that houses the trophies and pictures of the great teams and great players of Thornton history. There is Caress' father sitting with Boudreau and the 1933 team. And there is his son Bob sitting with the 1961 team. And there is LaMarr Thomas and the 1966 state championship team.

"For our [1961] team to be considered with the great teams of Thornton history is so impressive. We were the next great thing after 1933," Bob Caress said. "Thornton tradition had legs. We felt we were the Yankees when we went to other towns. People would stare at us. It wasn't just our team, it was a feeling you got from being a part of the tradition. But you had to win to back it up. When you went to other schools, you felt they didn't have the same feeling. Other teams didn't expect to win. We always did."

But this is about football and Thornton has produced winning teams since the 1930s, when Jack Lipe coached football and basketball. Tiny Huddleston, Caress' coach, was 76–16–3 from 1951 to 1961. Frank Bauman, Thomas' coach, was 41–10–1 in six years, including a mythical state championship in 1965. And Bill Mosel is 153–77 in the past 22 years, including a state title in 1990 and a second-place finish in 1989.

When he assumed the dual role of athletic director last year, Mosel set about to elevate Thornton's football tradition. He is the only coach in the nation to have as many as eight former players competing in the NFL at the same time—Antwaan Randle El, Napoleon Harris, Jack Golden, Tai Streets, Sam Williams, Winfield Garnett, Barry Gardner, and Jermaine Hampton.

One of Mosel's first projects was to update the football history in the Boudreau Room by recognizing every All-Stater from the 1930s to the present. There are 29 of them—Ed Beinor (1935), Robert Bauman (1938), Frank Bauman (1941), Wayne Benson (1948), Rod Hanson (1953), Dick Binnot (1954), Chuck Truby (1955), Paul Jackson (1958), Allen Johnson (1959), Wilfred Henry (1960), LaMarr Thomas (1965), Mike Walker (1968), Jim Pala (1968), Stan Jackson and Fred Cooper (1969), Herb Simpson (1976), Andre Wright (1987), Rory Lee (1989), Stirling Luckey (1991), Andrew Morgan (1992), Sam Williams (1993), Tai Streets (1994), Reggie Gage (1995), Napoleon Harris and Antwaan Randle El (1996), Stafford Owens (1999), Mike Berry (2001), Tim Jamison (2003), and Terrance Jamison (2004).

Ironically, there were no All-Staters on the 1990 squad that finished 12–2 and beat Downers Grove North 31–21 for the state championship. "There wasn't a big name in that group," Mosel said. The stars were running backs David Wright and Melvin Roberts. Other major contributors were Stirling Luckey, who would be an All-Stater in 1991, Mario Cole, Fred Price, Kyle and Kelly Johnson, Eric Jones, and Henry Calderone.

The Wildcats lost to unbeaten Homewood-Flossmoor (H-F) 42–21 in Week 7, and then came from behind to win all five of their playoff games. They beat Carl Sandburg 43–22, avenged their earlier loss to H-F 44–32, then dispatched St. Rita 27–14, Loyola 13–8, and Downers Grove North.

Against Sandburg on Wednesday, Wright rushed for 260 yards and five touchdowns. On Saturday, he rushed for 400 yards and five touchdowns against H-F. Wright finished with 2,100 yards and 27 touchdowns. He averaged nine yards per carry. Roberts also rushed for 1,000 yards and quarterback Floyd Coleman passed for 1,000.

In the state final, Thornton trailed Downers Grove North 21–12 with six minutes to play. But the Wildcats rallied to win as Coleman threw a 13-yard touchdown pass to Barry Starks, Wright scored on a one-yard run after Thornton recovered a fumble at Downers Grove's 21 and Kyle Johnson scored on a 72-yard interception return.

"I felt vindicated," said Wright, a Harvey native who transferred to Thornton after spending his freshman year at St. Francis de Sales. "We had lost to East St. Louis 55–8 in the state final in 1989 and no one thought we had a chance to do anything in 1990 because Rory Lee was gone. No one knew about me but the people who played with me. Everybody asked, 'Who will fill Rory's shoes?' Rory had put Thornton back on the map. The buzz was back."

Roberts said Mosel lit a fire under his players that never went out. "He is a bulldog who comes off the porch and chases you down the block to prove he can take you. He doesn't just stay on the porch and bark," he said.

But Mosel insists the most talented team he ever coached was the 1996 squad led by Randle El, Harris, and Hampton that lost to Lincoln-Way Central and UCLA-bound quarterback Corey Paus 19–6 in the state quarterfinals and finished 10–2.

"It was the hardest loss I have ever had," Mosel said. "We had three touchdowns called back. I still replay that game over in my mind every day of my life. That game sticks out above all others. I'm not over it yet. You always remember losses more than wins."

Randle El insisted it was more disappointing than losing three times to Peoria Manual and finishing 2–2–3 in the state basketball tournament in 1995, 1996, and 1997.

"It was the worst experience I've had in football," said Randle El, who was a Big 10 MVP at Indiana and played on the Pittsburgh Steelers' Super Bowl championship team in 2006. "Our team was better than the 1994 team with Jack Golden, Tai Streets, Curtis Randle El, and Reggie Gage. We had a 92-yard run called back and a 75-yard run called back. I threw a touchdown pass that was ruled offensive pass interference. At the end of the game, we looked at each other in disbelief, watching them celebrate, just shaking our heads."

But the 1965 team might have been best of all. LaMarr Thomas and Larry Snoddy were a pair of game-breaking running backs. Thomas was one of the most recruited players in the state. Other standouts were quarterback Butch Meek, fullback Mark Callahan, linebacker Butch Davis, and linemen Clarence Kennedy, William Murphy, and Rick Jones.

The Wildcats were dominant. Their closest games were 27–7 decisions over Thornridge and Joliet. They crushed archrival Bloom 47–17. They were recognized as the mythical state champion, a rarity for a south suburban school.

"We read about Chicago Public League, Chicago Catholic League, and Suburban League teams but we weren't aware of how we compared to other schools," Thomas said. "We felt confident about ourselves because we kept winning and winning convincingly. But because we never played another ranked team and there wasn't a state playoff, we didn't think about what would happen if we played the Catholic League champion or Evanston or Mount Carmel. How good were we? We would have liked to judge how good we were in a concrete way rather than somebody's opinion."

Born in nearby Blue Island, Mosel knew about the Thornton tradition. A 1973 graduate of Blue Island Eisenhower, he had played football against Thornton. He joined Frank Esposito's staff in 1983, worked his way up the ladder, and became head coach in 1987. He still lives in Blue Island. But he is painted in Thornton purple.

"I came in at the tail end of the lean period from the 1970s to the 1980s, when the program wasn't winning as it had been," Mosel said. "I thought the talent was still there but they weren't producing on the field like they were capable.

"We started to bang home the Thornton tradition. I took them to the Boudreau Room and instilled a sense of pride and family. As we progressed, the old-timers started to show up again. LaMarr Thomas, Dale Mize, Antwaan Randle El, and Napoleon Harris came back to talk to the kids. When you have an opportunity to talk to older players, you can hear it in their voice and see it in their eyes. It was something special. We tried to get that across."

Mount Prospect:
Team of the New Millennium

When Brent Pearlman was named head football coach at Prospect High School in 1999, he was only 31 years old and, by his own admission, somewhat naïve. "I thought we could be a great team," he said. His first team was 4–5, his second 6–4. But he had a plan and he was determined and confident that he could pull it off.

"Once I got the job, I got a lot of calls from people, other coaches and friends, who said that I shouldn't take the job, that I can't win there," Pearlman said. "But I didn't get worried. It did provoke me to think quite a bit. How would I be as good as the great coaches before me, Joe Gliwa and Gary Grouwinkel, who also struggled at Prospect? How could I keep the program fresh and creative?"

Pearlman found some answers. In a six-year span from 2001 to 2006, he guided Prospect to three state championships and a record of 65–12. He went from 6–4 to 14–0 and 4–5 to 13–1. Not bad for a program that once won only nine games in 11 years and had 13 losing seasons in a row before Pearlman turned it around.

"I had been here for five years [as Jim Nudera's defensive coordinator] before I took over. I saw kids who could make a good football team," Pearlman said. "The kids weren't proud of what they were doing. The first thing that struck me was we had to get a sense of pride back in the kids. We had to make it worthwhile to play Prospect football. There have got to be payoffs for all that training."

Mike Anderson, one of the leaders of the 2001 championship team, remembers the way it was before Pearlman. "It was all about showing up to see the band at halftime and leaving before the football team came out for the second half. As a freshman, I didn't watch the games that much. They had good players but they didn't put it together as a team. The program had a long tradition of losing, like the Cubs. They were the doormat of the Mid-Suburban League, the loveable losers," he said.

But Anderson and his friends on the Mount Prospect Lions' eighth-grade team—George Smith, Pat Wilson, and Josh Flickinger—weren't used to losing. They were brash and confident and they boldly predicted, as incoming freshmen, that they would win a state championship before they graduated. Some classmates laughed. No one took them seriously.

They took their first step as juniors in 2000. They were 3–3 and had to finish 6–3 to have a chance to qualify for the state playoff for only the fourth time. They won their last three games, and then had to win a three-way coin toss for the last spot. In the opening round, they met top-seeded Bloomington and lost 41–35 in three overtimes.

"Most people say that game started the tradition," Anderson said. "It showed us that we could hang with the best teams in the state."

Pearlman was noted, above all things, for being a superb motivator. He surrounded himself with good coaches, including defensive coordinator Joe Petricca. His objective was to outwork other teams, to be in better physical condition than anyone else. And he emphasized execution. If he wasn't happy with the way a play was being run in practice, he'd run it over and over and over again.

He was superstitious to a fault. He would pick up grass from Prospect's playing field to put in his players' shoes for away games. He would park his car in the same spot on the day before a game and leave it there overnight. He prepared a video with a message to present to the team before a game and always wore an ugly striped purple and green shirt for the film session and to school on the day before a game. Anderson, a receiver, suffered a compound dislocation of a knuckle in summer workouts. He kept the tape on his hand for the entire 2001 season because the team was winning.

"He changed the mind-set," said Max Cherwin, a linebacker who starred on the 2005 state championship team and is described by Pearlman as the best and toughest kid he ever put on the field. "He made kids care about the program. His attitude was contagious, how strongly he felt about winning. He wanted things done a certain way and would stop at nothing to get it done."

Pearlman was looking for winners. He would scout the lower levels to discover kids who would develop their skills, kids who had a winning attitude. He had a plan. He told his players that Prospect wouldn't attract great talent so they had to be tougher and in better shape and find other ways to win, that opponents would be faster and more talented.

"He asked us, 'Do you want to be a 4–5 team, make the playoff or get by or barely beat teams or go for a state championship?' Then he'd come up with a plan to do it. It was pretty inspiring," said Jared Dall, who quarterbacked the 2002 state championship team.

The 2001 team put Prospect on the map, capping a 14–0 campaign with a 19–14 victory over Edwardsville in the state final. Leaders were Anderson, the 5–9, 145-pound Smith, Flickinger, Wilson, linebacker Nick Spizzirri, end Ben Coffman, running back Jason Rodriguez, junior offensive linemen Chris Bergner, Jimmy Argentine, and Brian Powers, and strong safety Nick Iovino. In the semifinals, they trailed Bolingbrook 15–0 in the first quarter but rallied to win 47–22.

But Pearlman insists his 2002 team, despite losing two games and finishing third in the conference, had the most talent and was better than his 2001 and 2005 champions. In Pearlman's new spread offense, Dall rushed for 1,000 yards and passed for 2,000. Iovino, Bergner, Powers, Argentine, and fullback Bryon Gattas returned from the 2001 squad and provided the bulk of the leadership in 2002. Gattas rushed for school-record 1,363 yards, including a career-high 194 in the 24–7 victory over Edwardsville in the state final.

But all agree that the turning point in the season came after Prospect lost to Buffalo Grove in Week 5, then lost to Hersey at homecoming in Week 7. Afterward, Pearlman entered the locker room and said a lot of players "don't have the right attitude," that they were talking about getting to the state title instead of focusing on what they had to do to get there. It was a very emotional time.

"You don't want to look back and regret that you had a poor attitude and didn't reach your full potential and you're wishing you were still playing football but the season is over," he told them.

Later that night, the team conducted a players-only meeting at Iovino's house. They searched their souls and recommitted themselves. On Monday, Pearlman had them watch a movie, "My Life" with Michael Keaton, the story of a man who is terminally ill with cancer while his wife is pregnant. In it, he tells his wife that he is living on borrowed time. But when he learns to enjoy life, he is happier.

"It became our theme," Iovino said. "We were 5–2 and living on borrowed time. The state playoff wasn't guaranteed to us. We had to enjoy the experience together and not waste it. That meeting was the turning point. Things started to turn around for us. It got our mental game back on track."

In the rematch with Hersey in the second round of the playoff, Prospect was tied at 7–7 and faced with third-and-28 with 1:30 to play. Dall threw a fade to Iovino for a 33-yard gain to the 18. Then Pearlman drew up a play on the sideline, a play he dubbed "the spoon route" that wasn't even in the playbook, the most important play of the season. Dall threw a game-winning touchdown pass to Iovino in the corner of the end zone to cap a 97-yard drive.

"I didn't think Iovino would be open," Dall said. "I looked for Scott Sprague to be open over the middle. Then I looked and saw Iovino behind everybody. I threw it up and he went up and got it. It was memorable how we came together. I didn't want it to end."

The 2005 championship was significant for two reasons: Prospect beat Mount Carmel 20–14 for the state title. And, after losing to Downers Grove North 41–21 in the opener, they proceeded to get better and better and won 13 games in a row. The leaders were Cherwin, linebacker Tony Baratti, quarterback Matt Bowman, and center Marcus Zusevics.

"Mount Carmel is an established program with great tradition. If we want that for our program, we have to beat teams like that," Pearlman said. "We didn't know how good we could be. We were down 41–7 in the third quarter to Downers Grove North. But that was the first team that got better and better all season long. Some kids held together with duct tape but refused to come off the field. It was such a driven group."

They were coming off a disappointing 4–5 season. They lost five games by a total of 16 points. The 2004 team was one of the most talented to play at Prospect but it didn't play together or believe in itself. In fact, when Pearlman gathered the squad at a preseason camp in DeKalb, he predicted it would finish 4–5 and miss the playoff. He had a knack for reading his players and he didn't have a good feel for the 2004 squad. But 2005? He could envision a state title.

The players had good vibes, too. Cherwin recalled a team meeting at nine o'clock on the night of the 2004 state final. They didn't watch the game. Instead, they viewed a video that Pearlman had put together that set the tone for 2005, a compilation of highlights and a preview of the following season. At the end, it said: "At this time, one year from today, a new state champion will be crowned and it might as well be us."

After the 2006 season, after Prospect lost to Lake Zurich in the state semifinals, Cherwin was so overcome with emotion that he purchased his No. 33 jersey and his helmet. He didn't want to hand them in.

"I still have the jersey hanging in my room," Cherwin said. "It was difficult to let it go. I knew I wasn't going to play college football. Prospect football was over. It was a lifestyle for me and the kids I played with, how we lived, the way we walked, the swagger we had, our way of life. Now it was over. My role in the program was over. My time was done."

Park Ridge Maine South: A Coaching Clinic

Jason Loerzel saw it coming. He was there when it was being built. He was part of the foundation. Even though he was gone when it finally happened, he wasn't surprised. He knew the pieces were in place, that the stars were aligned in the right positions. Maine South was like a freight train that couldn't be stopped.

Loerzel grew up on Chicago's Northwest Side. He played youth football for the Portage Park Eagles and Patriots and the Shabonna Park Saints. He thought he would follow his friends to St. Patrick. But his parents moved to Park Ridge so he could get an education at a bigger and better school in the suburbs.

"I didn't know anything about Maine South, except it was big," he said. "As a freshman, I was upset because my friends were going to St. Patrick. But after a year, I realized I wouldn't have accomplished what I did if I hadn't gone to Maine South. They always had quality coaches who had a background in college and studied hard and knew what they were talking about. After I left, the kids knew nothing but winning."

Maine South had experienced some early success. Marv Nyren was 8–0 in 1967 with *Chicago Sun-Times* Player of the Year Tom Spotts, and Bob Schmidt was 8–0 in 1968. Both teams featured Dave Butz, a three-sport giant whose legendary exploits still echo in the halls. But the Hawks were 1–8, 1–8, and 3–6 in the three years before Phil Hopkins became head coach in 1982. They've had only two losing seasons since, none since 1991.

"He built the program from the ground up," Loerzel said. "He is such a spitfire, high energy all the time, constantly grabbing and pulling someone aside to give him a talk about what he was thinking about last night, how we can get better. I wanted to be one of those people. He was the best motivator of any coach I've ever had."

Loerzel was the *Chicago Sun-Times'* Player of the Year in 1994, the Central Suburban League's MVP on offense and defense. His team lost to Palatine 7–3 in the state quarterfinals. But he could see that the junior class, headed by quarterback John Schacke, receiver/kicker Brian Schmitz, linebackers Tom Carroll and Matt Braun, defensive back Ben Wilson, and lineman Brian Czerwinski, had the makings of a championship team.

Hopkins had served on Schmidt's staff for 13 years before he got his opportunity. He had been passed over several times, once at Maine South, once at Glenbrook South, twice at Maine West. He didn't want to be locked into power football, Schmidt's system. He wanted to do it his way. He wanted to throw the ball.

He felt he had to make changes to be competitive in a conference that featured New Trier, Deerfield, Glenbrook North, and Glenbrook South. Maine South had won 19 in a row when the Roodhouse, Illinois, native arrived in Park Ridge. But the program fell on hard times after Schmidt retired. Other programs had caught up. The best athletes in the school played basketball, not football. The basketball team was a state power in the 1970s, winning a state championship in 1979.

"I saw potential," Hopkins said. "I felt if we ran a strong off-season conditioning program and threw the ball, we could be good. A coach we played in my last year said, 'You really can't scout them because they'll come out with something you've never seen anyway.' That was a compliment, what I wanted to do. We had a huge package, a lot of sets. It was a fun offense to coach and fun to run. The kids thrived in it."

Hopkins attended Illinois' spring practice to learn Coach Mike White's passing schemes. He surrounded himself with knowledgeable assistants, including Dave Inserra, Charlie Bliss (offense), Carl Magsamen (defense), and his son, Rick. He also installed an off-season conditioning program that emphasized speed and jumping and explosion. In fact, Maine South athletes were working on speed drills before speed camps were popular.

Loerzel's foresight notwithstanding, Schacke and Schmitz didn't have high expectations for 1995. The senior class was 1–8 as freshmen. Hopkins wasn't sure which offense to run. He opened with a wishbone formation with two tight ends. Schmitz broke a leg in the opener against York and missed four games. The Hawks started 2–2, rallying from a 21–3 deficit to edge York 22–21 but lost to Evanston 35–28 and Waukegan 6–0. Then they got on a roll as Hopkins switched to a pass-oriented offense.

They won nine in a row, including a 24–21 semifinal victory over Fenwick on Schmitz' 27-yard field goal in overtime. It set the stage for a dramatic championship game against heavily favored Mount Carmel. Maine South won on Schmitz' 37-yard field goal with eight seconds to play. He had missed a 58-yarder but a roughing-the-kicker penalty gave him another chance.

Bliss remembers that the entire 2000 season rested on a fourth-and-11 play against Lincoln-Way Central in the semifinals, when quarterback Shawn Kain ran up the middle for 11 yards and a first down, then threw a 60-yard scoring pass to Joe Sergo, and Maine South finally won 35–34 in overtime. In the final, Kain passed for 175 yards and one TD and Kevin Sherlock rushed for 181 yards as Maine South beat Glenbard North 27–8.

"I coached Sean Price and Tyler Knight and John Schacke and Charlie Goro— and Schacke set the tone for everything else. He is the quarterback that everyone is measured to," said Bliss, the architect of the four-wide-and-let-it-fly offense. "But no one was a better competitor than Kain. People don't speak of him like the other quarterbacks because of his statistics. But he had a great playoff run."

Hopkins retired after the 2000 championship season. In 19 years, he won 74 percent (149–52) of his games. Inserra, his successor, has won 88 percent (90–12) of his games in the past eight years. He settled for second-place finishes in the state playoff in 2003, 2004, and 2005 but won the Class 8A championship in 2008 by overwhelming Hinsdale Central 41–21.

In 2003, Price passed for 4,751 yards and 55 touchdowns, including 460 yards and six touchdowns against Deerfield, and Albert DeCicco caught 110 passes but Maine South lost to Lockport 48–27 in the state final.

In 2004, Price suffered a broken collarbone in Week 4 and Tyler Knight stepped in. But the Hawks lost to Downers Grove North 33–13 in the state final.

In 2005, Knight and tight end Adam Fee were standouts but Maine South lost to Lincoln-Way East 30–24 in two overtimes to finish second for the third year in a row.

But quarterback Charlie Goro, the *Chicago Sun-Times* Player of the Year, junior running back Matt Perez, wide receiver/safety Joey Orlando, two-way lineman Zach Timm, and linebackers Corby Ryan and Nick Catino led Maine South to a 14–0 record in 2008.

Goro completed 74 percent of his passes for 3,171 yards and 38 touchdowns and rushed for 665 yards and 12 touchdowns during the season. Perez rushed for 1,145 yards and 22 touchdowns and Orlando accounted for 925 yards in pass receptions. They averaged 45 points per game.

"It was like backyard football, lining up with four wide receivers, passing out of the spread, four wide and let it fly," Price said. "You couldn't wait for Friday night or Saturday afternoon to come around. It was so much fun. How could you not want to throw more than 40 passes in a game and have success with it, doing it all with your friends, guys you played with in elementary school in recess?"

To this day, Loerzel recalls the life lessons he learned at Maine South through sports. "I learned how you had to fight for what you wanted, learned to be competitive, learned that if you want something, you have to work for it," he said.

"Every time I come back to Park Ridge, when I drive past the stadium, I get tingles. I was part of it. They started winning after I left but I was part of laying the foundation. By the time we were done and thought of what we had done for the program, we were a bunch of 17- and 18-year-olds who were very emotional."

Peoria Richwoods:
The "Rich Kids" School

Rick Telander, an award-winning wordsmith and former football player who has delighted a generation of readers by relating sports stories in two books, *Sports Illustrated*, and the *Chicago Sun-Times*, has never forgotten his roots, the life lessons he learned while growing up in Peoria, and playing football for Coach Tom Peeler.

"High school football means the coming of age as a man," Telander said. "You recognize it is something you will do once in your life. You'll never again play tackle football in front of people cheering wildly for you. I still hear 90-year-old men talking about it—the physical pain, aggressiveness, the beauty of the game.

"There is nothing sadder than your last game in high school. Things won't be the same again. Yes, I was excited to move on to college. But the innocence is gone forever, your buddies that you grew up with. It's a whole separate thing in college. That's the business side of the game. I could have walked through the stands at Richwoods and known everyone. But I didn't know anyone in college."

Telander attended Peoria Richwoods, one of eight high schools in a sports-crazy town. Opened in 1957, Richwoods was known as the "rich kids" school. It was built as the baby boomers were growing, the first wave of children whose fathers were veterans of World War II. Basketball was a big attraction but football was even bigger in the 1980s, when Richwoods won two state championships and settled for a second.

In an attempt to be competitive with cross-town rival Peoria Manual, which had a dominant program in the 1950s, Richwoods hired Tom Peeler. He had produced an unbeaten team at nearby Canton in 1963 and arrived at Richwoods in 1965, Telander's junior year. In 1969, Peeler's 10–0 team was rated No. 1 in Illinois. From 1968 to 1972, his teams were 46–3–1.

"Tom Peeler is one of those guys who may come into your life once if you are lucky," Telander said. "He was what Peoria was. He was a young man who decided to coach in high school and didn't look to go to college or the NFL. He said this is a good life, be a teacher, build a program, and have your own issues to work out.

"I didn't need a father figure. I needed someone to teach me how to play the game, have confidence in me, and put up with my quirks. He is what high school sports are all about. You are blessed to have him. I thought he was a 70-year-old man who had been there for 50 years. That's how it seems when you are 16 or 17. I didn't realize we were setting the tone for future years."

Telander was wide receiver on Richwoods' 8–2 team in 1965. He was a skinny 165-pounder who wore long underwear under his jersey. He said he was a terrified 16-year-old. After the season, Peeler said he wanted to convert Telander into a quarterback. In 1966, he ran a wing-T, scored 12 touchdowns on bootlegs and sneaks, called the plays, earned All-Conference recognition, and guided Richwoods to a 7–3 record.

"I'm a little different and Peeler sensed that in me. He could tell I could be distracted easily," said Telander, who was recruited by Northwestern as a defensive back. "I was a problem in school. I was bored. I needed to do stuff, even though I had good grades. At halftime, I'd be staring out the window. It angered him but he tolerated it because he knew it was me. He knew all teenage boys were nuts.

"I'm 17 and playing in front of big crowds at Peoria Stadium. He could give you such a sense of calm and you knew he knew what he was doing. He made me have confidence about everything I would ever do. It was the greatest education I ever had."

After producing unbeaten teams in 1969, 1971, and 1972, Peeler experienced seven losing seasons in the next 10 years as basketball emerged as a dominant sport in Peoria. But he responded in 1984 by producing a 13–0 state champion that swept Mount Vernon 27–0, Marian Catholic 13–7, Joliet Catholic 27–15, and Deerfield 21–14 in the state playoff.

In becoming the first Peoria team to win a state title, Richwoods averaged 36.3 points while allowing 4.6. The offense was triggered by quarterback Greg Peeler, the last of the coach's five sons, and fullback Kevin Hattendorf. Linebacker Perry Danier, cornerbacks Todd Glispie and John Kennington, and end Matt Weeds anchored the defense. After the season, Tom Peeler closed his 30-year career. In 21 years at Richwoods, his teams were 135–72–1.

Peeler was succeeded by Rod Butler, who had assisted him for seven years before becoming head coach in 1985. In nine years, he was 90–15. He produced a 10–2 state quarterfinalist in 1986, a 13–1 state runner-up in 1987, and a 14–0 state champion in 1988. From 1985 to 1990, he was 69–6.

"I was a cheap imitation of Tom Peeler," Butler said. "I inherited the program from him. The kids said, 'Same words but different voices.' We are close to being family without being family. When we coached together, we lived three doors apart."

Eddie Sutter, who starred on Butler's 1987 state runner-up and later played at Northwestern and spent seven years in the NFL, insists Butler is being too humble. Yes, he learned a lot from Tom Peeler. But he was his own man. He was structured and disciplined and always said he didn't want to come back to a 10th reunion and hear former players say how soft the coach was.

"I played for Bill Belichick in Cleveland and Butler was every bit as intense," Sutter said. "On a scale of 1 to 10, Butler was 10-½ on intensity. The fundamentals I learned at Richwoods I took with me throughout my career. The teaching that Butler gave me is why I was able to play so many years."

In the 1987 state final, Richwoods led Joliet Catholic 13–0 in the first quarter but lost 14–13. Sutter missed an extra point conversion after the second touchdown. His teammates included quarterback Jeff Schwarzentraub, tackle Malcolm Hooks, linebacker Greg Bradshaw, and end Marty Reno.

"Among all the games I've played, that's the one I struggle with the most," Sutter said. "It's disappointing to close your high school career with a one-point loss."

The 1988 team, with Schwarzentraub returning at quarterback and sophomore fullback Darrel Taylor launching a brilliant career that saw him rush for 4,500 yards in three years, didn't figure to finish 14–0 but it did. Even Butler was surprised. They returned only three starters on offense, one on defense. The defensive line averaged 178 pounds, the offensive line 179.

"We won our first five games and were happy to know we had a winning season," Butler said. "It was the biggest example of a team having grit. They were overachievers but they were very confident, more than the coaching staff, and they felt they were doing what they thought they could do. They weren't as good statistically as the 1987, 1989, and 1990 teams but they were my best team, the only team to win 14 games."

In the 1988 playoff, Richwoods disposed of Bloomington 35–16, Rich South 6–0, Mount Vernon 28–0, Reavis 21–6, and Belvidere 29–26. In the final, Belvidere set a state record by rushing for 442 yards and Richwoods trailed 26–21 in the fourth quarter but rallied to win as Schwarzentraub threw a 44-yard scoring pass to Kevin Carpenter with 5:45 to play. Daras Adams and Brian Senn blocked a 22-yard field goal attempt with nine seconds remaining to preserve the victory.

Doug Simper was an important part of the Richwoods program from 1975 to 2007. He served as Tom Peeler's assistant until Peeler retired in 1984, assisted Butler until Butler retired in 1994, then was head coach until he retired after the 2007 season. In 14 years, his teams were 95–47, including 43–11 in his last five seasons.

"I ran the same offense and defense that Peeler ran when he came to Richwoods in 1967," Simper said. "I tried to continue the same standards and discipline and make the game fun to play. I learned under Peeler and Butler. That's all I knew and what to coach. I didn't try to change anything, including our winning ways. From 1983 to 1996, we made 13 straight playoff appearances. It wasn't the rich kid syndrome that people think."

Springfield Sacred Heart-Griffin: Downstate Power

Ken Leonard sometimes wonders where he would be if Chris Andriano, who had been offered the job as head football coach, hadn't turned it down to stay at Montini in the Chicago suburb of Lombard. Leonard was coaching at rural Gridley at the time and he was the second or third choice on Springfield Griffin's priority list.

"I knew it was a great program, that they had had previous success," Leonard said. "I was young and ambitious and stupid enough to think I could do it, coming from a small school. It was a Catholic school, tough kids, good football players.

"The problem that scared people away was it was independent. You had to schedule nine games. They were booted out of the Capitol Conference with the other Springfield schools. But now people look at us as a Downstate football power, arguably one of the top three or four programs outside of Chicago."

Since he was hired in 1984, Leonard has built one of the most successful and most exciting programs in the state. In 25 years, he has logged a record of 236–51, a .822 winning percentage. He won state championships in 2005, 2006, and 2008 and finished second in 1995 and 2003. In the past nine years, his teams were 103–10. He has suffered only one losing season. In 2006, he was selected as the National High School Coach of the Year.

Springfield Griffin had established a football tradition before Leonard arrived. George Fleischli produced a state runner-up in 1975 and had a five-year record of 45–12, a .789 winning percentage. Robin Cooper was 38–6 in four years, finishing second in 1982. But Leonard put a new face on the program.

At Gridley, he installed a passing game, Dennis Erickson's three-drop system. It has been the staple of his offense ever since. In 1999, he went to shotgun formation, then to a spread offense designed by Florida's Urban Meyer and Michigan's Rich Rodriguez. The result has been a 90–9 record, two state titles, and a second.

"You fit your system to your personnel," Leonard said. "We run a four-wide-and-let-it-fly offense. But with Eric Peterman (2003, 2004), we were 75 percent run. With Bobby Brenneisen (2005, 2006), we were 75 percent pass."

Run or pass, the program has set a standard for success. It is the only sport in the school that has drug testing, a program that Leonard implemented five years ago "to help kids to have a reason to say no, to help kids who might need help."

"It was a football school," said Peterman, who was a receiver at Northwestern. "There were quarterbacks I looked up to—Johnny Sundquist, Brad Sellinger, Derek and Brad Leonard. On game day, when we walked on the field, you could feel something different. When the other team saw our jersey, they knew we meant business. In the three years I played, we never lost a conference game."

But Leonard wasn't all Xs and Os. He said he wanted to make sure that his players knew the difference between football goals and purpose in life. A man of faith, he related things that happened on the football field to what happened to Christ. His program was about developing character, instilling core values, and involving the parents.

"The night before a game, we had a team meal at a local restaurant or in the school cafeteria. Then we had a lock-in that night," Peterman recalled. "We'd go to the stadium and sit in his office, watch a movie, play cards until 10 o'clock, then go home. He wanted to be sure that nobody went to parties or goofed off on the night before a game.

"He always made sure we were in bed, too. He made calls to the house. He would surprise you. You didn't know if you would get a call or not. He kept us on our toes. You were in big trouble if you weren't home when he called."

He was emotional and motivational, too. Brenneisen, who first met Leonard when he was a team water boy at age six, recalled his opening game as a senior when Griffin trailed Montini 15–7 at halftime.

"He was wearing a state playoff ring from the previous year," Brenneisen said. "I thought he'd throw it away. He took it off and didn't wear it for the rest of the season. The talk he gave opened us up and we played at a whole different level in the second half. He really inspired us."

Griffin, which merged with Sacred Heart in 1988, began a glorious five-year run (only three losses in 65 games) in 2002, losing to Belleville Althoff 35–31 in the state quarterfinals. But the 2003 team, led by Peterman, wider receiver Tony Nevins, running back Curtis Robinson, and center/linebacker Steve Edwards, averaged 48 points in winning its first 13 games and appeared primed to claim the school's first state title.

It didn't happen. Joliet Catholic built a 24–7 lead with seven minutes to play. Peterman, who completed 16 of 24 passes for 197 yards, threw two touchdown passes to J. C. Bland in the last five minutes but they weren't enough and Joliet Catholic prevailed 24–21.

"It was a crushing loss," Peterman said. "We had so much talent but we couldn't get the right play calls and execute the right play. We couldn't click on offense. We had a great team but we couldn't get the job done. It was very disappointing."

So was 2004, Peterman's senior year. Sacred Heart-Griffin finished 10–1, losing to Jacksonville 21–14 in the second round. Peterman passed for 1,500 yards and rushed for 1,500 yards and, in his view, had no state title to show for it. "It was harder than the previous year," he said. "It was hard to realize we were done playing high school football. It was like hitting a brick wall. It was very difficult to deal with."

Brenneisen felt the pain, too. He was a sophomore wide receiver on the 2004 squad. He made an illegal block in the back on a screen pass that nullified a 95-yard touchdown in the Jacksonville game. "I felt terrible about it," he said. "I thought we were going to win state."

With only Brenneisen and four other starters returning in 2005, Sacred Heart-Griffin figured to stagger through a rebuilding year. Brenneisen was switched to quarterback with pressure to replace Peterman. Senior leadership was provided by Jeff Sanders and James Davis. There were a lot of question marks but lack of confidence wasn't one of them.

"We weren't the most talented team but we had heart and we believed we could win," Brenneisen said. "It didn't matter that other people doubted us."

In the opener, Montini returned the kickoff 98 yards for a touchdown but Sacred Heart-Griffin rallied to win. They got on a roll. In the playoff, they beat Chatham Glenwood 28–21, Morton 55–7, Kankakee Bishop McNamara 34–28, North Chicago 29–19, and Rock Island Alleman 28–21. In the final, Brenneisen completed 29 of 40 passes for 351 yards and two touchdowns.

"We were the first team at Griffin to win a state title," Brenneisen said. "It was more than a memory to us. Being able to take a knee at the end of the championship game was an awesome feeling."

"Why did we win that year and not the other years?" Leonard said. "Our guys didn't get hurt. McNamara returned a fumble 100 yards to make it 34–21, then recovered a kickoff and closed to 34–28. Then our kids buckled down and ran out the clock. You have to win games like that. In the past, we lost them. There is always a game or two that you should have lost but won to be a champion."

The 2006 team was Leonard's best. Brenneisen shattered all of the school passing records. Chris Peterson and Josh Gossard were the leading rushers. Wide receiver David Kavish was the leading receiver. Tackle Matt Mast anchored the line. Linebackers Mike Edwards and Andrew Collins and safety Keenan Gilpin keyed the defense.

They got past Montini by one touchdown, then dominated the remainder of their opponents to complete a 14–0 sweep. In the playoff, they dispatched Mattoon 49–0, Kankakee Bishop McNamara 22–8, Cahokia 42–6, Metamora 19–6, and Marian Central of Woodstock 35–14. In the final, Brenneisen closed his brilliant career by scoring once and completing 18 of 25 passes for 295 yards and one touchdown.

"We were seniors. We had played together for so long. It meant a lot to go out on a good note. Mast and Kavish were my best friends," said Brenneisen, who passed for 6,369 yards in two years, 11th highest total in state history.

"They achieved greatness because there were no egos on the team," Leonard said. "We don't give out any awards, no MVP or Mr. Hustle. That's how we promote the team. It was an unselfish team. It had great chemistry. They didn't care who scored or made tackles."

Leonard didn't play any favorites, either. Any list of his best players included Chris Ondrula, his first quarterback in 1985; center Doug Hembrough and defensive end Dan Dee in 1986; quarterback Bart Geiser, who was the *Chicago Sun-Times* Player of the Year in 1988; wide receivers Mike McGee and Mike Pilger, who broke several state passing receiving records in 1994; defensive tackle Matt Mitrione and defensive back Bill Bruney, who had 15 interceptions in 1995; quarterback Brad Svoboda in 1996; kicker Peter Christofilakos and punter Brian Stapleton in 1988; quarterback Derek Leonard in 1997; quarterback Brad Sellinger in 2000; wide receiver Matt Brewer, defensive tackle Josh North and fullback J. T. Wise; running back Kenni Burns, who rushed for 2,500 yards in 2002; defensive lineman Larry Luster in 2003; Sanders, Peterman, Kavish, and Brenneisen.

And how about 2008? After losing to Montini in their opener, the Cyclones won 13 in a row, beating Lemont 37–15 for the Class 6A title. Quarterback Tim Dondanville passed for 2,715 yards and 30 touchdowns, Gary Wilson rushed for 1,653 yards and 31 touchdowns, and John Lantz caught 70 passes for 1,237 yards and 18 touchdowns.

"Our philosophy is to have great communication between kids and the coaching staff and to make the young men better as men," Leonard said. "Their worth as a man has nothing to do with their worth as a football player."

Wheaton North: The Jim Rexilius Era

Chuck Long, Kent Graham, and Jim Juriga are the most celebrated graduates of Jim Rexilius' boot camp at Wheaton North. Each starred on state championship teams, had outstanding college careers, and played in the NFL. But none of them was the best player Coach Rex ever produced, and none ever played on the best team in school history.

The best player was Charlie Martin, who was the most highly recruited player of the Rexilius era along with Graham. A running back, Martin reminded recruiters of Ohio State and Green Bay Packers star John Brockington. A three-sport star, he signed with the Los Angeles Dodgers out of high school and later spent one year playing football at Colorado.

"Baseball was my least favorite sport. Football was my best sport but I liked playing basketball better than any of them. If I had been tall enough, it would have been my dream," Martin said. "I had many college offers for football. I had a letter from every major college that you could name. Colorado recruited me heavily. I had given a verbal commitment to Wisconsin."

But Martin opted for baseball because "my family didn't have a whole lot and I got a good money offer to sign in baseball." He was drafted in the 10th round by the Dodgers. He went to spring training but was cut on the last day. After two years, he decided to test his football legs at Colorado. After one year, he moved on with his life.

The best team was 1973, the year before the state playoff. Brent Musburger, then a Chicago television sports reporter, said it was the best team he had ever seen. Martin, a junior, and Bobby Sullivan each rushed for more than 1,000 yards. Other standouts on the 9–0 powerhouse were linebackers Jim Fletcher, Steve DeFalco, and John Friedery, linemen Keith Burlingame and Bob Graham, quarterback Steve Massman, and end Rick Jacobsen.

The 1972 team was 8–0 but the 1973 team was even better. Ten players went to Division I schools. The offense averaged 41 points per game and 6.5 yards per play. The defense allowed 49 points and only 1.9 yards per play. Only one opponent scored more than one touchdown. The Falcons permitted only 22 points in their last seven games.

"In my 18 years as a coach, I have never been associated with a better team. I can't remember a team being as consistent on offense and defense as my 1973 club," Rexilius said. "It's just too bad we couldn't have found out how good they were with the playoffs. Our closest game was our opener against West Chicago—and it was 27–8."

They were the teams that put Wheaton North on the map, the teams that set the tone for what was to come in 1979, 1981, and 1986. In a four-year period, the Falcons lost only four games and won two state titles. The program, which began in 1966, had gone from two rows of bleachers and a second-fiddle reputation behind Wheaton Central and its Red Grange image to being one of the most dominant in the state.

It probably wouldn't have happened, of course, if Rexilius had been selected to succeed retiring coach Harvey Dickinson at Hinsdale Central in 1968. But Gene Strode got the job and Rexilius, who said Dickinson was "the greatest football mind I ever saw," opted to accept athletic director Dick Helm's offer to coach football at Wheaton North rather than stay on as head basketball coach at Hinsdale Central.

Rexilius, who was Dickinson's assistant for five years, wanted to be a head football coach. He vowed if his basketball team beat Riverside-Brookfield in the regional final, he would continue to coach basketball. If he lost, he would go to Wheaton North. After losing, he mailed his acceptance on the way home from the gym.

It was culture shock. Rexilius went from the best of everything at Hinsdale Central to nothing at Wheaton North. Rival Wheaton Central was the big-name school. It played in a big-time conference, the Upstate Eight, and in a lighted stadium in downtown Wheaton. North had no lights and second-rate facilities and got no respect as a member of the Tri-County Conference. Central got the headlines. North was a footnote on the sports page.

In fact, the school board was so concerned that Wheaton North's football program wouldn't be able to compete fairly with more established Wheaton Central that it wouldn't permit the two schools to play one another until 1976. There was a genuine dislike between the two sides of town that continues to this day.

Rexilius set about to change attitudes and perceptions. He surrounded himself with outstanding assistant coaches, including George Turnbull, Larry Fox, Jack Schomig, Jim Jordan, and his son, J. R. Rexilius. He started a weight-training program and a summer recreation program for fifth through eighth graders. Deeply religious, he also started a chapter of the Fellowship of Christian Athletes in his basement that drew 30 to 60 kids weekly.

Most of all, Coach Rex, as he was known by one and all, was a disciplinarian, an ex-Marine who wore a crew cut and loved his drill sergeant persona. He ran his program with an iron fist. Players couldn't wear long hair and had to be clean-shaven. He didn't tolerate untucked shirts or profanity. If you swore, you ran a mile for every letter in the word.

"Not once did I ever hear him say hell or damn," his son said.

"He wanted to have an impact on kids' lives. After the season, he would sit down with each kid and interview him and set up goals and learn how he could help them. It was more important to help them spiritually than to send them to college."

On the field, Coach Rex was fanatical. He was such a control freak that he called both sides of the ball for a few years. At the end of his career, it drove him nuts just to coach the specialty teams. "Tradition never graduates" sums up his philosophy. He would challenge his players. "Who will be the next great player?" he asked. Everyone wanted to be the next great player or play on the next great team. Nobody wanted to fail.

"He always had the interests of his kids at heart, academically and spiritually," said Turnbull, who coached the 1981 state championship team when Rexilius left for Wheaton College for two seasons. "He wanted to build a top-notch program based on strong faith, morals, and integrity. He never wavered from the standards that he set."

Rexilius had a slogan. He called it his banana slogan. "He wanted the whole banana. That was his goal—to win the whole banana," Turnbull said.

The 1979 squad achieved the goal. Rexilius described them as "a bunch of no-name lunch-bucket carriers" who thrived on competition and always chanted their theme, "Play to win," at practices and games. Long and Dave Burshtan were the most celebrated players, but most agreed that the "heart of the team" were running back/linebacker Shawn Young, 5–8, 165-pound guard/linebacker Rich Stachniak, and 5–10, 210-pound defensive tackle Bob Reis.

The Falcons lost their opener to Forest View 14–13 in overtime and got past West Chicago 3–0 in Week 4 on Marvin Carter's last-second, 40-yard field goal. But they shut out Wheaton Central 20–0 and allowed only two of their last 12 opponents to score more than one touchdown. They trailed Simeon 15–0 after 13 seconds in their opening playoff game but rallied to win 37–22. They beat top-ranked La Salle-Peru 14–6 for the state title.

"We had few seniors who played a lot. We weren't picked to win the conference. We came out of the fog to win the state title," Long said. "In the state final, I set a record for futility, one completion in four attempts for minus three yards. But it was a hard-nosed team, the type Coach Rex loved. He developed one of the best teams I've ever been around chemistry-wise."

In 1981, Rexilius was gone and Turnbull was in charge. The Falcons were coming off an 11–1 season in which they had lost to De Kalb 14–6 in the state semifinals. With 15 starters returning, nine on offense, they were eager to make amends. "It was the kind of season we anticipated. If we had lost a game, we felt we should have been fired. We had so much talent on both sides of the ball," Turnbull said.

They didn't lose a game. Juriga, 1,000-yard running backs Darryl Richardson and Lou Holland, quarterback Dan Graham, center Rich Morris, and tackle Rick Jordan keyed the offense. The defense allowed 64 points, only 14 in the four playoff games. In the state final, they blanked perennial state power Geneseo 14–0.

"I was on a Big 10 championship team and two seconds, played in three bowl games in four years, and went to three Super Bowls with the Denver Broncos," Juriga said. "But some of my fondest memories are going 13–0 and winning the state title in 1981. It was one of the highlights of my career. I recall the camaraderie and the teammates I grew up with, playing against Wheaton Central when their fans wouldn't let us on the field, playing in the mud against Benet in the state semifinal. Those are some of the best memories I have in sports."

Rexilius returned in 1983 after two years at Wheaton College and built another powerhouse in 1986. The Falcons, led by quarterback Kent Graham, the *Chicago Sun-Times* Player of the Year, overcame a 7–6 loss to Naperville Central in Week 3 and went on to beat powerful Deerfield and Glenbrook South in the state playoff before smashing Mount Carmel 34–14 for the Class 5A championship.

The team also featured Jack Schomig, Dave Kooser, Tom Reber, Doug Jorndt, Claudio Garcia, Joe Minniti, Mark Neibch, and David Neidballa. Kooser returned the opening kickoff against Mount Carmel 84 yards for a touchdown and Wheaton North never blinked. Schomig ran for three touchdowns and Graham threw a 34-yard scoring pass to Reber as the Falcons broke away in the fourth quarter.

Of all the games, Graham recalled an incident in the 6–0 semifinal victory over Glenbrook South that he felt said everything about what he had learned in four years in Rexilius' program.

"It was one of the most intense games we played all year, down to the wire, a real gut check," Graham recalled. "Eric Anderson [who later played at Michigan] ran me over and I got embarrassed and I got up and responded and shoved him. It was a real big thing. I had grown up with the program. All the guys on the team were in families of the last generation. I had grown up with older brothers who were on other teams. I wanted to live up to that tradition.

"Two months later, someone asked me if it had worn off. No, I said, it still feels really good. There is something about being state champions that is pretty special."

After coaching for 27 years, after taking nine teams to the state playoff, Rexilius retired in 1995. He died of liver cancer in 2003. He was 71.

Wheaton Warrenville South:
Red Grange's Legacy

Wheaton is steeped in football history. Have you ever heard of Red Grange? The Wheaton Iceman, remember? He started the tradition after World War I and went on to the University of Illinois to become the most celebrated college player in history. Later, Bob Horsley coached four unbeaten teams in the late 1940s and 1950s.

But Jeff Thorne probably has as much or more to do with the school's success in the past two decades—it was called Wheaton, then Wheaton Central, now Wheaton Warrenville South—as anyone you could name.

"We finally got our players to buy into our whole philosophy and that started happening when Jeff and his friends got into the program," said former coach John Thorne about his son. "They had a lot of confidence and trusted the coaches and were willing to work really hard. Before that, we couldn't get everything across to the teams, how hard they needed to work."

The Thorne family moved to Wheaton when Jeff was eight years old. Baseball was his first love. He wanted to be the next Bobby Murcer. He said he "hated" his first year of football. It was such an unpleasant experience, he took a year off. But it started to grow on him. He didn't know a lot about Red Grange but he attended a lot of games even though the team wasn't very good. Soon, he began to fall in love with football.

Jeff arrived at Wheaton Central in 1986 with a class of very good athletes—Marvel Scott, Greg Shelby, Devin Leftwich, Rob Seabrooks, Darren Bell, Tim Wojihowski, Bill Hess, Chris Dudek, Chuck Davito, Rich Sampson, and Chuck Moeaki. They set the tone for what was to come, one of the most glorious tales of success in state history.

"I think back and see how far the program has come," Jeff said. "The school hadn't done anything until we started to win in 1988 and 1989. Once you get something rolling and put the tradition in place and the kids know how to get it done, it makes it easier. Then kids want to be part of the football program. And the more players you have, the more chances you have for kids to develop into great players."

John Thorne, who grew up in tiny Milford, Illinois (he graduated ninth in a class of 60), was pink-slipped at Stanford Olympia in 1972 for lack of seniority, and opted to come to Wheaton Central over Danville Schlarman. He became head football coach in 1980. In his first eight years, his teams were 38–34. He wanted to make the game fun and wanted to play a lot of players. It wasn't fun at the time. But he came up with a new game plan.

"When I first got to Wheaton, we didn't match up very well. We weren't big and couldn't block people at the line of scrimmage," Thorne said. "We went to the veer for a long time because it helped us to play against teams that were more talented than we were. We loved throwing the ball, too. Our focus was to make certain we were asking our athletes to do something they physically had a chance to do and be successful."

Thorne discovered the right formula. From 1988 to 2001, when he resigned to become head coach at North Central College in Naperville, his teams were 143–31, won four state championships and two seconds. His successor, Ron Muhitch, who had served as his defensive coordinator for more than 20 years, is 69–16 with one state championship and a second in the past seven years.

The 1988 team, which started 0–3 but bounced back to win eight games in a row before losing to cross-town rival Wheaton North 19–13 in the state quarterfinals, was the catalyst. Until then, Wheaton North was the dominant program in town. Coach Jim Rexilius had raised the bar. The Falcons had strong teams in the pre-playoff years and had won three state titles in 1979, 1981, and 1986.

"When a program turns around, it needs a benchmark moment," Muhitch said. "Until 1988, we had a dysfunctional program. It took us seven years to get our act together. After our third game, when we were 0–3, Ron Shelby stood up in front of the kids. It was the first emotional moment I remember when a kid said enough is enough. He had two interceptions and we upset Naperville North. That was a turn-about moment."

"When we were 0–3, my dad almost gave up and resigned. He was totally discouraged," Jeff Thorne said. "We were supposed to be a really good team. Thankfully, we went on a streak and our class started to believe that we could win. Shelby was an interior lineman who said enough was enough. We tasted success in 1988. Our goal in 1989 was to go unbeaten."

It didn't happen. They had to settle for 11–2 after losing to Niles Notre Dame 6–3 in overtime in the state semifinals. But it was a start. They had momentum. They beat Wheaton North for the first time in six years. People around the state began to notice. They lost to Mount Carmel in the 1990 and 1991 state championships but beat Joliet Catholic 40–34 in double overtime in 1992 in one of the most memorable state finals of all.

The program was getting bigger than Wal-Mart. John Thorne recalled drawing barely 100 players when he became head coach in 1980. In the last five years of his regime, he had 275 candidates. Everybody wanted to be part of the success. He had to cut. He didn't have enough uniforms. It was difficult to budget.

"After we won in 1992, the principal said to pick a number and promise I would cut players if more came out," Thorne said. "I picked 225—80 on varsity, 60 sophomores, 85 freshmen. But more and more kids kept coming out.

"We had a string of great quarterbacks and hard-nosed running backs and linebackers. Of course, you can't have a great quarterback without great receivers. No senior class wanted to be the class that slowed us down. They all wanted to do better than the class before them."

The quarterbacks included Jeff Thorne, Tim Lester, Ben Klaas, Tim Brylka, and Jon Beutjer. Klaas led the 1992 championship team, Brylka guided the 1995 and 1996 kingpins, Beutjer set a national record for touchdown passes (60) while quarterbacking the 1998 powerhouse, and Michael Highland directed the 2006 champion.

"How many guys get to quarterback two state championship teams? I happened to be in the right place at the right time," Brylka said. "We don't have two or three kids going to Division I schools. We don't have a huge offensive line. We don't have big-name players with big-time talent. But we still find a way to compete against more established programs. We aren't intimidated by other schools. We expect to be successful every year."

Brylka's 1995 team outlasted Palatine and Mike Burden 21–18 in the second round, then avenged an earlier loss by stunning top-ranked Naperville Central and *Chicago Sun-Times* Player of the Year Tim Lavery 22–21 for the state title. Tom Schweighardt knocked down a two-point conversion pass in his end zone to preserve the victory.

In 1996, Wheaton Warrenville South was rated No. 1 in the preseason with Brylka and running back Kelly Crosby returning. The Tigers got past Dunbar and Rocky Harvey 30–22 in the second round, crushed New Trier and *Chicago Sun-Times* Player of the Year Mark Floersch 42–0 in the quarterfinals, then beat Lincoln-Way and Corey Paus 42–27 for the title.

"The big game was Dunbar at Gately Stadium. It was culture shock for suburban boys. We had never been to Gately before. It was very intimidating," Brylka said. "Dunbar was big and fast and it was cold, raining and snowing. Crosby pushed Harvey out of bounds on a two-point conversion attempt that would have put them ahead in the fourth quarter. Then, with 20 seconds left, Thorne called a hook-and-lateral play. I threw to Justin Penn, who flipped it to Crosby for over 70 yards and the winning touchdown."

John Thorne described wide receiver Jon Schweighardt of the 1998 squad as "the greatest athlete I ever coached." Phil Adler rushed for 186 yards and three touchdowns in the dramatic 1992 victory over Joliet Catholic. Dan Dierking, the *Chicago Sun-Times* Player of the Year, rushed for 2,300 yards while leading the Tigers to the 2006 state title and shattered all of Red Grange's school records along the way.

"All my friends and I looked at Beutjer and Schweighardt as superheroes. The 1998 team was like the Yankees," Dierking said. "We couldn't wait to play on the field. After the game, we would get autographs of the players. Winning the state title was like a dream. You couldn't ask to finish your high school career any better, winning a state title with all of your buddies."

Phil Hopkins coached Maine South to state championships in 1995 and 2000 and laid the groundwork for a program that has been dominant in the 2000s, winning a state title in 2008 and three seconds. Photo courtesy of the Illinois High School Association.

St. Laurence's Tim Grunhard (73) turns emotional as he attempts to energize his teammates during a 1985 playoff game. Grunhard later went on to star at Notre Dame and had a long and distinguished career in the NFL. Photo courtesy of Tim Grunhard.

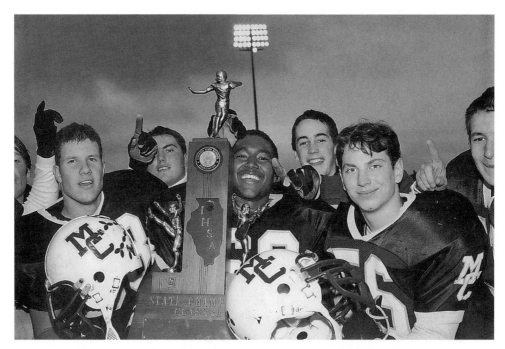

Mount Carmel players celebrate after winning the Class 5A championship in 1996, a 17–6 victory over Joliet Catholic that completed a 14–0 season. It was one of nine state titles won by Coach Frank Lenti's teams. Photo courtesy of the Illinois High School Association.

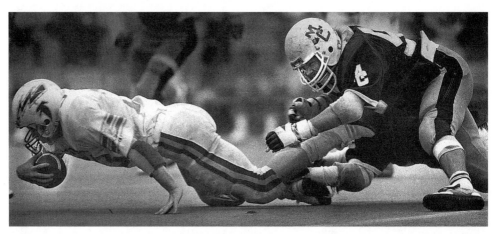

Wheaton North's Dave Kooser (left) stretches for an extra yard after being upended by Mount Carmel's Jonas Kujawa in the 1986 Class 5A championship game. Kujawa was credited with 11 tackles in the game but Wheaton North won 34–14 as Kooser returned the opening kickoff 84 yards for a touchdown. Photo courtesy of the Illinois High School Association.

Jim Rexilius came from Hinsdale Central and built a dynasty at Wheaton North in the 1970s and 1980s. He produced two unbeaten teams in the pre-state playoff era, then collaborated with George Turnbull to win state championships in 1979, 1981, and 1986. Photo courtesy of Scott Gibson.

Coach Tom Peeler built a successful program at Peoria Richwoods in the pre-playoff era. He produced four unbeaten teams. His last team went 13–0 and won a state championship in 1984. Photo courtesy of Tom Peeler.

Chuck Long quarterbacked Wheaton North to the Class 4A championship in 1979. Curiously, Long, who later was runner-up to Bo Jackson for the Heisman Trophy when he played at Iowa, completed only one of four passes for minus three yards in the state final. Photo courtesy of Scott Gibson.

Rod Butler (left), who coached Peoria Richwoods to a 89–16 record from 1985–1993 and produced one state champion and one state runner-up, congratulates one of his best players, linebacker Eddie Sutter, after the 1988 Illinois high school All-Star game at Illinois State University's Hancock Stadium. Sutter, who later played at Northwestern and in the NFL, was named the most valuable defensive player in the game. Photo courtesy of Rod Butler.

8

Fourth Quarter

State Playoff

In the early 1970s, a number of football coaches and athletic administrators from throughout the state began to lobby for a state playoff. Every other sport had a postseason tournament. Why not football? Other states conducted football championships. Why not Illinois?

It wasn't a new idea. In the early 1960s, Coach Warren Smith of Urbana had proposed a state playoff. He had a plan. But nobody would take it seriously. The argument from the Illinois High School Association (IHSA) officials was the plan lacked substance, no tangibles, no blueprint. Logistics wouldn't allow it.

But pressure began to build, especially after the newly formed Illinois Basketball Coaches Association successfully lobbied for a two-class format in the state basketball tournament, the IHSA's signature event.

"If they ever get serious about this, I have a plan in my desk drawer. I know exactly how we can do it," said Lavere L. "Liz" Astroth, who was second in command to IHSA executive secretary Harry Fitzhugh at the time.

Astroth was a former football coach and athletic director at Glenbard East in Lombard. He was the IHSA's supervisor for football. He bounced ideas off close friend Bill Duchon, the football coach at Glenbard West in Glen Ellyn, and several other coaches, including Smith, Champaign's Tommy Stewart, Pittsfield's Deek Pollard, Oak Park's Ed Zembal, and Geneseo's Bob Reade. And he discussed the issue with athletic directors.

The coaches began to get serious about the issue in 1970. They were in the process of organizing a state football coaches association. Coaches from all over Illinois met at the Drake Hotel in Chicago, site of a national football clinic. Zembal was a speaker. Smith, Duchon, Pollard, Loyola's Tom Powers, Downers Grove's Dick Carstens, Hinsdale Central's Gene Strode, Sandburg's Joe Devine, Morton's Ken Geiger, Carbondale's Joe Pollock, and East Moline's Gene McCarter were there.

There was an Illinois Coaches Association but no football coaches association. The Chicago Catholic League had a strong association. Suburban and Downstate coaches asked, "Why can't we have what they have?" With Geiger's leadership, they went to Peoria and East St. Louis to solicit Downstate support.

"We had to show we were viable," Zembal said. "Our goals were to establish an all-star game and a state playoff and a coaches' Hall of Fame. We also wanted to sponsor a clinic—but we had no money. We asked Coach Chuck Fairbanks of Oklahoma's national championship team to speak. But he was going to Europe. We ended up with Galen Hall, one of his assistants, Tom Osborne, Lee Corso, Alex Agase, and Abe Gibron."

Phil Salzer, secretary-treasurer of the Illinois High School Football Coaches Association since 1973, said Smith and Duchon were the driving forces behind the coaches' plan. They sat down with Astroth and did a lot of work. Astroth and Duchon were neighbors. Astroth's son, Jon, quarterbacked Duchon's unbeaten 1968 team.

Salzer said, "After looking at the original plan, Astroth once told me, 'The whole thing will fall through because coaches want more than six games. They want every school in the playoff in the beginning, like basketball. To do that, they have to reduce the regular season schedule to six games. Nobody wants to do that.' But Astroth had a plan."

"We talked all the time," Duchon said. "We copied a lot from the Texas plan. I was real excited about it. It was my No. 1 project to get through. The problem was some football coaches weren't as interested in the playoff as some of us were. If Liz had an issue, he'd call me and we'd talk about it. We saw it the same way."

While the Texas plan was predicated on counties, the Illinois plan was all about conference champions, a tournament of champions. But there were stumbling blocks to overcome. What about overtime to decide tie games? How many classes? How does a school qualify? How do you determine at-large teams? What about independent schools? It took the IHSA about five minutes to adopt a soccer playoff. It took nearly two years to agree on a football playoff for 1974.

Astroth felt the football coaches were dragging their feet, that they were more interested in organizing their own association. There was a lot of talk, not much movement. The principals, who ultimately would have to vote on the issue, were more interested in basketball. There was a bloc of people who didn't want to expand the football season, didn't want three games in a week as the playoff plan called for, and claimed that a conference championship was a fitting way to cap off the season.

"In the end, Astroth saw the handwriting on the wall and he came up with a plan that would suit everybody the best and they bought into it," said John Elder, former president of the football coaches association who coached at Alexis for 33 years.

"He was that kind of guy. That was his manner of operation. He said, 'This is what we're going to do.' And the coaches accepted it. It turned out to be workable. The coaches hated to lose the Thanksgiving Day games [Belleville–East St. Louis, Peoria Manual–Peoria Central, Benton–West Frankfort]. But when we went down that path in 1974, everyone got behind us. It generated so much interest in football, locally and statewide."

"Astroth wanted a playoff system for football but he didn't come out for it immediately," said Dave Fry, who went to work for the IHSA with Astroth on the same day in 1967 and succeeded Astroth as executive secretary in 1991.

"Class basketball was the greatest door opener for football. It showed we can change the structure of sport in this state without damaging the sport. When Astroth showed he could expand the football season without cutting into basketball, he had a plan that had really been thought through."

Astroth's bottom-of-the-drawer plan called for a functional playoff structure with conference champions and at-large selections filling a field of 128 schools. The season wouldn't have to start early and it would run to the Thanksgiving weekend for only the teams that advance to the championship games.

If the issue had been proposed 10 years earlier, Fry said it would have been met with huge objection. It would have been an isolated issue. But because Astroth incorporated the conference structure, making it the most important aspect of his plan, win your conference in order to guarantee a spot in the playoff, it was a key to acceptability.

Fitzhugh had reservations about the football playoff but had no hard reasons to oppose it. "If it works, it works. If it doesn't, it will fade away," he said. The only dissent came from administrators who argued that the playoff would interfere with school time and the winter sports season.

Another positive spokesperson for the playoff was Glenbrook North coach Harold Samorian, whose support was a sobering and convincing factor with administrators in the suburbs. He was highly respected and many critics who were skeptical of the plan changed their minds when he became a vocal supporter of the playoff.

When the polished plan was revealed to one and all, it was obvious that most, if not all, concerns were minimized. "There was no reason not to give it a shot," Fry said.

Ironically, the state playoff became an immediate smash hit when Samorian's team upset heavily favored East St. Louis 19–13 in overtime in the first state championship.

"That was the game that put the playoff on the map," Salzer said. "Even today, people ask, 'Do you remember that game?' That's the one game in the history of the state playoff that everybody remembers."

Prep Bowl

Many years ago, when football fans walked through the main gate at Soldier Field in Chicago, there was an enormous picture hanging high on the wall. It was a black-and-white photograph of the estimated record crowd of 120,000 people who attended the 1937 Prep Bowl game between Austin and Leo.

The memory of that picture—it has since disappeared and Chicago Park District officials don't know what happened to it—always has been a source of wonder. No other football game—high school, college, or professional—ever attracted more people. Not Army–Navy or Notre Dame–USC or Michigan–Ohio State.

But the game has changed. The Prep Bowl pairing of Chicago's Public and Catholic League champions that once drew annual crowds of 60,000 to 90,000 no longer attracts more than 5,000, only parents, family, friends, alumni, and students. Except for the Bears, football has ceased to be the only game in town.

What was so intriguing and magical about the Prep Bowl in those pre–state playoff years was that the crowds included more than just the followers of the participating teams. Other Catholic and Public League schools came to cheer for their representatives. It truly was an All-City championship.

No longer. Sure, city kids still dream of playing in Soldier Field, as suburban and Downstate kids dream of playing in Memorial Stadium in Champaign. But it isn't the same. Like the Prep Bowl since the 1960s, the state playoff attracts only followers of the participating schools. They come to see their team, then go home. The state playoff never has generated statewide appeal, as the state basketball tournament has.

For years, the Prep Bowl was the only game in town. It attracted bigger crowds than the Chicago Bears, who played at Wrigley Field. There were legendary players such as Bill DeCorrevont, Eddie Galvin, Babe Baranowski, Marty Wendell, Buddy Young, Dale Samuels, and Johnny Lattner; great teams such as Mount Carmel 1950, Fenger 1954, Leo 1956, Fenwick 1962, St. Rita 1963, Mount Carmel 1967, and St. Rita 1971; and great coaches such as Terry Brennan, Bill Heiland, Max Burnell, Chuck Palmer, Jim Arneberg, Bernie O'Brien, and Tony Lawless.

It all began in 1927 when the *Chicago Herald & Examiner* proposed a championship contest between the winners of the Catholic League and Public League. It was a competitive environment that was fueled by the political warfare of the time. In 1924, William Hale Thompson, an anti-Catholic, had defeated Irish Catholic William Dever in the mayoral race. Now the newspaper wanted to take the fight to the football field.

Mount Carmel beat Schurz 6–0 in 1927 and Tilden beat DePaul 12–0 in 1928. The Public League refused to play in 1929 and 1930, citing differing player eligibility rules. The Public League was agreeable in 1931, however, and a Harrison powerhouse led by future Notre Dame players Andy Pilney and Andy Puplis crushed Mount Carmel 44–6.

In 1932, Morgan Park refused to play Mount Carmel because, according to a Morgan Park parent who wrote a letter to the *Chicago Tribune*, the school stressed the overemphasis and commercialization of the game. "Football is being stressed all out of proportion to its proper values. It is becoming the reason for attending school," he said.

But the All-City game resumed in 1933. Mount Carmel avenged its embarrassing 1931 loss, beating Harrison 7–0. It was all very confusing because Mount Carmel (9–1–1) was designated as the Catholic representative even though Loyola finished 8–0–2. In an early season duel, the two teams tied 6–6. Today, a team picture with Loyola star Jack McCarthy holding the Catholic League trophy hangs in Loyola's Hall of Fame.

The following year, Chicago's new mayor, Ed Kelly, adopted the city championship as his own, ensuring the future of the event. There would be no more interruptions. The two sides could scuffle on and off the field but the game would go on. And it would help to raise funds for underprivileged children.

The game was known as the Kelly Bowl until Mayor Richard J. Daley moved into the fifth floor of City Hall in 1955. Until 1976, it was sponsored by the Mayor Daley Youth Foundation. But the concept was changed after the Illinois High School Association introduced the state playoff in 1974. Afterward, it no longer was the only game in town and it no longer pitted the best teams from the Catholic and Public leagues. Crowds declined and interest waned.

But from the 1930s to the early 1970s, the Prep Bowl commanded national attention. In the pretelevision era, it filled Soldier Field to overflowing. By any estimate, the biggest crowd in football history in this country—high school, college, or professional—attended the 1937 game between Austin and Leo. Even more than witnessed the Dempsey–Tunney heavyweight championship in the same venue 10 years earlier.

Bill DeCorrevont, who ranks with Centralia's Dike Eddleman as one of the most celebrated high school athletes in history, ran for three touchdowns and passed for another as Austin smashed Leo 26–0 before a crowd that was estimated by everyone from city officials to policemen to independent sources to Andy Frain, the city's chief usher, between 115,000 to 130,000. The "official" count was announced at 120,000 and nobody disputed the figure.

Crowds of 75,000 to 80,000 were common in following years. In 1962, a crowd of 91,328 saw Jim DiLullo rush for 224 yards and five touchdowns as Fenwick overwhelmed Schurz 40–0.

There were many exciting games. Loyola edged Vocational 20–14 in 1966 when sophomore Jack Spellman scored in the fourth quarter and Jim Rianoshek and Ken Krajchovich broke up a pass at the goal line to preserve the victory. St. Rita overcame an 8–6 halftime deficit to nudge Lane Tech 12–8 in 1970. Billy Marek's 85-yard run keyed St. Rita's 18–12 decision over Morgan Park in 1971. And Vocational, behind Ronald Pinnick and Frank McKinnie, stunned St. Rita 13–6 in 1976 for the Public League's first triumph since 1959.

Chick Cichowski, who later played at Indiana and in the NFL and the Canadian Football League and coached at New Trier for 20 years, started as a sophomore defensive back for Lane Tech against Mount Carmel's 1950 powerhouse.

"I'm 15 years old," Cichowski recalled. "It was an unbelievable experience, playing against Mount Carmel and Tim McHugh in Soldier Field. I run out for the pregame warm up and I'm in awe, so many people, I'm only a sophomore. Never did I realize how many great players were on the field. I was All-State as a senior but we never got back to the Prep Bowl. It was so disappointing."

Since the Catholic League began dominating the city series and the state playoff has become the focus of everyone's attention, Public League coaches and officials such as Lexie Spurlock, Roy Curry, J. W. Smith, Rich Rio, Glenn Johnson, Elton Harris, Calvin Davis, and Mickey Pruitt have attempted to rekindle interest in the Prep Bowl. They argue they have one venue that every kid in the city wants to play in.

"It is more exciting to play in Soldier Field," Spurlock said. "Sure, everyone wants to go to Champaign, to play in the state championship. But the Prep Bowl has such historical significance. It goes back farther than the state playoff. A lot of kids love the Prep Bowl. It's a big thrill for them to play in the game. I'm convinced if the powers-that-be would publicize it year-round, it could return to the way it was."

John Potocki has seen it from both sides. He played football for Frank Maloney at Mount Carmel but most of his friends from his neighborhood went to Vocational and hung out with Dick Butkus. Later, he succeeded the legendary Bernie O'Brien as head coach at Vocational, produced an unbeaten Prep Bowl champion in 1976, and then assisted Frank Lenti at Mount Carmel from 1989 to 1995.

"To me, the public schools had better athletes but the Catholic schools were more fundamentally sound, had better facilities, and more coaches," Potocki said. "You didn't move on from A to B unless you were known very well in the Catholic League. The fundamental drills we did at Mount Carmel in the preseason of 1989 were the same drills we did before the state championship game. I did the same thing at Vocational."

Perhaps more than anyone else, J. W. Smith is responsible for rebuilding the football program in the Public League to the point where some programs, especially Hubbard, Morgan Park, Lane Tech, Simeon, and Robeson, have become competitive with parochial and suburban opponents.

Now retired, Smith coached at Julian from 1975 to 1989, then served as executive director of the Chicago Board of Education's sports administration from 1995 to 2003. He won two Prep Bowls—1979 against Joliet Catholic and 1989 against Fenwick. And he lost twice—1987 to Gordon Tech and 1988 to Loyola. He produced several outstanding players, including Danny Walters, Howard Griffith, Carl Boyd, Larry Mosely, Corwin Brown, Andre Gilbert, and Torrance Garfield.

But Smith saw how Public League football was struggling, how the prestige of the Prep Bowl had declined, and how more kids in the city were playing basketball than football. He was determined to do something about it. As a Chicago Board of Education administrator, he was in a position to do it. He organized a football program in the elementary schools designed to train youngsters much as Catholic Leaguers learned how to play the game in the old parish leagues.

"So often you get a kid who, when he gets on the field, you have to tell him how to put on his pads," Smith said. "It is tough to compete with the private and suburban schools that have lower-level football and come to the varsity with three or four years of experience. When you lose to a private or suburban school, it is the finer points of the game that usually make the difference."

Smith started with four teams. He outfitted them and brought them to Gately Stadium for controlled scrimmages. He got some funding, put together a staff, and expanded his program to include eight teams and scheduled games in the second year. Later, he established two levels, one for fifth and sixth graders and the other for seventh and eighth graders.

"Since 1995, it has been beneficial," Smith said. "It has worked. It was a developmental league, to prepare kids for the next level. It wasn't supposed to be a win-at-all-costs program. It was going to help because we didn't have it. Look at the kids who are getting scholarships now. A great percentage of them started in the developmental league."

Chicago Catholic League

Bob Foster and Tom Winiecki are what the Chicago Catholic League is all about. They were teammates on Leo's 1956 Prep Bowl championship team. Foster went to Purdue, Winiecki to Michigan State. Later, Foster returned to Leo as a teacher, coach, counselor, athletic director, and chief administrator. Winiecki coached at Gordon Tech for 31 years.

Leo had emerged as a city powerhouse in the 1930s and early 1940s under coach A. L. "Whitey" Cronin. The Lions won Prep Bowls in 1941, 1942, and 1956 and lost in 1934, 1935, 1937, 1940, and 1947. Johnny Galvin, Babe Baranowski, Ed Ryan, and Rich Boyle were South Side heroes.

Foster grew up three blocks from Leo. His three older brothers went to Leo. His dream was to coach at Leo. When other kids played with tinker toys, he chewed on Leo yearbooks. When even his closest friends advised him to leave the school because it was destined to close because of declining enrollment and lack of financial support, Foster remained at the helm, never wavering in his commitment to his alma mater.

"I was the only individual who believed the school would survive," Foster said. "Some people said they'd bury me here. But I just love the place. We always had a mission, to help working-class people, from Irish Catholic to blue-collar to African American, downtrodden, underdogs. When you are blessed, you have to return that blessing."

Winiecki was the first member of his family to obtain a college education. His father, a steelworker, wanted him to go to Harvard and become an accountant. Tom didn't think about coaching until he was influenced by Leo coach Jim Arneberg. Later, Michigan State coach Duffy Daugherty persuaded him to become Larry Bielat's line coach at Gordon Tech. He became head coach in 1966 and retired in 1996.

"To this day, when I talk to guys who played and coached in the Catholic League, there still is a camaraderie when you meet old Catholic Leaguers," Winiecki said. "Coaches coached because they loved coaching. Money was never an issue. There were great rivalries, great intensity. Coaches would meet at Johnny Lattner's restaurant at Marina City or meet at Film Processors on Grand Avenue in the Loop to pick up their film after Sunday games, then eat chili next door. You made lifetime friends."

But even old-timers like Foster and Winiecki admit the Catholic League isn't what it used to be. Lattner's is gone. So is Film Processors. So are spring practice and Sunday afternoon games at Gately Stadium. So are St. George, Mendel, and Weber. St. Francis de Sales is hanging on. Leo, Gordon Tech, and St. Laurence aren't what they used to be. Alumni have moved to the suburbs and send their children to suburban public schools or Providence or Joliet Catholic.

"It was a neighborhood league," said Tom Powers, who coached at St. George and Loyola. "All the schools were close together and grade school kids had choices of where they could go to school. They would go with their friends. There was scholarship aid for some needy kids. Competition was brutal. Coaches were products of the league. They grew up in the schools, played there, and went on to coach there."

How competitive was it? In the early 1960s, St. Rita coach Ed Buckley once loaded up a school bus with eighth graders and put them up in a hotel so they couldn't go to other schools to take entrance exams. Some schools clipped scoring plays from their game films. Some schools offered free tuition, free books, and free transportation to lure promising athletes.

There was a glamour about the Catholic League that no other conference could equal. Great coaches built great programs—Cronin at Leo, Tony Lawless at Fenwick, Max Burnell at St. George, Pat Cronin at St. Rita, Tom Kavanagh at St. Laurence, Tom Winiecki at Gordon Tech, Bob Naughton and Bob Spoo at Loyola, Lou Guida at Mendel, Tom Mitchell at Brother Rice, and Frank Lenti at Mount Carmel.

And who could forget Catholic League playoff games, the Prep Bowl or St. Rita–St. Laurence in Soldier Field and Sunday afternoons at Gately Stadium when Big Ten officials like Jerry Markbreit, Don Hakes, Tom Quinn, Frank Strocchia, and Mike Sheehan, who might have worked Michigan–Ohio State the day before, showed up to work a Mount Carmel–Brother Rice game.

It all ended in 1974 when school officials opted to join the Illinois High School Association. Schools were expanding their sports programs. Football and basketball no longer were the only games in town. They wanted their students, boys and girls, to compete for state championships in swimming and track and other sports. And they wanted them to participate in other extracurricular activities such as band, debate, and speech.

The Chicago Catholic League is the oldest still-existing high school athletic conference in Illinois. It has been in operation longer than any other league and there is little doubt that its tradition is unsurpassed.

Loyola and Mount Carmel (then St. Cyril) were charter members when representatives of eight parochial schools met at Chicago's Great Northern Hotel on October 3, 1912, to form the Chicago Catholic High School Athletic League. Other original members were DePaul, St. Philip, St. Ignatius, De La Salle, Cathedral, and St. Stanislaus.

The schools participated in only basketball and indoor baseball in the first year. Football followed in 1913, track in 1916. Later, swimming, golf, tennis, cross-country, wrestling, and water polo were added. But they built a reputation as the most competitive football conference in the nation.

"It was a conference of great rivalries and great coaches," said Bob Spoo, a 1955 graduate of St. Rita who coached Loyola to the 1969 Prep Bowl championship. "I lived in the same Marquette Park neighborhood as kids going to St. Rita, Mount Carmel, and Leo. Later, coaching at Loyola were the happiest years of my career."

Fr. James Arimond has observed how the Catholic League has changed. In fact, he was a part of it. In 1971, at the age of 32, he became headmaster at Loyola, the youngest ever at a Jesuit school. He served as president of the league's board of principals for nine years. He was involved in discussions with the IHSA and oversaw the league's 11–0 vote with one abstention (Mount Carmel) in favor of joining the state association.

"I'm the new guy on the block in the fall of 1971," Fr. Arimond recalled. "In 1972, Fred Wright [Loyola's athletic director and head of the league's athletic directors] started to push for the league to get into the state. It wasn't a popular topic with the principals, who were still living the Lawless era and loved their independence."

There were three major obstacles—lightweight basketball and spring football (longtime staples in the Catholic League), and coaches who didn't have teaching certificates. There were some holdouts. One sticking point was tradition. Fenwick didn't want to give up the lightweight basketball program.

"Lawless called me a young whippersnapper," Fr. Arimond said. "We wanted to get in for the state playoff. We saw down the line that the Prep Bowl wouldn't be what it used to be, that it wouldn't be the only game in town. We were forward enough thinking that if the state starts a playoff, we have to be in it.

"We hated dropping Sunday football with the Big Ten officials. It was the only game in town. But it has worked out tremendously for the league. It isn't just about football championships. The Catholic League isn't what it used to be. We began losing our identity when we lost the luster of the old Catholic League in the late 1980s, when it merged for several years with the East Suburban Catholic and Joliet Catholic."

Today, the league is divided into three divisions. The Blue is the headliner with Mount Carmel, St. Rita, Brother Rice, Loyola, and Providence. Leo, Gordon Tech, and Hales Franciscan are in the Green. Fenwick, De La Salle, St. Laurence, and St. Ignatius are in the White.

The Blue is the premier football conference in the state, having won more state championships than any other league. Mount Carmel has won 10 titles, Providence 9, St. Rita 2, and Loyola and Brother Rice 1 each.

"But it isn't the same," said Fr. Arimond, who currently is alumni chaplain at Loyola. "When the neighborhoods started to change, priests didn't change their mission. They kept educating kids like they were white Irish and Polish kids. They lost the spirit of the school and the religious orders closed them.

"Now when I go to the Catholic League's Hall of Fame dinner, I notice that the coaches don't come any more. Some coaches never missed. But a lot of today's coaches don't have a sense of tradition that the old-timers had."

Chicago Public League

Walter Stanley was typical of most youngsters who grew up on Chicago's playgrounds in the 1940s through the 1970s. He had no interest in football. He loved to play baseball. In his era, kids drew boxes on the sides of buildings and played a game called strikeout. They played as often as they could.

Stanley liked to play basketball, too. So did many of his friends. Other kids enjoyed softball. They heard stories from old-timers about Nat "Sweetwater" Clifton, who carved a legend on the city's softball fields before becoming one of the first African Americans to play in the National Basketball Association.

While the Chicago Catholic League built a national reputation in football, the

Public League, founded in 1913, couldn't keep pace. Everybody conceded the public schools were filled with talented athletes, but it was apparent that they lacked quality coaches, adequate facilities, equipment, and a firm commitment from the Chicago Board of Education. In the city, head coaches are paid $4,000. In the suburbs, they are paid $10,000 to $12,000. Freshman coaches earn $4,000.

The Kelly Bowl or Prep Bowl provided a measuring stick. Which system was better? Public or Catholic? After being competitive in the 1930s, 1940s, and 1950s with players such as Bill DeCorrevont, Buddy Young, Dale Samuels, Jack Delveaux, and Mike Lind and programs such as those of Austin, Lindblom, Tilden, and Fenger, the Public League rapidly fell behind.

"We're getting better but we're still behind. We're a decade behind. It will take 10 years before we can catch up," said Roy Curry, who coached at Robeson from 1969 to 2000 and later became the Public League's football supervisor.

"We used to be that all of our coaches were physical education teachers. They went through training on how to teach sports. Now coaches come off the street and teach math and science. They don't know the game and that is killing us. They don't understand the game like the old-timers who were physical education teachers. Taking physical education out of the schools [it is required for only two years] has hurt."

The quality of the football program also suffered because more and more kids opted for basketball. The rise of AAU competition allowed youngsters to play basketball on a year-round basis. It not only drew kids away from football but baseball and track and field as well. Public League programs in the spring sports haven't been the same.

"It will be difficult to change the mind-set from basketball to football," Curry said. "The AAU program is so glorified because the kids have their expenses paid [by shoe companies] and they travel from city to city. They get a lot of national exposure and an opportunity to get a college scholarship. Basketball players would rather sit on the bench than play football. It will be difficult to get them away from basketball."

In the late 1950s and 1960s, the Public League built a reputation for producing blue-chip football players such as Dick Butkus, Al MacFarlane, Jim Grabowski, Otis Armstrong, and Darryl Stingley. And after the Public League entered the state playoff in 1979, Robeson made an impact by finishing second in 1982. But the league hasn't sent a team to the championship game since.

Stanley admits it is "weird" when he explains how he got into football. His family moved from Hyde Park to the South Shore area when he was in sixth grade. All of the kids in his new neighborhood played two-hand touch football on asphalt in the playground. It was more difficult than one-hand touch and flag football. He didn't put on pads until his sophomore year in high school.

His friends tried to persuade him to try out for South Shore's freshman team. But he refused. They persisted. Finally, close friend Tony Bailey convinced him to join the sophomore squad. He started at receiver and was moved to running back. He learned the fundamentals from coaches Homer Turner and Glenn Johnson.

"I was 14 years old, five-feet eight-inches tall, and weighed 150 pounds at the time," Stanley recalled. "On the first day of practice, I was amazed at what I could do. I impressed the coaches with my hands, then my speed. I saw I had potential to run and catch the ball out of the backfield. As we started to play games, we began to be a dominating team. In some games, I never touched the ground."

He rushed for 1,500 yards as the sophomore team went 8–0. On the varsity as a junior, he ran for 2,200 yards as South Shore won the Blue Division. As a senior, he rushed for 2,900 yards but South Shore lost a one-pointer to Tilden, which went on to win the Blue Division title. His team was never eligible to play in the Prep Bowl playoff. He played in Soldier Field as a professional but never as a high school player.

It didn't matter that Stanley didn't play for one of the elite programs in the Public League. College recruiters came from everywhere—Illinois, Michigan, Michigan State, Minnesota, LSU, Colorado, Northwestern. But his mother made the decision for him. Her son was going to Colorado.

"She felt it would benefit me more to leave Illinois and explore other areas, to find out what life was like on another campus in another state. She wanted me to grow a little bit," Stanley said. He didn't argue with her.

As a freshman, Stanley started at wingback. After his junior season, he declared for the NFL draft and was chosen in the third round by the Green Bay Packers. He played for the Packers for six years, the Lions for two, the Redskins for two, and the Patriots for one, then retired in 1997.

"Sports is a big fraternity. It's the best experience anyone can have in life, a dream come true," he said. "Football taught me how to compete at all levels. Now I'm in the banking business. I'm very competitive on a daily basis. Like sports, you have to show you are better, you have to be creative, be a go-getter, and build a cohesive team."

Robeson (then Parker) was a basketball school in the 1950s with Tommy Hawkins. When Curry became head coach in 1969, the team won one game. But they won the Blue Division title in 1970. In 1982, Robeson defied the odds—the Raiders had seven players going both ways and only 25 on the varsity roster—by becoming the first and only Public League team to advance to the state final.

Led by Mickey Pruitt, Vincent Tolbert, Tim Spencer, Jimmie Spraggins, and Tiffany Hamilton, Robeson (11–2) had lost to Tilden and Dempsey Norman 7–6 in the regular season (Tilden went on to upset top-ranked Deerfield in the first round of the state playoff) but ousted Antioch 18–16 in a semifinal at Soldier Field on Spencer's last-minute touchdown pass to Tolbert.

In the state final against Rockford Guilford, Robeson was leading 12–9 and trying to run out the clock. However, on a handoff from Spencer to Pruitt, Guilford linebacker Larry Brasfield forced a fumble and teammate Joe Francis recovered at Guilford's 38 with 2:35 to play. Quarterback Jeff Anderson completed passes for gains of 16, 9, 10, and 20 yards, then ran to the 1 before Credell MaGee scored the winning touchdown with 45 seconds left.

"It was the most devastating loss of my career," Curry said.

"After the game, we were told that they had never seen a team from the city that was so well coached. That's the problem today. Coaches today aren't as good as they used to be and they have so much to work with. When I came along, there was Bernie O'Brien, Al Manasin, Carl Bonner, Sherman Howard, Joe Stepanek, Al Scott,

Terry Lewis, J. W. Smith, and Frank Esposito. All of them had been in the game for a long time. They knew the game. Today, we have a lot of young guys who don't know the game. Maybe in time they will get better."

Morgan Park's Lexie Spurlock and Hubbard's Elton Harris are two of the "young" coaches who are trying to make a difference. They have produced some outstanding players, sending as many as eight to Division I colleges in one year, and guided their teams to the state semifinals. But they agree with Curry's assessment. They have a lot of obstacles and mind-sets to overcome.

"We're getting better and better with the help of the elementary school programs that push football and save the lives of a lot of kids," Spurlock said. "Instead of 5 or 10 kids going up and down a basketball court, you have 22 kids playing football. Kids have to understand there are more opportunities for them in football.

"Now we're getting better coaches and more coaches. They are going to clinics and upgrading their coaching skills. We are still far behind with facilities but we are moving. A lot can still be done. We are competing with the great football programs in the Catholic League and the suburbs.

"What's the next step? People love to coach but when they get into it they find out it is tougher than they think. It takes a long period of dedication beyond a dollar bill to build a successful program. The trick is to find coaches who are willing to dedicate their time to the kids, go away from their wives and families, and work with someone else's child—without monetary reward."

Tom Kavanagh built one of the strongest programs in the state at St. Laurence in the 1970s. The Vikings won three Prep Bowls in a row in 1973–1975, won a state championship in 1976, and finished second in 1979 under Mike O'Neill. Kavanagh was recognized as a visionary, one of the first high school coaches to employ the new wishbone offense. Photo courtesy of St. Laurence High School.

Coach Lexie Spurlock (left), with quarterback Demetrius Jones (8), has built Morgan Park into a power in the Chicago Public League. More importantly, few high school coaches have sent more players to Division I colleges in recent years than Spurlock. Photo courtesy of Lexie Spurlock

Index

Taylor Bell, a graduate of the University of Illinois, covered high school sports in Illinois for more than forty years, mostly for the *Chicago Daily News* and the *Sun-Times.* He has covered professional sports as well, but found his niche in traveling the state to cover high school sports. He is the author of *Sweet Charlie, Dike, Cazzie, and Bobby Joe: High School Basketball in Illinois* (UIP 2004).

The University of Illinois Press
is a founding member of the
Association of American University Presses.

———————————————

Composed in 9.5/13 ITC Cheltenham Light
with Meta display
at the University of Illinois Press
Manufactured by Sheridan Books, Inc.

University of Illinois Press
1325 South Oak Street
Champaign, IL 61820-6903
www.press.uillinois.edu